D1243399

An

INTRODUCTION

to

Black Studies

An INTRODUCTION to Black Studies

Eric R. Jackson

UNIVERSITY PRESS OF KENTUCKY

Scholarly publisher for the Commonwealth, serving Bellarmine University, Berea College, Centre College of Kentucky, Eastern Kentucky University, The Filson Historical Society, Georgetown College, Kentucky Historical Society, Kentucky State University, Morehead State University, Murray State University, Northern Kentucky University, Spalding University, Transylvania University, University of Kentucky, University of Louisville, University of Pikeville, and Western Kentucky University. All rights reserved.

Editorial and Sales Offices: The University Press of Kentucky
663 South Limestone Street, Lexington, Kentucky 40508-4008
www.kentuckypress.com

Library of Congress Cataloging-in-Publication Data

Names: Jackson, Eric, 1965- author.
Title: An introduction to black studies / Eric R. Jackson.
Description: Lexington, Kentucky : The University Press of Kentucky, [2023] |
    Includes bibliographical references and index.
Identifiers: LCCN 2022043805 | ISBN 9780813196916 (hardcover) | ISBN
    9780813196923 (pdf) | ISBN 9780813196930 (epub)
Subjects: LCSH: African Americans—Study and teaching (Higher) | African
    Americans—History.
Classification: LCC E184.7 .J28 2023 | DDC 973/.0496073—dc23/eng/20220915
LC record available at https://lccn.loc.gov/2022043805

Member of the Association
of University Presses

This volume is dedicated to my wife (BJ)
as well as the millions of people of color
who continue to persevere during these troubled times.

Contents

Preface

On February 20, 2012, Florida resident George Zimmerman shot and killed an unarmed Black seventeen-year-old, Trayvon Martin, claiming that he felt threatened. Even before Zimmerman was acquitted at trial, activists were concerned about how Martin's death was handled by the local police department, especially the delayed reporting of the crime and the resultant delayed notification of Martin's parents. The tragedy provoked outrage, not just over Martin's death but over a past whose effects, both covert and overt, are yet to be fully addressed. It also prompted organized action to address racism and inequality in the United States in the form of the Black Lives Matter movement. The movement first became nationally recognized for the street demonstrations it organized in 2014 following the deaths of Michael Brown in Ferguson, Missouri, and Eric Garner in New York City. Initially organized by Alicia Garza, Patrisse McCullors, and Opal Tometi as a hashtag call to action, the movement involved informal, peaceful, local protests to bring about cultural change, particularly police reform. A few nonprofit organizations formally adopted the Black Lives Matter slogan and operated under the name. But, by the time of the murder of George Floyd by a Minneapolis police officer on May 25, 2020, racial tensions in the United States had risen to a new level, and Black Lives Matter had grown into one of the largest decentralized protest movements in US history.

In the wake of all this upheaval, fresh legs were given to the concept of critical race theory, a social theory developed in the post–civil rights era that seeks to demonstrate how racist attitudes and unjust laws have served as the foundation of behavior, policy, and power structures in the United States and how deeply these systemic problems are rooted in society. Some of its pioneering scholars are Kimberlé Crenshaw and the late Derrick Bell. Critical race theory also provides a framework for the 1619 Project, a prize-winning series of articles seeking to recontextualize slavery as central to the history of the United States. The project originated when Nikole Hannah-Jones and other journalists collaborated on several pieces for the *New York Times* and the *New York Times Magazine* in August 2019, the four hundredth anniversary of the arrival of enslaved Africans at Jamestown, Virginia. In short, the 1619 Project argues that the establishment of the United States served the purpose of protecting the institution of slavery—and, indeed, that the very existence of the United States depended on slavery. On this view, the nation's history began not in 1776, but in 1619.

Many of the ideas embraced by the Black Lives Matter movement, by proponents of critical race theory, and by contributors to the 1619 Project first emerged in the 1960s and 1970s, during the early years of the Black studies movement, if not earlier. *An Introduction to Black Studies* aims to trace the history of such ideas and the role they played in empowering African Americans to challenge the status quo and fight for the rights that other Americans take for granted.

1

The Nature, Scope, and Construction of Black Studies

Born in Chicago on January 14, 1927, Nathan Irvin Huggins was the son of an African American father, Winston J. Huggins, a waiter and railroad worker, and a Jewish mother, Marie Warsaw. When Winston left the family, Marie moved twelve-year-old Nathan and his sister to San Francisco, California, but died two years later. Having been left in charge, Nathan divided his time between school and work, taking jobs as a longshoreman, a porter, and a warehouseman. He was drafted at the age of eighteen, near the end of World War II, but saw little action. While in the service, however, he managed to finish high school, and at the war's end, he enrolled at the University of California, Berkeley, under the GI Bill.

At Berkeley, Huggins studied with the renowned historian Kenneth M. Stampp, focusing on African American history, particularly the experience of slavery and its aftermath, following Stampp in taking a revisionist approach to American history. After graduating from Berkeley in 1954 with a bachelor's degree, he enrolled at Harvard University, becoming one of the very few African Americans to pursue a doctorate in history at a predominantly White institution of higher education. Because few colleges and universities recognized African American history as a legitimate field of inquiry, he worked hard to establish himself, not as an African American historian, but as a historian pure and simple. Therefore, working with the Pulitzer Prize–winning historian Oscar Handlin, he wrote his dissertation on the influence of Protestant ethics and values on charity organizations in Boston in the nineteenth century, receiving his doctorate in 1962.

After leaving Harvard, Huggins taught at California State College at Long Beach, Lake Forest College, the University of Massachusetts at Boston, and Columbia University, publishing two important books during this time. The first, *Harlem Renaissance* (1971), was an intellectual and cultural history of Harlem's arts movement during the 1920s and early 1930s. The second, *Black Odyssey: The Afro-American Ordeal in*

Slavery (1977), assessed the impact of the Middle Passage as well as that of slavery on both enslaved people and enslavers. In 1980, Huggins joined the Harvard faculty as the W. E. B. Du Bois Professor of History and Afro-American Studies and the first permanent director of the university's W. E. B. Du Bois Institute for Afro-American Studies.

Although he appreciated the singularity and power of African American history, Huggins rejected the approach to African American studies that tied academic work to community activism, thus reducing the discipline to a therapeutic search for an exploitable past or the undergirding of a political agenda. Instead, he viewed African American history as intertwined with American history generally, a central part of the American experience. Thus, during his time at the Du Bois Institute, he sought to establish the legitimacy and intellectual respectability of the discipline of Black studies. In the end, he concluded that the American experience and African American experience were one and the same. This perspective helped Huggins achieve a number of personal and professional firsts for a person of color in the field of history. For example, he served on the Program Committee and the Executive Board of the Organization of American Historians and on the editorial boards of the *Journal of American History*, the *American Historical Review*, and the *Journal of Ethnic History*. Huggins died on December 5, 1989.

Patterns of Black Studies Ideologies

The push for Black studies programs was part of a larger reform movement led by students on campuses nationwide during the modern civil rights movement of the 1950s and 1960s. (The civil rights movement in the United States—the decades-long campaign to end institutionalized discrimination, disenfranchisement, and segregation based on race—can be broken down into three periods: 1865–1896 [the Reconstruction and post-Reconstruction eras], 1896–1954 [the Jim Crow era], and 1954–1968 [the period from *Brown v. Board of Education,* the landmark Supreme Court decision declaring racial segregation in public schools to be illegal, to the Fair Housing Act of 1968, which banned discrimination in the sale or rental of housing]. When this text discusses the *civil rights movement,* the third period is meant unless otherwise indicated.) Black students seized on this movement because they sensed that change was in the air, focusing specifically on race relations. The

Black studies movement emerged within this environment. However, the movement was not a monolith. Those involved held many different views about how Black studies programs should be organized and run, but they can be characterized as falling into three general groups: integrationists, Black Power separatists, and cultural nationalist separatists.

While all three groups agreed that more courses examining the African American experience were needed, integrationists rejected the argument that Black studies programs should be separate, autonomous institutions, whether inside or outside the academy. For starters, they believed that few White faculty and administrators were racist and that they would therefore treat their Black students and colleagues fairly. They also felt it to be imperative that Black students learn to operate within the existing social system despite its flaws. Isolation within the academy would result in an academic ghetto, a situation that would benefit no one, allowing White faculty and administrators to dismiss their Black students' and colleagues' academic endeavors, and depriving Black students of the training and credentials necessary to function in any institutional setting. Separatism was seen as self-defeating.

Integrationists therefore felt that Black studies courses should be offered, not as a separate program of study, but scattered throughout the general college or university curriculum, as were other interdisciplinary programs, and overseen by faculty from a variety of programs and departments. They also felt that those courses should not be taught only by Black faculty. Yes, the African American experience was unique and would bring a useful perspective to the classroom, but it was not the only useful perspective.

Integrationists—students and faculty alike—were not troubled by what segregationists saw as their alienation from the Black community generally as they did not see academic and professional success as a rejection of a Black American identity. In fact, they saw too close an association with segregated programs and institutions as a hindrance to that success. They preferred to maintain their independence and to have both White and Black friends. Unfortunately, during the 1950s and 1960s, the state of race relations—which had never been good—became worse, making holding an integrationist position increasingly difficult.

The Black Power movement of the 1960s signaled an ideological and philosophical shift within the overall civil rights movement, especially the student-led faction. The voices of individuals such as the activists Stokely

Carmichael, H. Rap Brown, and Malcolm X and groups such as the Black Panther Party for Self-Defense became much louder and more potent during this time. This new position claimed that, by conforming to the demands of the predominantly White higher education institutions, Black Americans were allowing their values, strategies, and goals to be defined by their White allies and supporters and that Whites—even well-intentioned liberals—were opposed to the thought of power resting in the hands of African Americans. They would give Black Americans everything except for power and the self-respect that comes with it and abandon them whenever doing so was in their own interests. In allying themselves with Whites, Black Americans had denied themselves leadership opportunities, and the Black Power message was, therefore, one of separatism. Community building and race consciousness were seen as the essential first steps in the establishment of racial equality. Black Americans had to become economically and politically self-reliant before they could gain real power. Otherwise, they would always be dependent on White Americans.

The notion of self-reliance powered the push for autonomous Black studies programs. It all came down to the question of independence. Would a higher education institution give a Black studies program the independence it needed to thrive? The notion of self-reliance also led to the demand for separate Black dormitories, student centers, libraries, and so on. Such structures were seen as essential if students of African descent were to come together as one. From the Black Power perspective, Black Americans had the right, the ability, and the obligation to create their own academic structures on their own terms, just as White Americans had always done.

Black Power separatists worked within the existing system. That is, they believed that it was possible to negotiate with White Americans when it came to power relationships. Cultural nationalist separatists did not. Instead, they took community building—both inside and outside the university setting—even further and worked toward the establishment of two permanent and separate nations and cultures within the nation, one Black and one White.

Overview of the Field of Black Studies

The field of Black studies explores the past and present experiences, characteristics, accomplishments, issues, and problems of people of color living in the United States whose family history traces back to Africa, as well as their ancestral culture. It also focuses on what distinguishes those of African descent from other Americans and how they relate to other Americans. In other words, Black studies is a concentrated analysis of the factors and conditions that have shaped African Americans and the African diaspora. It is especially concerned with the development of new approaches to and tools with which to study the experiences of people of African descent. The end goal is to inform the creation of social policies and programs that will improve the lives of all Black Americans.

To understand the scope of Black studies, one has only to review the various titles that are currently used in the academy to identify it. Besides *Black studies,* some of the most common are *African American studies, Afro-American studies, African American and African studies, Africana studies,* and *Pan-African studies,* each giving a clue as to the difference in scope of the program in question. For example, the University of Cincinnati's Africana Department is described in its current handbook as "using a variety of approaches to explore and better understand the experiences of African, African American, Afro-Latin, Afro-Caribbean and Afro-European populations in a global context," its main objective being to empower students to "employ analytical tools from fields such as sociology, psychology, literature, anthropology, politics and history to explore important social issues facing people of African descent, from continental Africa and throughout the African Diasporas." A similar perspective can be found outlined in Alphonso Simpson's study *Mother to Son,* which the author states seeks to create a "supplement for those seeking to better understand the interdisciplinary scope of African American Studies" (p. xiv). In short, it can safely be said that the field of Black studies develops academically and pedagogically within a broad interdisciplinary framework, but it is essential that it focus primarily on eight major disciplines: history, sociology, psychology, religion, Black feminism, education, political science, and the arts.

To understand the purpose and rationale of Black studies, it is important to understand that the body of knowledge with which it is concerned has traditionally been excluded from the formal American education system, creating a lack of understanding and thus critical divisions between Black and White Americans that will persist as long as Black studies is kept out of the mainstream. Indeed, the current, hypersensitive state of race relations in the United States can arguably be attributed to the exclusion of this field, which seeks to challenge and correct the myriad distortions, stereotypes, and myths about people of African descent that have been and continue to be perpetuated in the American education system at the same time as it fills in the many gaps in knowledge about them and their communities. Black studies ultimately benefits all students, regardless of race or ethnicity.

Philosophical Framework

Black studies does not find its inspiration in classic European philosophy, much of which traditionally upheld the existence of a natural hierarchy among humankind: the lighter skinned at the top and the darker skinned at the bottom. Instead, it is Afrocentric. But it is not necessarily the study of Black philosophers. Rather, it is the study of the experience of people of African descent living in a hostile, oppressive environment and of how, from that experience, those people have created a group identity. By providing the appropriate intellectual framework, one that recognizes how social position affects public perception, Black studies validates that identity.

Historically, there never has been a unified African American philosophical or intellectual tradition to which all people of color have subscribed. Different life experiences have led to the articulation of different philosophical positions (Black Power, Black nationalism, voluntary segregation, etc.). Black studies seeks to contextualize these positions properly in order to understand them better. To that end, it takes into consideration the thought and work of anyone—regardless of race/ethnicity or national origin—whose goal is the edification, uplifting, and emancipation of Americans of African descent.

Such philosophical positions—preoccupied as they are with power relationships, social mobility, and economic wealth and, thus, protest, survival, and liberation—have until recently, however, been largely dismissed by the academic community in general as irrelevant because politically based. As a result, the experience of people of African descent rarely figures in the discourse on American political and social theory. Black studies means to reclaim that experience. Its subjects may not be—and often are not—formally educated. But the life, the work, the thought of Phillis Wheatley, Jupiter Hammons, and Harriet Jacobs is just as important as that of Frederick Douglass, Booker T. Washington, W. E. B. Du Bois, and Alain Locke if we are to understand the daily experience of African Americans.

Important Organizations

The 1970s and 1980s saw the consolidation and growth of Black studies programs, marked especially by the creation of national professional organizations that helped define the character and chart the course of the discipline. For example, the African Heritage Studies Association (AHSA) was founded in 1969 in the aftermath of 1964's Freedom Summer (also known as the Mississippi Summer Project, a voter registration drive) and the struggle of African American scholars generally during the 1960s. It emerged from a year-long discussion within the Black Caucus of the African Studies Association (ASA) of the lack of people of color in the organization's leadership positions. Those involved openly challenged the paternalistic assumptions embedded in the work of their White colleagues and decided to create a new, truly Afrocentric organization, one that would embrace the work of scholars of African descent and use that work to forge a connection between academic Black studies programs and Black communities generally. The AHSA also set out to create a research center for scholars of African descent worldwide, establish links with scholars in Africa through their home countries' embassies, and encourage full participation of all its members, both academic and lay scholars, in its annual conference. The first AHSA conference was held in Washington, DC, in June 1969. Under the leadership of its first president, the historian John Henrick Clark of the City University of New York, the organization launched several important initiatives, including a regular newsletter, a mentoring program for young faculty, the scholarly journal *African Heritage Studies,* and several international research projects. The organization continues to thrive today.

Another organization that emerged shortly after the AHSA and helped strengthen and promote the field of Black studies was the student-established and student-led National Council for Black Studies (NCBS). Founded in 1975, the NCBS has become the discipline's preeminent organization. Bertha Maxwell, the chair of the Department of Afro-American Studies at the University of North Carolina at Charlotte and the organization's first female president, called on African American scholars nationwide to participate in a dialogue on the most important issues faced by Black studies programs. The next year, the NCBS held a national conference, the deliberations of which yielded its two major objectives: the formalization of the study of the African/African American world experience and the expansion and strengthening of Black studies programs. The organization also continues to thrive today.

One last and very important organization that predates the AHSA and the NCBS by decades—though it is not normally associated with Black studies programs—is the Association for the Study of African American Life and History (ASALH). Founded in 1915 under the leadership of the historian Carter G. Woodson in response to the lack of attention paid to the accomplishments, history, and plight of people of African descent not just in the United States but globally, the ASALH was designed as a research and publishing outlet for scholars of African descent. It established the scholarly *Journal of Negro History* in 1916 and the *Negro History Bulletin* (a monthly bulletin for mostly elementary and high school teachers) in 1937, both of which gained public support nationwide. (The former became the *Journal of African American History* in 2001 and continues to be published today.) In 1926, the organization declared the second week of February to be Negro History Week—the week was chosen because it coincided with the birthdays of Frederick Douglass and Abraham Lincoln—a celebration that, in 1976, became Black History Month. Today, the ASALH continues, according to its website (asalh.org), to "promote, research, preserve, interpret and disseminate information about Black life, history, and culture to the global community."

Conclusion

One of the problems facing the early proponents of an Afro-centered Black studies movement was the development of new research paradigms. Those involved were convinced that the dominant and supposedly value-neutral and unbiased research methodology employed at that point by scholars generally was based on the norms of White, middle-class society and, thus, involved racist assumptions that invalidated its application to the issues on which Black studies was meant to focus. In order to bring about social, economic, and political change in the lives of people of color, the status quo was rejected, at least by those scholars who did not see the goal of Black studies as assimilation. And new paradigms had to take account of both the commonalities and the differences among the various communities of people of color, locally, regionally, nationally, and internationally. Thus, innovation has, as we will see, always been welcomed in the Black studies community.

Black studies programs in their many forms have over the years established themselves as vibrant and vital parts of both the academy and the African American community generally. For the most part, they concentrate on history, culture, and the arts (and rarely on the sciences). And because they rarely constitute entire academic departments, the faculty teaching in them must be cherry-picked from more traditional departments, so the programs are usually offered only at the undergraduate level. Still, the 1980s saw the rise of a number of Black studies doctoral programs, spurred by increased interest in Afrocentricity and Black feminism.

The result of these developments has already been a significant dismantling of myths and stereotypes about people of African descent worldwide. Most notably, the discourse on slavery has been forever changed. Led by scholars such as Molefi K. Asante and Angela Y. Davis, the field of Black studies will no doubt remain relevant as it continues to develop.

2

The Origin and Development of Black Studies as a Field of Analysis

Born on April 9, 1933, Nathan Hare spent his early years on a sharecropper's farm near the Creek County, Oklahoma, town of Slick, where he attended the segregated L'Ouverture Elementary School. When he was eleven, his mother (a single parent) moved her family (Nathan was one of five children) to San Diego, where she obtained a job as a civilian janitor at the local naval base. Once World War II ended, however, her job was eliminated, and the family moved back to Oklahoma, this time to McAlester, where Nathan attended L'Ouverture High School, also segregated.

While Nathan had aspired to become a professional boxer and, thus, put to use the skills he had acquired on the streets of San Diego, the return to Oklahoma put an end to that dream. But then, thanks to the result of a standardized test in English composition, he was chosen to represent his high school class at the statewide "interscholastic meet" of Black students held annually at Langston University, a historically Black college located in nearby Langston, Oklahoma. After winning first place in the competition, he set his sights on enrolling at Langston after high school. During his years there, he studied under Melvin B. Tolson, a celebrated poet whose teaching style was portrayed in the 2007 Denzel Washington film *The Great Debaters*. But, ultimately, he obtained his undergraduate degree in sociology and went on to receive his master's and doctorate in sociology from the University of Chicago.

In 1961, Hare began his career as an assistant professor of sociology at Howard University in Washington, DC. (Among his most highly motivated and intelligent students there were Stokely Carmichael and Claude Brown, both of whom would go on to become key figures in the Black Power movement.) However, he was fired in 1967 after a strident letter in which he was highly critical of the then university president James

Nabrit's plan to increase the non–African American student population to 60 percent over the next few years appeared in *The Hilltop,* Howard's student newspaper. In 1968, he joined the faculty at San Francisco State College (now known as San Francisco State University) and subsequently became the program coordinator and director of the university's Black studies program, the first of its kind in the nation. As a result, he is considered by many scholars to be the father of Black studies.

In this new role, Hare coined the term *ethnic studies* to replace *minority studies.* But, as a result of numerous academic and administrative battles in which he became embroiled, he left the university in 1969. Looking for a venue in which to express his views on racial issues, he established *The Black Scholar: A Journal of Black Studies and Research* and served as one of its principal editors. Also in 1969, he published "Questions and Answers about Black Studies," an article outlining the "two phases" into which he thought a Black studies program should be divided. First came the "expressive phase," emphasizing ways in which to build a sense of pride and self-worth in young Black Americans. That was followed by the "pragmatic phase," which would, through courses in such disciplines as political science, economics, science, and communications, develop in students the skills with which to deal with the racist society in which they lived.

In 1975, Hare left *The Black Scholar* and pursued a second doctorate, this time in clinical psychology. He subsequently opened a private practice as a clinical psychologist. In 1979, he went into private practice in San Francisco and, with his wife, Julia Hare, founded the Black Think Tank, which was meant to address the various problems plaguing the African American community at the local, regional, and national levels. During the next several years of his career, Hare served as a consultant and lecturer. He also authored several books, such as *The Black Anglo Saxons* (1965) and, with his wife, *The Endangered Black Family* (1984) and *The Miseducation of the Black Child* (1991), and received a number of prestigious awards, including the Joseph Hines Award for Distinguished Scholarship from the National Association of Black Sociologists, the Scholar of the Year Award from the Association of African Historians, the Lifetime Achievement Award from the National Black College Alumni Hall of Fame, and the National Council for Black Studies National Award. Even now he continues his work with his private practice and the Black Think Tank.

Learning Objectives

▼ ▼ ▼

1. Why were the early pioneers of the field of Black studies so important?
2. What role did the modern civil rights movement play in the development of the field of Black studies?
3. What factors motivated college students to become involved in the Black studies movement?
4. How were Black studies programs institutionalized in the academy?
5. How did the development of Black studies programs reflect a change in the nation's university education system?
6. What are the most important concepts and approaches within the field of Black studies?
7. What factors led to changes in the names of some Black studies programs?
8. What are some of the preeminent academic Black studies organizations today?
9. What is the current state of Black studies as a field of inquiry?

▲ ▲ ▲

Early Black Studies Scholars

Black studies rests on the cultural and historical experiences of people of African descent in the United States. Nevertheless, there never has been and still does not exist one unified African American worldview. Different experiences have prompted different philosophical responses. The field of Black studies seeks to examine and clarify these responses, whether the "philosophers" in question are intellectuals, artists, activists, or ordinary people. In fact, some of the most important responses come from people with little or no formal education and date back to the eighteenth century, if not earlier. What ties them all together is that they were formulated within an independent, African-centered perspective.

Consider, for example, Phillis Wheatley. Born in Senegal (around 1753), and brought to the British North American colonies at the age of eight, Wheatley was forced to learn a new language, embrace a new religion, and adopt an entirely new way of life, an experience of cultural disruption common among people of African descent at that time. Nevertheless, she adapted quickly and went on to become the first published African American writer in the United States. More importantly, her work—particularly during the American Revolution—embraced her Africanist views on religious and community life and political ideology, thereby establishing the foundation on which other African Americans, especially Black American women, would build in later decades.

Harriet Jacobs was another such example. In her 1861 autobiography *Incidents in the Life of a Slave Girl: Written by Herself*, Jacobs, born into slavery in Edenton, North Carolina, in 1813, discusses how the experience of slavery, horrific in general, was far worse for Black women than it was for Black men. Both men and women had to endure the continuous daily oppression and lack of control of their own bodies that a lifetime of bondage brought with it. But women also had no control over their own reproductive life and the destiny of their children. Speaking for the thousands of enslaved women living in the United States, Jacobs proclaimed that, for the "slave girl," there was "no shadow of law to protect her from insult, from violence, or even from death" (p. 19).

In 1832, Maria W. Stewart, a free Black woman from Connecticut with abolitionist, feminist, and religious convictions, delivered a series of lectures in Boston. The first took place at the African-American Female Intelligence Society. She was likely the first Black American woman to speak in public about the civil and political rights of women. In this and subsequent lectures, she discussed issues relevant to the African American community: for example, abolition, education, economic empowerment, racial solidarity, and self-help. But she was at her most powerful when she was exhorting Black women to abandon their socially assigned gender roles and actualize their potential by acquiring a formal education and then pursuing careers outside the home.

Another important figure who emerged during this time period was Ida B. Wells-Barnett, a dedicated advocate of African American civil rights, women's rights, and economic rights. Born into slavery on July 16, 1862, in Holly Springs, Mississippi, Wells-Barnett was the oldest of Jim Wells and Lizzie Warrenton's eight children. When, in 1878, a yellow fever epidemic swept through Holly Springs and took Jim and Lizzie as well as their nine-month old son, Stanley, sixteen-year-old Ida took on the responsibility of caring for her surviving siblings. Eventually, after training at Shaw University, she passed the local teacher's exam and in 1878 was hired by the local school, earning $25.00 a month. Then in 1881 she moved to Memphis with two of her younger sisters and secured a teaching job in the Shelby County school district. Once settled in Memphis, Wells became a community activist. She contributed articles to such national newspapers as the *New York Age* and the *Indianapolis World* as well as writing for her own periodical, *Free Speech.* The topics she addressed included the substandard living conditions of and poor educations received by most African Americans, how lynching was simply a racist tactic meant to maintain White supremacy, and how the right to vote was the key to economic, social, and political equality for Blacks generally and Black women in particular.

Both echoing and building on the work of Wells was Anna Julia Cooper. Born into slavery on August 10, 1858, in Raleigh, North Carolina, Annie Julia Haywood attended the Saint Augustine Normal School and Collegiate Institute. (It is not known when she graduated, but she enrolled in 1868.) She next attended Oberlin College, earning a bachelor's degree in 1884 and a master's in 1887, and then the Sorbonne in Paris, earning a doctorate in 1925. While at Oberlin, Cooper began to see herself as an advocate for race and gender equality. However, it was the publication in 1892 of *A Voice from the South,* the first book on the subject of African American feminist thought, that made her one of the most influential writers and speakers on the experience of Black women in America. By 1900, when she addressed the Pan-African Conference in London, she had become an international figure. Cooper consistently expounded Black feminist ideas in her speeches and writings, especially the notion that Black women should and must play an important and unique role in uplifting the entire race, declaring in *A Voice from the South:* "Only the Black Woman can say when and where I enter, in the quiet, undisputed dignity of my womanhood, without violence and without suing or special patronage" (p. 31).

There was also during the antebellum years a cadre of African American men whose work complemented that of activist women. One such example is Martin R. Delany, born in 1812 in Chambersburg, Pennsylvania, the son of a free mother and an enslaved father. In his work, Delany targeted the expanding Black middle class, proclaiming that education, self-help, racial solidarity, racial equality, and race pride were goals ordained by God, and linking them with the concepts of cultural preservation and liberation found

Stereograph showing a crowd of African American students on the lawn of Howard University near Miner Hall. (Photo by J. W. and John S. Moulton, published between 1867 and 1920. Courtesy of the Library of Congress: LC-DIG-stereo-1s07887.)

in his Christian faith. In his most important work, the 1852 *The Condition, Elevation, Emigration, and Destiny of the Colored People of the United States, Politically Considered,* he contended that all African Americans must "become elevated men and women, worthy of freedom" (p. 3).

Another example is David Walker, best known for the 1830 pamphlet *An Appeal in Four Articles; Together with a Preamble, to the Coloured Citizens of the World, but in Particular, and Very Expressly, to Those of the United States of America.* Born to free parents in Wilmington, Ohio, in 1785, Walker moved to Boston in 1827, where, outraged by the evils of slavery, he quickly became a well-known orator and also contributed to the first African American newspaper, *Freedom's Journal.* He urged Black Americans to use various tactics, including both violent and nonviolent resistance, to obtain their freedom. Specifically, as he noted in the *Appeal,* as Christians, enslaved African Americans should first try moral persuasion, but, if that did not work, more violent methods were justified.

During this same period, on a seemingly ordinary day in 1838, Frederick Douglass—born into slavery as Frederick Augustus Washington Bailey in February 1817 or 1818 in Talbot, Maryland—escaped the Baltimore, Maryland, plantation where he was living at the time, fleeing north. Once free, Douglass, who had taught himself how to read and write, continued the process of self-education, joined a local African American church, and began attending abolitionist meetings. At one such meeting, he met William Lloyd Garrison, the prominent abolitionist and publisher of the weekly anti-slavery newspaper the *Liberator*. The two men soon became good friends and worked closely together to bring about the abolition of slavery. Encouraged by Garrison, Douglass gave one of his first antislavery speeches at the Massachusetts Anti-Slavery Society's annual convention in Nantucket in late 1841. He eventually grew into one of the most powerful and influential speakers of the nineteenth century, always championing racial and gender equality.

Black Studies and the Modern Civil Rights Movement

Black studies developed as a self-conscious, organized, university-based academic field within the context of the 1960s civil rights movement and intellectual practices rooted in the social visions and struggles of the period. But, while it developed a uniquely twentieth-century self-awareness both as an area of intellectual study and as an instrument for social change, central to its concerns is the tradition of activism that, as we have seen, dates back at least to the nineteenth century. This lineage is evident in the three main focal points of Black studies as we know it today: cultural relevance, academic excellence, and social responsibility. Still, equally important is the mid-twentieth-century experience of African Americans.

In the run-up to World War II, the rise in fascism and racism in Europe alarmed not just African Americans but also progressive Whites, who viewed fascism as antipathetic to democracy and the individual freedoms it brought with it. Thus, the quest for racial justice became an integral part of the general struggle for economic, political, and social progress in the wake of the Great Depression. For example, President Franklin D. Roosevelt's 1941 Executive Order 8802, which prohibited ethnic or racial discrimination in the nation's defense industry, and the subsequent creation of the Fair Employment Practices Committee, represented a significant victory for the Black American working class.

As radical as the wartime-era changes seemed, the social retrenchment in the United States that followed victory in Europe and the Pacific resulted in a climate that was, oddly, both hospitable and hostile to the notion of civil rights. Radicals such as Paul Robeson and W. E. B. Du Bois found themselves ostracized, and only more moderate individuals and organizations were able to pursue the goal of racial equality within the ideological and legal context of the American political system. They met with some success (e.g., the *Brown v. Board of Education* decision in 1954). However, racism and even segregationist practices persisted (especially in the South), spurring such important actions as the 1955 Montgomery bus boycott, the 1960 sit-ins, the Freedom Rides of 1961, and the 1963 March on Washington. These and similar events ultimately forced the hand of the federal government, which, beginning in 1964, enacted a series of important civil rights acts prohibiting discrimination on the basis of race, color, religion, sex, or national origin.

Ultimately, however, what allowed Black studies to take root was the Black Power movement, which developed in the wake of the harsh brutality and urban violence of Freedom Summer. The Black Power movement reframed the discourse around power relations and the position of people of African descent, positing racism as the defining feature of American society. Its proponents argued for self-determination, cultural relevance, quality public education, and real economic opportunities for all African Americans.

One of the first Black studies initiatives to emerge was organized in 1966 by African American students at San Francisco State College (known today as San Francisco State University). The program—organized, as we have seen, by Nathan Hare—offered a number of experimental courses and also involved community service. But the university's board of regents at first declined to recognize it as an official department, doing so only after the Third World Liberation Front, a coalition of minority student groups calling for campus reform, mounted a campuswide protest. Soon, similar programs began to materialize on campuses nationwide.

The Precursors of the 1960s Black Studies Scholars

Alongside Phillis Wheatley, Harriet Jacobs, and the other figures discussed earlier there were also scholarly precursors who questioned the prevailing racism of the nineteenth and twentieth centuries. The most significant of these academics was W. E. B. Du Bois. Du Bois was born in Great Barrington, Massachusetts, on February 23, 1868, obtained a bachelor's degree from Fisk University, and then went on to earn a second bachelor's as well as a doctorate from Harvard University, the first African American to do so. He worked for several years as a professor of Latin and Greek at Wilberforce College in Ohio and at the University of Pennsylvania. He also held the position of professor of economics and history at Atlanta University for many years. Overall, his meticulous research and well-written studies—the best known of these being *The Philadelphia Negro* (1899), *The Souls of Black Folk* (1903), *Black Folk: Then and Now* (1939), and *The World and Africa* (1946)—set the standard for future Black studies scholarship. But other scholars also made significant contributions.

One such figure was Carter G. Woodson. Born in 1875 in Buckingham County, Virginia, Woodson was the son of a sharecropper born into slavery in Virginia. Although the Woodson family was extremely poor, the Woodson children were taught to value education. And, even though when he was seventeen Carter followed his older brothers to West Virginia to work in the mines, three years later he moved back into his parents' home in Huntington, Virginia, where he entered Frederick Douglass High School and graduated in only two years. Subsequently, he earned a bachelor's degree from Berea College in Berea, Kentucky, bachelor's and master's degrees from the University of Chicago, and, in 1912, a doctorate in history from Harvard University, all while teaching full-time. In 1915, Woodson published his first book, *The Education of the Negro prior to 1861.* In September of the same year, he founded the Association for the Study of Negro Life and History in the belief that education was an important catalyst of social change.

Woodson's most influential contemporaries were a pair of progressive White scholars, the sociologist Robert Park and the anthropologist Franz Boas. Park was among the first to teach courses about African Americans at a predominantly White university, and Boas continuously challenged the prevailing notion of White supremacy. Park, at the University of Chicago, and Boas, at Columbia University, trained a generation of scholars who would make influential contributions to the field of Black studies. These included the notable African American sociologists Charles S. Johnson, E. Franklin Frazier, and Horace Cayton, the writer Zora Neale Hurston, and the anthropologist Elsie Clews Parsons. By the mid-twentieth century, interest in the nascent field of Black studies began to increase, and both African American and White scholars began to investigate the multiple facets of African American life more vigorously and objectively. The important scholarly works produced during this period included Melville Herskovits's *The Myth of the Negro Past* (1941), Gunnar Myrdal's *An American Dilemma* (1944), and St. Clair Drake and Horace Cayton's *Black Metropolis* (1945), but equally important were Richard Wright's novel *Native Son* (1940) and John Hope Franklin and Evelyn Brooks Higginbotham's classic textbook *From Slavery to Freedom* (1947), a book that remains in print and is still used today.

From Outsider to Institution

The growth of Black studies programs in the late 1960s was a product of three cultural trends. The first of these was the increasing number of African American students attending predominantly White colleges and universities in lieu of the historically Black colleges and universities (HBCUs). The second was the fact that, responding to changes in prevailing social attitudes about race relations, many predominantly White higher education institutions intentionally began to incorporate the study of Black Americans into their curricula. The third was the growing strength of the notion of Black Power (or Black consciousness) within the larger civil rights movement. This led to the radicalization of increasing numbers of African Americans, both within and outside the movement, who began to recognize that most academic institutions disregarded their values and cultural norms, the study of which would aid their understanding of their own, individual identities and possibly bring about needed social change in the process. The City College of New York and Kent State University in Ohio offer two examples of the effects of such radicalization.

On June 28, 1968, after a massive demonstration at the City College of New York (CCNY) led by students and community leaders calling for the development of a more relevant curriculum, the college's administration submitted a proposal to the Board of Higher Education of the City of New York for the creation of an urban and ethnic studies program, seeking to avoid the violent protests that had broken out on campuses nationwide. An ad hoc committee was then appointed to draft a plan for the development of the program in accordance with the recommendations of the school's faculty senate, a plan that was quickly approved. But that program not only had an urban studies emphasis. It was also meant to cover all ethnic and minority groups in New York and was, thus, clearly unworkable, as soon became apparent.

Enter Leonard Jeffries, who joined the CCNY faculty in 1972 only to discover that the program the university had set in motion was in disarray. Jeffries, who had graduated from Columbia University with a degree in political science and had been greatly involved in the development of Black studies programs throughout New York State (and who was a founding member of the Black studies program at San Jose State University in California), had one clear objective in mind: making Black studies a stand-alone department at CCNY and, in the process, one of the leading Black studies departments in the country. The newly constituted Black studies department that Jeffries established had as its goal articulating—in intellectually valid and also constructive terms—the complex life experience of people of African descent, not just in America but also in the diaspora. Under his leadership, the department attracted some of the most prominent Black studies scholars in the country, and, with the addition to the faculty, the program experienced enormous growth in terms of both numbers of students enrolled and variety of courses offered.

Compare the situation at Kent State University, where the Deacons of Defense and Justice—an armed group formed in 1964 to protect civil rights workers from racist attacks—inspired a group of students to organize the activist group Black United Students (BUS) in the spring of 1968. At the same time, recruiters from the Oakland Police Department appeared on campus. Further moved by the assassinations of Medgar Evers, Malcolm X, and Martin Luther King Jr., Black students were spurred to action. A student walkout was organized in November 1968, the result of which was 58 percent of the university's African American students leaving campus and setting up their own university in the nearby Black American community of Akron. They returned to Kent State only when their demands were met, the most important of which was the creation of an autonomous Black studies institute. In the spring of 1970, the Institute for African American Affairs offered its first courses.

Many new Black studies programs were developed through the early 1970s, but not all survived their first year or two because of issues such as the casualties of the period's economic uncertainty: faculty turnover, budget cuts, and downsizing. During the late 1960s and early 1970s, few Black studies programs were well thought through. Most simply drew on whatever faculty were available (and willing) and could be retained—often part-time or temporary instructors—and the courses they brought with them, and the resulting curricula were not always coherent. Further complicating matters was, first, that most programs focused on history, culture, and the arts—the sciences were rarely included—and, second, that those individuals who were available were usually artists (musicians, dancers, writers). This lack of uniformity meant that there was no one, proven model on which fledgling programs could draw.

Also problematic was the fact that not all Black faculty were supportive of efforts to develop Black studies programs. While they did not actively oppose them, their silence on the topic spoke volumes. Thus, it was primarily up Black students themselves to push the faculty and administrators of their predominantly White institutions to establish Black studies programs.

The Current State of Black Studies Programs

Since the early 1970s, most Black studies programs have developed in one of three ways: as self-contained undergraduate programs, as self-contained graduate programs, or as academic or administrative organizations whose goal is to advance the field of Black studies by expanding the field of inquiry. All three developments are responses to the obstacles that the academy has traditionally placed in the way of Black students and the study of the African American experience. And all three therefore have as their goal autonomy.

The creation and maintenance of Black studies programs proceeded slowly but steadily, newer programs learning from both the successes and the failures of earlier programs. And it soon became apparent that one key to success was that programs rest on a Black perspective. This did not mean that the people who taught Black studies courses had to be of African descent (a popular misconception); it meant simply that they had to understand and appreciate the African American perspective. The first self-contained graduate program was the doctoral program at Temple University, established in 1988. Several years later, the University of California, Berkeley, and the University of Massachusetts Amherst created doctoral programs in Black studies. The first Black studies research institutes were developed in the late 1960s—for example, at Kent State in 1969—initially embedded within already-established institutions. Many such centers are in operation today and are based at such institutions as Columbia, the University of Michigan, and the University of California, Los Angeles.

Some Current Concepts and Approaches in the Field of Black Studies

From its inception, the primary purpose of the field of Black studies has been twofold: preserving African American culture and promoting the welfare of African American communities. But Black studies programs cannot focus solely on the Black experience in America. If they did, they would become studies in victimization benefiting no one. They must also take into consideration the larger, dominant society, within which social and political change must be brought about if the position of Black Americans is to be improved. And they must also take into consideration and learn from oppressed peoples and liberation movements worldwide. And the goal of promoting the welfare of African Americans also involves enhancing the professional, scientific, and technical skills of people of color, allowing them to tackle on their own the problems facing their communities.

Over the years, a number of ideological and philosophical frameworks have been developed in furtherance of these ends. One such example is Kawaida, developed by Maulana Karenga. Born Ronald McKinley Everett on a farm in Parsonsburg, Maryland, on July 14, 1941, Karenga was the youngest of fourteen children born to the Baptist minister Levi Everett and his wife, Addie. Young Ronald excelled academically, by 1964 earning bachelor's and master's degrees in political science and African studies from the University of California, Los Angeles, where he fell under the influence of Malcolm X. While he began a doctoral program at UCLA in 1965, he stepped away from it when the Watts riots occurred that same year because he wanted to help rebuild the region. At the same time, he changed his name to Maulana (meaning "master teacher") Karenga (meaning "keeper of the tradition"). One year later, in 1966, he formed Organization Us, also known as the US Organization, a Black-nationalist group devoted to social change and educational reform. And it was during this time that he formulated the idea of Kawaida.

Kawaida, Karenga proclaimed in his book *Introduction to Black Studies,* was "an ongoing synthesis of the best of African thought and practice in constant exchange with the world" (p. 173). Central to the philosophy were the Seven Principles (or Nguzo Saba): Umoja (unity), Kujichagulia (self-determination), Ujima (collective work and responsibility), Ujamaa (cooperative economics), Nia (purpose), Kuumba (creativity), and Imani (faith). In general, these principles served as the basis for the African American and Pan-African holiday known as Kwanzaa, a weeklong celebration observed annually from December 26 to January 1. Karenga concluded that such an ideological and philosophical framework was needed because the cultural consciousness of African Americans had been enormously damaged over the centuries by the dominance of European society and must be restored.

Related to Kawaida is the concept of Afrocentricity, a more intellectual approach to the African American experience. Although Afrocentricity has existed in some form in the United States since the eighteenth century, it came into its own academically with Molefi K. Asante, who in *Afrocentricity* (1980) describes it as "a way of viewing and interpreting the universe from an African historical and cultural perspective" (p. 3). Asante was born on August 14, 1942, in Valdosta, Georgia, to Arthur Lee and Lillie B. Wilkson-Smith, the fourth of sixteen children. He earned an associate's degree from Southwestern Christian College in 1962, a bachelor's degree from Oklahoma Christian University in 1964, a master's degree from Pepperdine University in 1965, and a doctorate in communications from the University of California, Los Angeles, in 1968. While working as an assistant professor in the Department of Communications at Purdue University, he published (with Arthur L. Smith) *Rhetoric of Black Revolution* (1969) and was a founding editor of the *Journal of Black Studies.* He returned to UCLA, where he served as the first permanent director of the Center for Afro-American Studies and created the center's master's degree program. In *Afrocentricity*, Asante expounds his idea that Black studies must be viewed as an extension of African history and culture, beginning with the classical African civilizations.

The notion of Afrocentricity has always been controversial. In its simplest form, it is an academic and worldly perspective that contends that people of African descent should create and assert a sense of agency that is based in an African worldview. In its academic manifestation, where it appeared in nascent form in the work of W. E. B. Du Bois and Carter Woodson as early as the 1930s and 1940s, it is an attempt to look at information from a Black and not a White perspective. But recently it has been challenged by a small but influential group of White scholars—most prominently Martin Bernal and Mary Lefkowitz—who consider it coun-terproductive and racist at its core.

Black Studies vs. African American Studies vs. Africana Studies vs. Pan-African Studies

Black studies has always suffered from the imprecision of being characterized as *Black* studies. For starters, some proponents of the field viewed it as solely the study of American history and culture. But others sought to portray it as the systematic study of people of color not just in the United States but worldwide, and, to indicate this, a variety of names have been (and still are) employed. The idea was not simply to present African/African American–related material in courses with *African, African American, Afro-American,* or *Black* in their titles. Rather, it was also to dismantle the White, Eurocentric content areas that dominated the academy through the 1950s.

Other factors further muddied the waters. The terms *Black, Afro,* and *African* became in the 1960s essentially interchangeable, not just in the academy but also in the broader culture. (Many African American stu-dents began to call themselves and one another *brother* and *sister,* the Afro hairstyle was becoming very popular, the phrase *Black is beautiful* started to be used more regularly, and the notion of Black Power was being articu-lated more frequently by thousands of Black Americans and some of their White progressive supporters.) They also came to represent the past and present unity of people of color in the United States with people of color worldwide, not just in Africa. The end result was that early distinctions between Black studies, Afro-American studies, African American studies, and African studies programs—and later Africana studies and Pan-African studies programs—began to fall by the wayside.

Some Important Black Academic Organizations

Having been firmly established by the end of the 1960s, Black studies pro-grams strengthened their position and expanded their field of inquiry in the 1970s and 1980s. During this time, several developments determined both the course and the character of Black studies. One of the most important changes during this time was the creation of professional organizations.

As we have seen, the earliest was the African Heritage Studies Association (AHSA), which emerged in 1969 from an intense, year-long discussion within the Black Caucus of the African Studies Association (ASA), the goal being to develop a more directly African- and African American–led organization. At issue were the lack of people of color in ASA leadership positions and the openly dismissive and superior attitude some White scholars took in discussions of African history and culture. The envisioned new organization would focus on challenging the until now unquestioned assumptions of White colleagues; linking Black studies programs to African and African American communities locally, regionally, nationally, and internationally; creating a research center for all scholars of African descent; networking with Africanists worldwide; and encouraging the participation of both academic and lay scholars in its conferences. Following its formal establishment, the AHSA held its first conference in Washington, DC, in June 1969. Its first initiatives included launching a newsletter, the *ASA News*; two scholarly journals, *History in Africa: A Journal of Method* and *African Studies Review*; a mentoring program for young faculty; and several international research projects.

In 1975, six years after the AHSA was established, the National Council for Black Studies (NCBS) was founded. As discussed, its goal was to bring together African American scholars to participate in a dialogue about the issues faced by Black studies programs nationwide. Its first major conference, held in 1976, formulated two major objectives: to formalize the study of the African/African American world experience and to expand and strengthen academic and community Black studies programs, especially fledgling programs. The NCBS has since become the preeminent organization in the field of Black studies, to which it has given much-needed direction through national conferences, workshops, symposia, and community programs.

Another important organization—one that has not normally been associated with Black studies but that shares the discipline's research agenda and many of its objectives—was the Association for the Study of African American Life and History (ASALH). As discussed, the ASALH was founded in 1915 under the leadership of Carter G. Woodson in response to the lack of information on the history and accomplishments of people of African descent in the United States and globally as well as the challenges they have faced. In 1916 and 1937, respectively, it established the *Journal of Negro History* and the *Negro History Bulletin* as outlets for the publication of research focused on what would come to be known as *Black studies*. In 1926, it initiated the celebration of Negro History Week (as of 1976 Black History Month)—which was timed to honor the February birthdays of Frederick Douglass and Abraham Lincoln—now viewed as one of the most important aspects of Woodson's legacy. Today, the mission of the ASALH has expanded greatly, and the organization states its goal as follows: "to promote, research, preserve, interpret and disseminate information about Black life, history, and culture to the global community" (asalh.org).

Conclusion

By the middle of the 1970s, Black studies had proved to be a vibrant and vital field of inquiry, and Black studies programs had been firmly institution-alized at colleges and universities nationwide. Still, even today Black studies figures in higher education in the form of not departments but programs, the faculty teaching in them having appointments in more traditional departments, and those programs' target constituency continues to be mostly undergraduates. Nevertheless, some true Black studies departments have been established and are flourishing at some of the nation's most prestigious institutions. And, perhaps more importantly, scholarship about people of African descent has increased exponentially in the past fifty years, greatly expanding our knowledge base.

The years since the 1980s have seen important developments in the field of Black studies. One of the most significant of these was the rise of doctoral programs at some of our nation's most prestigious higher education institutions. Also important has been the rise of both Afrocentrism and Black feminism. The latter especially has challenged certain assumptions of traditional Black studies that were, it is alleged, based primarily on the insights and views of African American men. Consequently, some of the most perceptive work in Black studies recently has been that of African American women bringing their unique and crucial historical and cultural perspective to bear on issues long thought settled, thereby ensuring the vitality and relevance of the field of Black studies for many generations to come.

3

The History of African Americans in the United States

From Enslavement to the Civil War

Lemuel Haynes, born July 18, 1753, to an African father and a Scottish mother, was raised as an enslaved person of color by John Haynes of Hartford, Connecticut, until he was five months old, when he was indentured to Deacon David Rose of Granville, Massachusetts. Rose was a farmer, but he was also a newly ordained Congregational minister. Thus, not only was Lemuel taught to read and write; he was also imbued with religious fervor. Haynes's ultimate goal was to join the clergy, but that goal was put on hold by the coming of the American Revolution.

Despite living in a frontier region—he stayed on with the Rose family even after his period of indentured servitude ended—Haynes could not escape the radical political ideas circulating in the colonies. Newspapers, pamphlets, and public speeches spread reports of developments in the impending conflict to even the most remote areas of the soon-to-be United States and, with them, the notions of freedom, equality, and natural rights underlying the revolt. Haynes was spurred to military service, joining first the minutemen of Massachusetts soon after the Battles of Lexington and Concord, next General George Washington's army during the 1775 attack on the city of Boston, and finally a regiment that fought in the 1775 Battle of Fort Ticonderoga. Indeed, these experiences had a profound impact on his political consciousness and philosophical makeup. All these experiences prompted a burst of literary activity.

In 1775, after returning from the Battle of Boston, Haynes wrote a political ballad titled "The Battle of Lexington," in which he proclaimed that the British colonies in North America had been corrupted, manipulated, and oppressed by the tyranny and self-centeredness of King George III and Parliament. More importantly, after returning from the Battle of Fort

Ticonderoga, he wrote the electrifying essay "Liberty Further Extended," in which he claimed that the "unalienable Rights" proclaimed by the Declaration of Independence—"Life, Liberty, and the pursuit of Happiness"—applied to all the colonies' citizens: "An African, or in other terms, . . . a Negro may Justly Chalenge [slavery], and has an undeniable right to his freedom and liberty" (quoted in Bogin, p. 95).

After the American Revolution ended, Haynes devoted the rest of his life to spreading the gospel throughout the new nation. He was ordained in 1785 and appointed to the first of his ministerial positions. His last post—which he accepted in 1822—was at the Granville Congregational Church in New York State, where he remained until his death in 1832.

Learning Objectives

▼ ▼ ▼

1. Why are ancient African civilizations important?
2. What were the Atlantic slave trade and the Middle Passage?
3. Who were the peoples of the North American colonies?
4. What did the American Revolution mean to African Americans?
5. What were the characteristics of early African American communities?
6. How did the massive increase in cotton production affect the lives of African Americans during the antebellum period?
7. What were the demographics and characteristics of the various African American communities during the antebellum years?
8. How did racism and violence affect the antislavery and abolition movements?
9. How did African Americans respond to the outbreak of the American Civil War?

▲ ▲ ▲

Setting the Stage

It is now generally accepted that early humans first evolved in Africa beginning about 6 million years ago and began migrating into first Asia and then

Europe beginning about 2 million years ago. While these facts were defin-
itively established only in the twentieth century, speculation to this effect
began in the nineteenth century, most importantly in Charles Darwin's 1871
The Descent of Man. Despite Darwin, however, most Europeans continued
to cling to the belief that Africans and their descendants constituted a separate, inferior race and that true human life had arisen in Germany, where
fossilized human remains had been discovered in 1856. Current scientific
thinking is that the species *Homo sapiens*—modern humans—evolved in
Africa between 120,000 and 160,000 years ago.

It is also generally accepted that one of the first great world civilizations
arose in North Africa when what we now know as ancient Egypt coalesced
around the upper reaches of the Nile River ca. 3100 BCE, the result being
a kingdom that survived for over three thousand years until it was conquered by Rome in 30 CE. European scholars have long maintained that
the Egyptians were not true Africans, that is, not Black, and that Egypt was
properly associated with Eurasia, not Africa. This position has, however, been
contested, most recently—and most famously—by the Cornell University
professor Martin Bernal. In his three-volume *Black Athena* (1987–2006),
Bernal claimed that White scholars have consistently downplayed and even
dismissed the role Black Africans played in the origin and development of
the ancient Greek civilization. And here he was talking about the Egyptians, asserting that, among other things, they invented mathematics and
philosophy and developed certain religious concepts, all of which laid the
foundation for classical Greek society and, by extension, Western society
in general. Bernal's ideas aroused such a strong response that, even before
the second volume of *Black Athena* appeared, the collection *Black Athena
Revisited,* edited by Mary R. Lefkowitz and Guy MacLean Rogers, which
debunked Bernal's ideas, was put in motion. Bernal's position is still not
generally accepted, but it does have antecedents.

As early as the eighteenth century, some scholars began to refer to
Egyptians as *Ethiopians,* thus identifying them as Black. By the nineteenth
century, Afrocentrists and Africanists were claiming that the Egyptian civ-
ilization had its origins in Ethiopia, that that country was the cradle of
civilization, and that Egypt had close ties to other African cultures as well.
In *The World and Africa,* for example, W. E. B. Du Bois contended: "In
Ethiopia the sunrise of human culture took place, spreading down into the
Nile Valley. Ethiopia, the land of the Blacks, was thus the cradle of Egyptian

civilization" (p. 170). By the 1870s, some historians of African America were even claiming that some Black Americans could trace their family lineage back to Egypt. Today, there still is a heated debate over whether ancient cultures thought in terms of race and ethnicity. This debate—epitomized by the question of whether Cleopatra, the last pharaoh, should be characterized as Black, White, or biracial—is ongoing, as is that about the influence that Egyptian culture actually had on Eurasian culture.

Given the persistent fascination with ancient Egypt, the many other African cultures and kingdoms that developed and flourished over the centuries tend to be overlooked. The Nubian kingdom known as Kush, for example, which was also centered on the Nile, developed roughly contemporaneously with Egypt and rivaled it in many respects. Much later—definitely by the eighth century CE and possibly as early as the fourth century CE—the Islamic kingdom of Ghana emerged in the western part of what is today Sudan, founded by the Soninke people. Ghana's kings were known across Europe and in parts of Asia, largely as a result of the important trading routes the kingdom controlled and its resulting wealth. Imports to Ghana included silk, cotton, glass, beads, horses, and salt; the country's exports included pepper, gold, and even enslaved people. The kingdom survived into the twelfth century, eventually brought down by internal political and religious conflict.

With Ghana on the decline in eastern North Africa, the empire of Mali, also Islamic, arose in West Africa, beginning probably in the eleventh century. Mali was larger than Ghana, stretching some fifteen hundred miles from the Atlantic coast to the Niger River, and at its height (1312–1337) controlling a population of some 8 million. Its wealth—greater than that of Ghana—was based on gold mining and, like Ghana's, trade. Its most important city was Timbuktu, established around the eleventh century along the Niger River. By the thirteenth century, Timbuktu had become a major outpost where gold, silver, salt, and enslaved people were traded. Mali survived—in diminished form—into the fifteenth century, its decline and eventual collapse, like Ghana's, the result of internal conflict. In the fifteenth century, the Islamic kingdom of Songhai arose in Mali's place, becoming at its peak (1549–1582) one of the largest states in African history. Songhai was, like Ghana and Mali before it, a great trading power, depending largely on gold, salt, ivory, and enslaved people. But, also like Ghana and Mali, it too gradually declined and eventually disappeared.

Common to all three societies was, as we have seen, slavery, which had been practiced in Africa since ancient times. But the system of human bondage that was practiced traditionally in Africa was different from that which prevailed after the continent was pulled into the developing trans-Atlantic slave trade. In order to understand that system, a review of the social and cultural practices that prevailed in West Africa before European merchants entered the scene is in order.

Life in West Africa was *lineage* (i.e., clan) based and centered on farming. Generally speaking, farm families collected in villages, self-sorting on the basis of lineage. A lineage could be either patrilineal or matrilineal (an ethnic difference). Polygamy was practiced in service primarily of the economic benefit of the whole, more than one husband or wife being seen as a way to generate more money for the nuclear family. The nuclear family existed only in the context of a broader community composed of grandparents, aunts, uncles, and cousins. In general, women were subordinate to men, even in matrilineal societies. However, West African women did enjoy a relative amount of autonomy and freedom, unlike Arab and European women. (In ancient Ghana, some women even held political office, and some women were able to inherit and own land.) Finally, although many West Africans lived in regions not organized as states, most were governed by a monarch who ruled by divine right. Although these monarchs did not have absolute power and authority, they did command the army, were able to tax commerce, and, thus, amassed enormous wealth. The various class systems that developed included as their component parts landed nobility, warriors, bureaucrats, blacksmiths, oral historians, peasants, and enslaved people. As for the latter, the system of human bondage was centered on those individuals (men, women, and children) captured in war and forced into slavery. Enslaved people became either servants in royal courts or soldiers. Thus, slavery functioned as a means of assimilation. Still, enslaved people were not dehumanized; that is, their value was more than purely economic. They were allowed to maintain family connections and, therefore, were able to retain their cultural traditions. It should also be noted that, before the involvement of the Europeans, there was no racial component to the slave trade.

The Atlantic Slave Trade and the Middle Passage

When the Portuguese first explored West Africa in the early fifteenth century, they were interested mainly in establishing bases in the region that would anchor oceanic trade routes to India and beyond. While in 1488 the Portuguese mariner Bartolomeu Dias was the first to sail around the Cape of Good Hope, at the southern tip of Africa, it was not until the 1497–1499 voyage of another Portuguese mariner, Vasco da Gama, that the first oceanic trade route to India was established. A similar desire led to the Spanish monarchy's investment in the voyages of Christopher Columbus. Columbus hoped that, by sailing west, he could establish a more direct trade route to the Orient, not realizing that the Americas blocked his path.

With their West African bases established, the Portuguese initially traded primarily in gold, ivory, and pepper. Only later did they become involved in the slave trade. Neither they nor other Europeans themselves captured and enslaved Africans, however. Instead, they purchased them from African traders. Such transactions can be dated to 1442, but they were formalized in 1472 when a Portuguese merchant gained permission from an African king in Benin to trade for human beings. Initially, most Africans were reluctant to sell other Africans to the Europeans, considering the practice unethical.

By contrast, the Spanish explorers in the Americas themselves enslaved many of the native people, who were forced to work in the fields and the mines. This workforce was not, however, unlimited. Those who did not escape died, either from European diseases to which they had no immunity or from being worked to death. The need for a steady supply of forced labor thus gave rise to the Atlantic slave trade. Initially, it was the cultivation of sugar that fueled the trade. But soon the cultivation of coffee in Brazil and tobacco, rice, and indigo in the North American colonies added to the already enormous demand for the labor of enslaved people.

The system of human bondage in the Americas was based exclusively on race. Only African and native peoples were enslaved. Most enslaved people in the Americas were males between the ages of fifteen and twenty-five who served as agrarian laborers.

During the early years of the sixteenth century, the Atlantic slave trade was dominated by the Portuguese and the Spanish. Initially, approximately two thousand Africans were shipped to the Americas each year, most going to Brazil. (By the time the trade had been abolished, this number had increased to approximately 12 million annually.) By the mid-sixteenth century, the profits had become so enormous that the Dutch, French, and English became involved. Eventually, two triangular trade routes—dominated by the English—developed. One involved traders carrying English goods to West Africa in exchange for enslaved people, whom they then carried to the West Indies and exchanged for sugar and tobacco, which they then took back to England. The other involved traders carrying North American rum to West Africa to trade for enslaved people, whom they then carried to the Caribbean islands and exchanged for sugar and molasses, which they then took home to turn into rum.

The most dangerous part of both routes was the so-called Middle Passage, the leg that carried the enslaved people across the Atlantic. The danger mostly involved their health, which was not good to start with, since they were casualties of the wars fought almost incessantly at that point in service of territorial expansion and state formation: the inhabitants of conquered towns or villages and the objects of raiding parties sold off to the Europeans. The farther from the coast these individuals were captured, the longer they were forced to march to reach the *factories,* as the areas where European traders waited were known. Those considered fit for sale were branded with the mark of the trading company that purchased them and could be held in a factory for weeks or months before being shipped across the Atlantic, a journey that could take up to three months. (Those considered unfit were released and left to their own devices.) On the slave ships (or *slavers*), which varied in size, anywhere between two and four hundred captives were placed in the hold, remaining chained together for most of the journey. Mortality rates were extremely high because of the overcrowded conditions, unsanitary environment, and threat of disease. Seasickness was also common. Overall, only about one-third of the African captives survived the Middle Passage. Nevertheless, the slave trade still earned fortunes for its principals.

African Americans in Colonial North America

It is generally accepted that approximately 75 percent of all the individuals crossing the Atlantic Ocean in the three centuries after the arrival of Christopher Columbus were African. But not all these Africans came as enslaved laborers. Some came as indentured servants.

The system of indentured servitude, which had existed in Europe for centuries, is a form of labor in which an individual is bound by contract to work for another person, a company, or a nation for a specific period of time in return for maintenance and sometimes travel expenses. It was brought to the British North American colonies with the establishment in 1607 of Jamestown, the first permanent English settlement in the Americas, by the Virginia Company of London, an English joint-stock company, which hoped to profit from the natural resources of the New World. But the venture got off to a shaky start, and it was only the introduction of the cash crop of tobacco that put it on a solid financial footing. Tobacco being a labor-intensive crop, and labor being in short supply, indentured servants—mostly Black Africans and North American natives—were employed in Jamestown from the 1620s.

Between 1640 and 1700, tobacco cultivation expanded north to Delaware and south to northern Carolina. At the same time, a social and demographic revolution took place. The colonial economy was transformed from a system based on the labor of (mostly White) indentured servants to one based on the labor of enslaved Black Africans. In Virginia, for example, where there had been only thirty-two people of African descent living in 1619, enslaved Africans constituted at least 20 percent of the overall population by 1700. One reason for this economic and demographic shift was the precedent for the enslavement of Africans set in the British Caribbean sugar colonies during the second quarter of the seventeenth century. In addition, slavery offered Virginia planters a cheaper source of labor than did indentured servitude, White indentured servants having become more expensive as they began to demand the better living conditions offered by the other British North American mainland colonies. Furthermore, fewer English citizens were agreeing to indenture themselves in return for passage to the British colonies.

The institution of slavery had for a while been resisted in the English North American colonies. For starters, unlike the Spanish and the Portuguese, the English had no laws governing and little experience with the institution of slavery. Consequently, the Black Africans brought to Jamestown were initially considered to be simply servants and treated as their White counterparts were. But also many Black Africans had had their names Anglicized on arrival in the New World, and, according to English customs and traditions, they could not be enslaved because they were considered to be Christians. But this societal arrangement did not last very long, and not just for economic and demographic reasons.

Notions of race and class also came into play. A number of instances of rebellion figured prominently in the change. Two examples will suffice. In 1640, the Black indentured servant John Punch attempted to flee Virginia for Maryland, but he was captured and sentenced to slavery for life. In 1675–1676, Nathaniel Bacon led an (unsuccessful) armed rebellion against Virginia's colonial government. What particularly disturbed the colony's upper class was that the rebel force was an alliance of European indentured servants and their African allies (indentured servants, enslaved persons, and freemen). The result was the hardening of race and class lines. There were also myriad laws passed in the Chesapeake colonies during the 1660s stipulating that the children of African females would be servants for life. All these and more set in motion the development of the institution of chattel slavery that would prevail in the American South until the Civil War.

Interestingly, slave codes and race relations developed differently in the North than they did in the South. For example, organized religion played a more important role in the northern colonies, and many religious groups espoused nonviolence and spiritual equality, if not racial equality, and, thus, opposed the institution of slavery. More important, however, was the cooler northern climate, which did not allow the emergence of a lucrative and, thus, dominant cash crop like tobacco or sugar or cotton. Instead, a much more diversified economy developed, one that found the existing White labor force on the whole sufficient. While the institution of slavery did develop in the North, especially in the middle colonies (New York, New Jersey, and Pennsylvania), the few people of African descent who lived there had a much easier time of it than did their southern cohorts, having access to more African American–led schools and social institutions.

African Americans during the Struggle for Independence and Its Aftermath

The struggle between the three European empires intent on expanding their influence in North America—England, France, and Spain—and the subsequent struggle between England and the North American colonists interested Black Africans in North America enormously. Conflict first broke out between the colonies of British North America (along the Atlantic seaboard) and those of New France (roughly the eastern half of what is today Canada and the central portion of what is today the United States) in 1754. Great Britain eventually prevailed—it even acquired Florida from Spain in exchange for Havana, which it had captured during the course of the conflict—and the French withdrew from North America.

Armed conflict ended in 1763, only to be replaced by the colonists' increased dissatisfaction with British rule. During the 1760s, Parliament passed a series of increasingly oppressive laws. For instance, a royal proclamation of 1763 limited colonial expansion westward. The Sugar Act of 1764 cut the tax rate imposed by the earlier Molasses Act (1733) but increased enforcement efforts. In 1765, the Stamp Act was passed, requiring many materials produced in the colonies to be printed on paper produced in London and carrying an embossed revenue stamp. The final straw was the 1773 Tea Act, which imposed no new taxes but did give the financially unstable British East India Company a monopoly over all the tea sold in the American colonies. The independence movement was born, and the organized resistance that ensued spread throughout the colonies, leading to the outbreak of the American Revolution in 1776.

African Americans who resided in the colonies—most of them in bondage—followed the events of the 1750s, 1760s, and 1770s closely. Each step toward revolution brought greater attention to the question of what rights and responsibilities Britain had with regard to its American colonies. Whether it had the political authority to tax the colonists, whether royal governors had the power to disband colonial legislatures—these things admittedly mattered very little to most African Americans. What did capture their attention, however, was the language the colonists used and their methods of resistance, which they took as models to emulate in their attempt to obtain their own liberty. The simplest form this resistance took was running away, a means by which hundreds of African Americans escaped slavery in South Carolina and the Georgia low country. But some protested. In January 1766, for example, a group of enslaved African Americans marched through the streets of Charleston, South Carolina, shouting: "Liberty, Liberty, Liberty!" And some even made a formal case for freedom. As early as 1701, an enslaved person from Massachusetts had gone to court and won his suit for freedom. As revolution approached, more and more African Americans began to use the arguments of White revolutionaries such as Thomas Paine and Thomas Jefferson to fortify their calls for freedom. In fact, a 1777 slave petition to the Massachusetts general assembly proclaimed: "Your Petitioners . . . have in Common with all other men a Natural and Unaliable Right to that freedom which the Grat Parent of the Unavers hath Bestowed equalley on all menkind" (Prince Hall, p. 2).

When the Revolutionary War began, African Americans were essentially opportunistic when it came to choosing between the English and the Americans, supporting whichever side they saw as most likely to offer them their freedom. Interestingly, despite having fought beside the rebels in several early skirmishes, they were forbidden to enlist in the military, whether free or enslaved, when General George Washington organized the Continental Army in July 1775. Soon, all thirteen colonies had followed Washington's example, banning them from joining state militias. Of course, the British used the opportunity to recruit Blacks, the most famous appeal being the proclamation issued by the royal governor of Virginia in November 1775 offering freedom to enslaved persons who fought for British or Loyalist units. (Some one thousand African Americans joined the British in response.) In December 1775, Washington reversed his decision, and, owing to troop shortages, several state governments followed suit by the end of the next year. However, a few southern states (including North and South Carolina and Georgia) held firm to the ban despite the fact that hundreds of southern Blacks served in military units in other states. Overall, of the roughly 300,000 men who fought on the colonists' side, about 5,000 were Black.

Owing to the willingness of Blacks to risk their lives in combat for the American cause, many northern legislatures began to manumit, or free, enslaved African Americans no matter where they resided. And, owing to the conducive cultural and economic environment in the North, many state governments had by the late 1770s begun to debate abolition. Consequently, by 1784, except for New Jersey and New York all the northern states had immediate or gradual emancipation plans on hand, as did Delaware, Maryland, and Virginia. Some states in the Deep South even encouraged plantation owners to free their enslaved. Soon, dynamic communities of free Blacks began to appear. A separate and distinctive Black American culture had existed in the United States since the colonial period, and these communities coalesced around an educated African American elite and were sustained by a variety of institutions.

One of those institutions was freemasonry, which appealed to African American men because it espoused the ideals of liberty and equality. But existing lodges were segregated, so Black lodges were founded. These were particularly important because of the connections established between lodges in different cities. Another popular institution in Black communities was the mutual aid society—a foundation of social welfare at the time—whose function was to provide relief from various difficulties. Patterned after similar White organizations, these societies were more like benevolent groups or insurance companies. They provided their members with a variety of services: for example, medical care, burial assistance, and help for widows and orphans. But churches were the true center of most Black communities. Not only did they provide spiritual sustenance; often pastors became communities' social and political leaders. The churches also housed schools and provided a meeting place for a variety of social groups and events (e.g., antislavery meetings).

African Americans and the New Nation

During the decades that followed the War of Independence, the abolition movement began to take hold in the North and the Chesapeake region, its roots, as we have seen, traceable to revolutionary notions of natural rights, the evangelical Christian revival, and especially economic conditions. As for the latter, although slavery was widespread in the North, it was never an economic necessity there. Farming was more efficient when workers were hired only during the planting and harvesting seasons, thus obviating the need for year-round slave labor. In addition, while White Europeans continued to emigrate to the new nation, most settled in the North, not the South. Thus, slavery became difficult to defend in the North. And its demise in the region was certainly hastened by the crusades mounted by such organizations as the Pennsylvania Society for Promoting the Abolition of Slavery and the American Convention for Promoting the Abolition of Slavery and Improving the Condition of the African Race.

Still, in the North, the abolition movement proceeded at different rates in different states. The New England states moved more rapidly—in particular, Vermont, which abolished slavery in 1777 when it was still a colony. New York and New Jersey, by contrast, adopted gradual emancipation, the process taking from 1799 to 1827 in the former and from 1804 to 1865 in the latter. Not surprisingly, while the first US census, conducted in 1790, found no enslaved people in Massachusetts and Vermont, 150 enslaved African Americans still resided in New Hampshire as late as 1792.

At the same time, movement of White settlers into the Northwest Territory during and after the Revolution—some bringing enslaved persons—prompted the newly established US Congress to limit the expansion of slavery, the goal being to avoid conflict with Native American tribes and the few remaining British troops stationed in the area. (Britain had ceded the Northwest Territory to the United States in 1783 but maintained a presence there through the War of 1812.) The Northwest Ordinance, which approved the orderly sale of land, free public education, a territorial government structure, the eventual formation of several new states, and the immediate ban of slavery in the region, was passed in 1787. And whether Congress had the power to ban slavery became a hotly contested issue, especially after 1803, when President Thomas Jefferson acquired the Louisiana Territory.

At the same time, several factors led to the strengthening and expansion of the "peculiar institution," as slavery was known, especially in the South. The most important was the US Constitution itself, which went into effect in 1789. Not only did it prohibit Congress from abolishing slavery until 1808. It tacitly encouraged the expansion of slavery: the Three-Fifths Compromise allowed states to count three-fifths of their slave population toward their total population (on which representation in the House of Representatives was based). And, in fact, more enslaved Africans were brought to the United States from 1787 to 1808 than at any other time in American history. Also important was the passage of the Fugitive Slave Act of 1793, which allowed slaveholders or their representatives to pursue fugitives across state lines, capture them, and take them before a magistrate to regain legal custody of their property.

The Cotton Kingdom

The cotton gin, invented by Eli Whitney in 1793, made cotton the most profitable and thus the most important crop in the United States until the outbreak of the Civil War, driving the southern economy. And the expansion of cotton production into the Louisiana Territory, Texas, and the Great Plains during the 1830s and 1840s was key to the expansion of slavery.

From 1790 to 1860, the enslaved African American population in the region stretching from the Atlantic coast to Texas grew almost six times, from roughly 700,000 to roughly 4 million. Agricultural laborers made up 75 percent of the South's enslaved population, but they were not equally distributed across the region. For example, very few enslaved people resided in western North Carolina, Eastern Tennessee, western Virginia, or Missouri. The fastest-growing slave populations were to be found in Alabama, Mississippi, South Carolina, and Virginia. Ownership of the enslaved was also unevenly distributed during these years. For instance, of the entire White southern population, only about 36 percent owned enslaved persons in 1830, a figure that dropped to 5 percent by 1860. Of slave owners in 1860, about half owned fewer than five enslaved, only 12 percent more than twenty, and just 1 percent more than fifty.

About 55 percent of the enslaved population of the South cultivated cotton, 10 percent grew tobacco, and 10 percent grew rice and hemp and produced sugar. About 15 percent were house servants, and the remaining 10 percent worked in a trade or in industry. Tobacco remained the most important cash crop in Kentucky, Maryland, North Carolina, Virginia, and parts of Missouri. Tobacco was a very difficult crop to produce, requiring a long growing season and very careful cultivation. In comparison, rice production was dominant in the low country of South Carolina and Georgia. Sugar production was restricted to southern Louisiana.

Despite the economic significance of tobacco, rice, and sugar, by 1860, cotton exports accounted for 50 percent of US exports, bringing in $1 billion annually, and about 1.8 million of the 2.5 million enslaved people in the United States were involved in cotton production. But the nature of cotton production meant that laborers were required in the field only at harvest time. Cotton production therefore changed the nature of slavery somewhat, a plantation's enslaved workers being hired out or leased during the off-season. Most of the skilled laborers who were hired out worked in southern towns and cities, where they had the opportunity to interact with free Blacks. They also interacted with their urban counterparts, who served as artisans, domestics, waiters, and general laborers, meaning they did the work that White immigrants refused to do. What was different about their situation, however, was that many urban slaveholders let their captives buy their freedom over a set period of years to reduce the likelihood of their becoming runaways.

Regardless, whatever a slave's situation, the peculiar institution was, by definition, a forced system of labor maintained by the threat of physical violence. Many slaveholders denied that they mistreated their enslaved workers, conceiving of themselves as benevolent fathers. And, even if they resorted to harsh treatment, correcting the behavior of servants in this manner was justified by the Bible. Nevertheless, fear of the lash was effective.

Despite the expansion of slavery, the African American family endured. The enslaved developed their own semiautonomous communities that had at their core the family. Although marriages of enslaved people were not legally recognized or protected, many took place anyway and endured for decades. Couples usually lived together in cabins on their master's plantation. Within these quarters, families, both nuclear and extended, lived, loved, and played. Parents instilled in their children the importance of being able to rely not only on grandparents, aunts, uncles, and cousins but also on biologically related members of the household in the face of physical assault, especially of women and girls, and other indignities.

The Lead-Up to Civil War

In the 1790s, a new wave of evangelical Christian revivals motivated hundreds of Americans to move their moral crusade into the political world. Commonly known as the Second Great Awakening—the First Great Awakening swept Britain and its North American colonies in the 1730s and 1740s—the movement lasted through the 1830s. Its message of spiritual equality—that all men and women can have a personal relationship with God and all souls can be saved—greatly influenced the establishment of independent African American churches. But, while Whites did begin welcoming Blacks into their churches as their spiritual equals, most still did not consider them their social and political equals. So Blacks created their own churches. In the South, these churches tended to be separate but not independent. That is, separate Black congregations were established, usually headed by a Black minister, but still under the umbrella of a White denomination. It was only in the North that a truly independent Black church movement emerged with the creation in the early nineteenth century of such denominations as the African Methodist Episcopal Church and the African Methodist Episcopal Zion Church. Naturally, these churches became part of the larger antislavery movement that was spreading throughout the country.

The effort to end slavery in what became the United States can be traced back to at least the 1730s, a crusade that intensified as a result of the American Revolution, the French Revolution (1789–1799), and the Haitian Revolution (1791–1804). The latter was especially inspiring—to

Black Americans at least—as it resulted in a government led by people of color. Of course it terrified White slave owners, who already lived in constant fear of rebellion. That fear was not unwarranted. Several planned slave revolts were discovered and suppressed in the first three decades of the nineteenth century. But it was the 1831 revolt in South Hampton, Virginia, led by Nat Turner, a privileged, enslaved African American—a revolt during which some fifty-seven White men, women, and children were killed—that marked a turning point, hardening views among both abolitionists and proponents of slavery.

Collaboration between Black and White abolitionists had always been sporadic and limited, largely owing to their differing aims. Black abolitionists, of course, sought immediate and unqualified emancipation and equality under the law. White abolitionists, however, favored gradual emancipation (to protect the economic interests of the slaveholders) and did not believe that Black Americans should be accorded equal rights with Whites. Whites in general, moreover, took the position known as *scientific racism,* which held that Blacks were physically, intellectually, and culturally inferior to Whites and that slavery was, therefore, justified. As a result of Nat Turner's Rebellion, a wave of racially motivated violence erupted, led and organized by federal and state government officials and White vigilantes. From the 1830s to the Civil War, White mobs regularly attacked African Americans, even in their own neighborhoods, and the offices of abolitionist newspapers. In fact, urban race riots targeting Blacks were common in the 1830s and 1840s. Nevertheless, Black and White abolitionists continued to work together. In some regards, African Americans who were involved in the antislavery movement found in Whites some of their most loyal allies and friends.

This is not to say that there were not disagreements. Particularly contentious was *colonization,* the emigration of free Black Americans to Africa. Paul Cuffe, a successful Massachusetts shipowner of African American and Native American ancestry, was an early advocate of colonization. In 1816, a year before his death, he even took thirty-eight Black Americans to Sierra Leone at his own expense. Most African Americans (whose families had lived in the Americas for generations) and abolitionists were opposed to the project of colonization. Some Whites who were in favor of it saw it as a way of ridding the nation of Blacks, who would, they claimed, be happier in Africa, where they would not experience racial discrimination. Others saw it as a means of Christianizing and civilizing Africa. Even some Blacks supported the project, their perspective based on a Black nationalist position that, because Blacks had never been truly integrated into American social, economic, and political structures, emigration to Africa was the only remaining option. Ultimately, because of the efforts of the American Colonization Society (a largely White group), roughly thirteen thousand Black Americans settled in Liberia. But this did little to calm fraught American race relations in the United States.

In response to the various abolitionist positions in general and the charge that slavery was inherently sinful in particular, the argument that slavery was not a necessary evil but a positive good emerged. It rested on three main points. Slavery was the natural and proper status for a race that was by nature inferior. It was, in fact, sanctioned by the Bible. It was humane because the enslaved were treated as members of the larger plantation family.

Compounding matters, the issue of slavery also got caught up in the issue of westward expansion and the notion of Manifest Destiny—the widely held cultural belief that the American nation was destined to span the continent. Victory in the Mexican-American War (1846–1848) gave the United States control of Texas (which it had annexed in 1845) as well as California, Nevada, Arizona, Utah, and Colorado and parts of Oklahoma, Kansas, New Mexico, and Wyoming, prompting a confrontation in Congress between slave and free states over the status of these newly acquired territories. The Compromise of 1850, a package of five separate bills passed by Congress, temporarily settled the question. Most pertinent to our concerns here are the Fugitive Slave Act of 1850, which bolstered the Fugitive Slave Act of 1793 and was strongly proslavery, and a statute prohibiting the slave trade, but not slave ownership, in Washington, DC, which southerners vigorously opposed as setting a bad precedent.

The Compromise of 1850 averted civil war, but only temporarily. Enslaved persons escaping to the North and freedom via the Underground Railroad; Bostonians attempting to liberate Anthony Burns, a fugitive slave who had been recaptured; the creation of the nativist Know Nothing Party; the enormous popularity of Harriet Beecher Stowe's *Uncle Tom's Cabin* (1852); the ratification of the Kansas-Nebraska Act (1854), which repealed the Missouri Compromise (which outlawed slavery in territories north of latitude 36°30' north) and triggered the series of violent confrontations between anti- and proslavery forces known as Bleeding Kansas; the concept of popular sovereignty, which held that the residents of territories should themselves be allowed to vote on whether to allow slavery; John Brown's attack on Harpers Ferry; and the election of Abraham Lincoln as president in 1860—all these events led to the secession of the southern states and the outbreak of the Civil War in 1861.

African Americans and the Civil War

Faced with first the threat and then the actuality of civil war, President Lincoln's main concern was always the preservation of the Union at all costs. Slavery was, at best, of secondary importance. Indeed, after the April 1861 attack on Fort Sumter, the first armed North-South confrontation of the war, Lincoln ordered state militia and military personnel to suppress slave revolts and turn back all runaways. In fact, he attempted to minimize the issue of slavery as much as possible, determined to keep the border states of Delaware, Kentucky, Maryland, and Missouri in the Union, and initially authorized the acceptance of only White men for military service.

It would take Lincoln almost two years to change his mind, not just about allowing Blacks to serve in the military but also about tying the war directly to the issue of slavery. Several factors influenced his thinking. One was the fact that abolitionists in the North, both Black and White, were deeply disappointed in the decision to exclude African Americans from the military. Another was the desire of African Americans themselves to assist in the preservation of the Union. (Sensing the change that must inevitably come, African Americans in cities such as New York, Boston, and Philadelphia began to form their own military units on the outbreak of hostilities.) Yet another was the fact that the Union Army began to use some of the hundreds of enslaved persons who had fled to the North after the outbreak of hostilities as laborers and spies. Finally, there was the perception that the government cared more for the interests of Confederate slaveholders than it did for the interests of the Blacks in bondage. The pressure led first to an interim step, the passage in August 1861 of the First Confiscation Act, which declared that any property that belonged to Confederates and was used in the war effort could be seized by Union troops. The act stopped short of freeing the enslaved—they were still considered property, only now in the care of the federal government. But it was a start.

It was only after the first year of the war (which did not go well for the Union) that Lincoln began to move away from the position that the long-term solution to slavery was the financial compensation of slave-holders for emancipation and the forced emigration of the newly freed African Americans to the Caribbean, Latin America, or West Africa. Finally concluding that the issue of slavery was the instrument that would hasten the end of the war and restore the Union, on January 1, 1863, he issued the Emancipation Proclamation, which ordered the release of the roughly 4 million enslaved African Americans still in bondage in the Confederate states. The Emancipation Proclamation also authorized the service of African Americans in the Union Army. (The Thirteenth Amendment to the Constitution, which abolished slavery and involuntary servitude, was passed by Congress in January 1865 and ratified by the states in December 1865.) Ultimately, over 180,000 African Americans served in the Union Army during the Civil War.

Conclusion

The North won the Civil War because it had a greater capacity to change, reorganize, innovate, and modernize than did the South. Its victory meant that the nation would progress without being half enslaved and half free. And African Americans, both free and enslaved, played a vital and pivotal role in the national transformation that started soon after the Constitution was ratified. The next chapter traces the progress made since the surrender of the Confederacy at Appomattox in April 1865.

4

African Americans in the United States from the Civil War to the Present

Sarah Breedlove—later known as Madam C. J. Walker—was born on a cotton plantation in Delta, Louisiana, on December 23, 1867, to Owen and Minerva Breedlove, formerly enslaved persons. She was orphaned at the age of seven (Minerva died first, Owen a year later), moving to Vicksburg to live with her sister Louvenia and her husband, and becoming a child domestic worker. In 1882, at the age of fourteen, partly to escape the cruelty of her sister's husband, she married Moses McWilliams. Sarah and Moses's daughter, Lelia (later known as A'Lelia), was born in 1885.

When Moses died in 1887, Sarah moved to St. Louis, Missouri, where three of her brothers (all barbers) lived, working at first as a laundress, sending her daughter to public school, and marrying John Davis in 1894. In 1904, the year after she left Davis, she became a sales agent for the Poro Company, owned by Annie Turnbo Pope Malone, an African American hair-care entrepreneur. It was common at the time for Black women to suffer from scalp ailments—brought on by a number of factors, including stress, poor diet, and harsh cleaning products of various sorts—and Sarah was no exception. When she noticed that she herself was showing early signs of balding, she learned more about hair care from her brothers and determined to develop her own line of hair-care products.

In July 1905, with $1.50 in savings, thirty-seven-year-old Sarah moved to Denver, Colorado, where she lived with a brother's widow and her four daughters. In 1906, she married again, this time a local newspaper salesman named Charles Joseph Walker. After taking her husband's name, Walker followed the traditional practice of female entrepreneurs, both Black and White, and became *Madam* C. J. Walker. With the help of her husband as her business partner and advertising liaison, Madam

C. J. Walker launched her hair-care business, selling her products first to her friends and then door-to-door. In the fall of 1906, Walker and her husband began an eighteen-month promotional tour, her daughter staying behind to oversee the orders that came in through the mail. Ultimately, she gained an excellent reputation among African American communities nationwide for her outstanding hair-care products and techniques.

In 1910, the Walkers moved their company to Indianapolis, at the time the largest inland manufacturing city in the nation, where it thrived. From 1912 to 1916, Walker traveled from coast to coast, promoting her business through lectures and presentations at local churches, schools, civic organizations, and fraternal associations. She also expanded her business outside the United States, traveling to Costa Rica, Cuba, Haiti, Jamaica, and Panama. Walker moved to Harlem in 1916 after she and Charles divorced, though her company's day-to-day operations continued to be run out of Indianapolis.

Walker's business philosophy rested on the notion of economic independence for African American women. As she noted in a 1912 speech: "The girls and women of our race must not be afraid to take hold of business endeavor and, by patient industry, close economy, determined effort and close application to business, wring success out of a number of business opportunities that lie at their very doors" (quoted in Bundles, p. 153). Putting her words into action, she regularly hired former maids, laborers, and schoolteachers to fill openings at all levels of her business. By the end of 1916, the Walker Company employed some twenty thousand people throughout the United States, Central America, and the Caribbean.

By 1919, Walker had been diagnosed with hypertension, the result of the constant stress of running her own business and keeping up a hectic travel schedule. When she died on May 25, at the age of fifty-one, she was the wealthiest African American woman in the United States and the first self-made African American millionaire, noted for her philanthropy. More importantly, however, she was a role model of racial uplift and female empowerment at a time when few such role models were available to African Americans.

This 1920s hair-care advertisement describes the history and successes of Madame C. J. Walker, the first African American millionaire. (Courtesy of the James Weldon Johnson Collection in the Yale Collection of American Literature, Beinecke Rare Book and Manuscript Library.)

Learning Objectives

▼ ▼ ▼

1. What did freedom mean to the nearly 4 million formerly enslaved people of African descent?
2. What factors led to the rise and fall of Reconstruction?
3. What were the political and legal methods used and the results of the attempt to redeem the southern states?
4. What methods did African Americans use to challenge White supremacy and racism in the post-Reconstruction years?
5. What avenues for advancement were open to African Americans during the early years of the twentieth century?
6. What factors led to the emergence of a new sense of empowerment for thousands of African Americans during the 1920s?
7. How did FDR's New Deal policies and programs affect African Americans?
8. How did African Americans use the crisis of World War II to protest racial discrimination and plant the seeds of the modern civil rights movement?
9. How has the modern civil rights movement changed the economic, political, and social lives of African Americans?

▲ ▲ ▲

What did freedom mean to a people who had endured over two hundred years of enslavement? For some, it meant that families could stay together. For others, it meant an end to sexual exploitation and physical abuse. It meant learning how to read and write. It meant being able to organize churches. It meant being able to move about freely without asking permission. It meant owning land. It meant hope. But it also meant uncertainty.

The Rise and Fall of Reconstruction

In March 1865, a month before the Civil War ended, what is now known as the Reconstruction Era was set in motion when Congress created the Bureau of Refugees, Freedmen, and Abandoned Lands, commonly known as the Freedmen's Bureau, in an attempt to assist the newly freed and others affected by the war in negotiating the next stage of their lives. That meant anything from helping them obtain land, gain an education, negotiate labor contracts, and settle legal disputes, to providing food, medical care, and transportation, to setting up refugee camps to house the displaced, a job made that much more difficult because Congress never funded the bureau adequately.

In July 1865, acting on General William T. Sherman's Special Field Order 15, the Freedmen's Bureau made its first attempt at land distribution, ordering its agents to set aside forty acres of land for each freedman. The order was, however, almost immediately revoked by Congress, which announced that even land confiscated from the rebels and distributed to formerly enslaved persons was to be returned to its former owners. The main reason for this reversal was that Andrew Johnson, who had become president after Abraham Lincoln's assassination on April 15, 1865, and did not believe that African Americans were in any way equal to White Americans, had adopted a policy of appeasement when dealing with the South and even begun to pardon former Confederate officials. Furthermore, the land that some southern Black Americans obtained as a result of the passage of the 1866 Southern Homestead Act was mostly worthless because it was unsuitable for farming, hence its affordability. Land distribution was a bust.

The negotiation of fair labor contracts between freedmen and local White landowners fared little better. Local Freedmen's Bureau agents, for example, created a situation in which Blacks were regularly forced to accept oppressive contracts. Out of these conditions eventually developed the system of sharecropping, an arrangement whereby a landowner allowed a tenant to use his land in return for a share of the crops produced.

In the face of these setbacks, Black southerners turned to the African American church as a safe haven. During the enslavement period, the lives of Blacks had centered on family and religion. After Emancipation, African American men and women began to organize their own churches, struggling to save the money to buy the land on which to build them. Most of these churches were Baptist and Methodist, denominations that tended to be more autonomous and thus less influenced by outsiders. Their services were more emotional and spiritual and thus appealed to more recently freed African Americans. By contrast, the Presbyterian, Congregational, and Episcopal Churches appealed to more established members of the African American community. Their services tended to be more formal and quieter. The Roman Catholic Church also made a few inroads during this period.

Black southerners also turned to education, feeling that to remain illiterate was to remain enslaved. People were especially eager to read the Bible for themselves. Even before Emancipation, some Black Americans began to establish their own schools. With the end of the Civil War, northern religious organizations, in cooperation with the Freedmen's Bureau, organized hundreds of day and night schools. Classes were held in stables, homes, former slave quarters, taverns, and churches. In 1866, the Freedmen's Bureau budgeted roughly $500,000 for education, and, in 1869, it was involved in the operation of some three thousand schools and the education of approximately 150,000 students.

Many White southerners responded to the efforts of African Americans to learn to read and write with disbelief, dismay, and even violence. For decades, most Whites had viewed people of African descent as inferior and their efforts at self-education as ludicrous. Schools were burned to the ground, and hundreds of teachers were threatened and even lynched. Furthermore, most Whites refused to allow their children to attend school with Blacks. Not surprisingly, no integrated educational facilities were established in the decades following Emancipation.

Despite the best efforts of Andrew Johnson, however, the political winds of change for a time favored African Americans. In the aftermath of the war, Black Americans and radical Republicans watched in disbelief as Johnson appointed former Confederates to positions of power in the southern states. The result was the enactment of the so-called Black Codes, which sought to ensure the creation and maintenance of a subservient, mostly African American laboring class controlled by Whites. The codes also permitted Black children between the ages of two and twenty-one to be apprenticed to White southerners and barred Blacks from loitering, being vagrant, using alcohol, fishing, raising livestock, and owning a firearm. While Blacks could legally marry, sign contracts, purchase property, sue or be sued, and testify in court, they could neither vote nor serve on juries.

Alarmed by these measures and the upturn in violence against Blacks, the radical Republicans—determined that African Americans assume their rightful place in the nation's political and economic life—began to take action. For example, in late 1865, Thaddeus Stevens introduced a bill in Congress calling for confiscating 400 million acres of land from the wealthiest 10 percent of the southern population and distributing it to free people of color. The measure failed, but largely because even those Republicans

Judge, lawyer, and US senator Lyman Trumbull. The Illinois senator was coauthor of the Thirteenth Amendment. (Photo by Matthew Brady, 1850s or 1860s. Courtesy of the Brady-Handy Photographs Collection, Library of Congress Prints and Photographs Division: LC-DIG-cwpbh-03888.)

(moderate or radical) who wanted fundamental change considered the confiscation a gross violation of individual property rights. Next, also in 1865, the radical Republicans supported a measure calling for voting rights for African American men, who, the thinking went, needed to be able to vote in order to achieve real power. It too failed. Moderate Republicans did not want to lose the White southern vote, and the thought of African American suffrage horrified Democrats North and South. In early 1866, Senator Lyman Trumbull, a moderate Republican from Illinois, introduced two major bills in Congress. The first sought more funding for the Freedmen's Bureau and the extension of the bureau's authority. The second was the first civil rights act introduced in Congress. It made any person born in the United States a citizen (except Native Americans), thereby according Blacks equal protection under the law. Congress passed both bills, and President Johnson vetoed both.

Johnson's vetoes stunned Republicans. Incensed, the radical and moderate camps of the party closed ranks and overrode them. (The Republican-led Senate impeached Johnson in 1868, but the attempt failed by one vote.) In order further to secure the legal rights of African Americans, the Republican-led Congress also passed the Fourteenth Amendment to the Constitution, which compelled states to accept all Black Americans as residents and guarantee that their rights as citizens would be protected. The radical Republicans then proposed the first of four reconstruction acts. The First Reconstruction Act called for the former Confederate states to be divided into five districts under military control (Tennessee excepted because it had already been readmitted to the Union). It required the states to craft new constitutions guaranteeing universal male suffrage and ratify the Fourteenth Amendment, which granted citizenship and equal civil and legal rights to African Americans and the formerly enslaved. Only after these two conditions were met would a state be readmitted to the Union. The act was approved over the objections of White southerners and Johnson's veto.

For the first time ever, African Americans were true participants in the American political process. And they did not just vote. They served as delegates to political conventions and even ran for public office. During the next ten years, roughly fifteen hundred Black American men were elected to public office in the South, including 2 US senators, 14 US congressmen, 6 lieutenant governors, 112 state senators, and 683 state representatives. Not surprisingly, there was a backlash among White southerners, who sought to restore White Democrats to power by any means. Ultimately, they were successful, gaining control of Congress by 1877. Reconstruction was dead, and most African Americans found themselves little better off than they had been before the Civil War.

African Americans in the Post-Reconstruction South

Between 1875 and 1900, African Americans in the South were gradually disenfranchised. The process of disenfranchisement took several forms. The most overt was direct political action. Gerrymandering on the part of southern White Democrats—crafting election districts in such a way that one party has a distinct advantage—diluted the strength of the Black vote, thus limiting the number of African Americans sent to Congress. But there were other ways to manipulate voter registration. State legislatures created voting hurdles: for example, literacy, property, and residency requirements and proof of payment of all taxes (including poll taxes). Louisiana even adopted a grandfather clause stipulating that only men whose fathers or grandfathers were entitled to vote on January 1, 1867, could vote.

Violence was also employed as a means of voter suppression. Lynching—putting someone to death (most commonly by hanging) by mob action without legal approval or permission—was the most extreme form of violence, an act of terror meant to spread fear. Between 1889 and 1932, 3,745 people were lynched in the United States. Other forms of intimidation were employed as well. White men routinely harassed, abused, and raped Black women. And White mobs rioted regularly. While Black men continued to serve in Congress, state legislatures, and local governments and received appointments to post offices and custom houses, they had all but disappeared from the political scene by 1900.

What became known as the *Jim Crow* system gradually took hold in the South. Officially, laws were passed mandating racial segregation in all public facilities, including transportation. Blacks were seated separately in theaters, restaurants, concert halls, and waiting rooms. They were forced to stay in separate hotels and boardinghouses and travel in segregated train cars. The rationalization behind this system was that Blacks were more comfortable around other Blacks than they were around Whites. After all, they lived in their own communities and had developed their own churches and social organizations. And, anyway, segregation represented an improvement over exclusion. Ultimately, in a landmark decision in the *Plessy v. Ferguson* (1896) case, the Supreme Court recognized the constitutionality of Jim Crow laws. The underlying principle thus affirmed is now known as *separate but equal.*

Unofficially, a system of racial etiquette was established that reinforced the subservience of Blacks toward Whites. Blacks and Whites did not shake hands. When addressing Whites, Blacks were never to look directly into their eyes but instead to stare at the ground. Black men were to remove their hats in the presence of Whites. Blacks were to enter White residences only through the back door, never the front. In stores, White customers were always taken care of first, even if a Black customer had actually arrived first. Black women could not try on clothing in a White-owned business. Whites did not have to use the titles *Mister, Missus,* or *Miss* when addressing Black adults. Instead, they used first names, *boy* or *girl,* or even *nigger,* and older Blacks were sometimes called *auntie* or *uncle.* Most Blacks having been relegated to menial agricultural jobs or domestic labor, which left them poor and dependent on Whites, little resistance was offered.

Not surprisingly, from the 1870s through the 1890s, record numbers of Blacks fled the South—but not for the North. Some struck out for Africa. But most—some forty thousand—moved west, mostly to Kansas, Oklahoma, and Colorado. These settlers were known as the *Exodusters* because their journey was considered an exodus in search of a new Promised Land.

African Americans Challenge White Supremacy and Racism

The challenges facing African Americans were both social and economic. Socially, racist attitudes still held sway and were even strengthened, bolstered by theories such as Social Darwinism (which took the biological concepts of natural selection and the survival of the fittest and applied them to sociology, economics, and politics) that were founded on pseudoscientific evidence. Economically, an extended agricultural depression meant that many Black southerners lost their jobs and fell into extreme poverty. For those Blacks for whom migration was not an option, there was no social safety net. They were on their own. But how were they to revitalize their lives and communities?

A traditional route out of poverty has always been education. But, for southern Blacks, acquiring even a rudimentary education was not easy. All public schools, Black and White, were underfunded. Rural Black schools usually operated for no more than thirty weeks per year, and Black children were rarely able to attend regularly owing to the demands of field work. Moreover, most Black schools were one-room, dilapidated shacks without plumbing and electricity, and teachers were poorly paid and trained and lacked appropriate teaching materials. The only other option was the private schools that operated in many Black communities, but only the most prosperous families could afford the tuition.

Even among Blacks who valued education, the most appropriate form was usually considered to be industrial or domestic training, which would impart to students skills that would make them productive members of their communities. This point of view led to the establishment of what are known today as historically Black colleges and universities, founded mainly to educate teachers. Few of these institutions expanded their focus beyond vocational training to offer classes in the liberal arts. There were, however, dissenting voices championing the teaching of literature, history, philosophy, and foreign languages as a way of elevating the race.

The military is another traditional route out of poverty, and it was one that many Blacks chose to take. Even though, after the Civil War, the US Army was reduced in size to fewer than thirty thousand troops and Congressional Democrats sought to exclude Blacks entirely, the Army Reorganization Act of 1866 created six new, colored regiments. These were reduced (through consolidation) to four under the Army Reorganization Act of 1869 and sent west to serve on the frontier for the next three decades. Here, the Buffalo Soldiers—a nickname given them by the Plains Indians against whom they fought so fiercely—proved their mettle despite the fact that they were poorly equipped and provisioned.

Despite the outstanding performance of the Buffalo Soldiers, Whites still treated Blacks in the military badly. Probably the best example of this is the so-called Brownsville Affair of 1906, when three companies of Black troops stationed in Brownsville were summarily dismissed from the army by President Theodore Roosevelt for defending themselves against an unprovoked attack by a group of local Whites and Mexicans. (Only in 1972 were they cleared of wrongdoing and awarded posthumous honorable discharges.) Despite constant discrimination, Blacks continued to serve in the armed forces, putting in outstanding performances in such conflicts as the Spanish-American War, the Philippine Insurrection, and the Battle of Cuba.

Some Blacks did manage to earn professional degrees. But even these lucky few faced obstacles. Black doctors and nurses were rarely allowed to practice in White hospitals, limiting their prospects. Black lawyers, on the other hand, could not be excluded from federal, state, or local courtrooms. Still, they were not welcomed by their fellow White lawyers or by White judges. As a result, many Black defendants hired White lawyers, and many Black lawyers thus had a hard time making a living at their chosen profession. The American Bar Association also refused to admit Blacks. (The National Negro Bar Association was not organized until 1925.)

Another option that many Blacks pursued was the arts. Before the Civil War, choral singing had been popular among the enslaved, and, after Emancipation, traveling troupes specializing in spirituals began to be organized. Traveling troops also performed minstrel shows, though few Black Americans enjoyed these demeaning, caricatured performances. Most importantly, however, Black musicians were developing the unique American art forms of ragtime, jazz, and blues.

An athletic career was yet another option. Black athletes encountered more prejudice than did Black musicians, who often performed for interracial audiences, whereas sports were largely segregated. Still, Blacks made a particular mark on boxing in the twentieth century. They also made their mark on baseball. The first Black professional baseball team—the Cuban Giants—was formed in 1885, and the first Black professional baseball league—the National Colored Base Ball League—was established in 1887.

African Americans during the Early Twentieth Century

As the twentieth century approached, the political atmosphere began to change. Rapid industrialization and urbanization, increased immigration, and rampant political corruption—causes of concern for many Americans—sparked a period of social activism now known as the *Progressive Era*. But that social activism went only so far. Progressives were, by and large, just as racist as non-Progressives. In fact, many enthusiastically supported the work of eugenicists, who sought the genetic improvement of the human population and promoted the propagation of those races considered to be superior. It was against this tide that Black political activists struggled.

Ezzard Charles, 1950s. Charles was recognized as both a heavyweight and light heavyweight world champion and was posthumously inducted into the International Boxing Hall of Fame. (Robert O'Neal Multicultural Arts Center [ROMAC] West End Collection. Courtesy of Toilynn O'Neal Turner.)

One controversial response was that of Booker T. Washington, the president of the Tuskegee Institute and one of the founders of the National Negro Business League. In a speech delivered at the Cotton States and International Exposition in Atlanta in 1895, Washington called on Blacks to pursue not political and civil rights but their own uplift and prosperity. Only economic success would convince Whites that they were worthy of such rights. The public response was mixed. Of course Washington's message appealed to Whites, but it also appealed to those Blacks who were uncomfortable with social agitation. Others in the Black community considered Washington a race traitor. Most prominent among them was W. E. B. Du Bois, perhaps the greatest scholar-activist in American history, who in his 1903 *The Souls of Black Folk* chastised Washington for having failed to stand up for the political and civil rights of African Americans, including access to higher education.

Du Bois was, for his part, committed to political action and convinced that the advancement of the race was the responsibility of the Black American elite, those he called the "Talented Tenth" (the upper 10 percent of the Black population): "My Talented Tenth must be more than talented, and work not simply as individuals" (p. 350). In 1905, he and William Monroe Trotter, a prominent Black newspaper editor and businessman, organized the Niagara Movement with the goal of opposing racial segregation and disenfranchisement. Despite some successes, the organization began to splinter, and what remained had by 1910 been absorbed by the newly created National Association for the Advancement of Colored People (NAACP). In its early years, the NAACP was a militant, integrated organization dedicated to the principle that Blacks could best obtain full civil and political rights through legislation and legal action. Its first major victory occurred in 1915 when the US Supreme Court in *Guinn v. United States* overturned Oklahoma's use of the grandfather clause as a violation of the Fifteenth Amendment, which guaranteed men the right to vote regardless of race.

Another response to the political environment was the foundation of activist Black women's organizations. While such groups date to at least the 1870s, initially they were mostly concerned with social, religious, and cultural matters. By the 1890s, a focus on politics had emerged. Most prominent among these organizations were the National Colored Women's League, founded in 1892; the New Era Club, founded in 1893; and the National Association of Colored Women, founded in 1896 when the

African American World War I infantry soldiers standing in front of a photographer's backdrop, 1914. (Courtesy of the Gladstone Collection of African American Photographs; Prints and Photographs Division, Library of Congress: LC-DIG-ppmsca-11422.)

National Federation of Afro-American Women and the National Colored Women's League merged. But these represent just the tip of the iceberg. There were thousands of these "colored women's clubs" spread throughout the country determined to tackle what were for Black Americans the most pressing issues of the day.

Nevertheless, racial violence continued and, in the early twentieth century, spread nationwide. The most horrifying of the race riots occurred in Atlanta (1906), Springfield, Illinois (1908), East St. Louis, Illinois (1917), Houston (1917), Chicago (1919), Elaine, Arkansas (1919), Tulsa (1921), and Rosewood, Florida (1923), but there were many others. And, in the midst of all this upheaval, the United States entered World War I.

Despite the meritorious performance of Black soldiers in previous conflicts, negative stereotypes of Blacks still had not been dispelled, and little was expected of them in the Great War. Black troops mostly served as stevedores and cooks or were deployed in labor battalions. Of the 380,000 African American men who served in the military during World War I, only about 42,000 saw combat. And, when the war ended, they returned home in segregated ships to very little fanfare.

These were also the years of the First Great Migration, the movement between 1910 and 1940 of roughly 1.75 million Black Americans from the rural South to the urban North seeking a better life. The most popular destinations were such metropolitan centers as Chicago, Detroit, Cincinnati, Cleveland, Kansas City, Indianapolis, Newark, New York, and Philadelphia. And in these cities Blacks did find some relief from racially based inequality and injustice. Most were able to vote and had access to better public schools and more public facilities. Yet segregation persisted, as did conflicts within Black communities themselves.

Black Americans and the 1920s

America's deep-seated racism continued to manifest itself in the 1920s. Social Darwinism was still going strong, and, thanks to D. W. Griffith's *The Birth of a Nation* (1915), Ku Klux Klan activity had increased. (*The Birth of a Nation*—a silent film directed by D. W. Griffith, starring Lillian Gish, and adapted from Thomas Dixon's 1905 novel and play *The Clansman*—is considered to be in some ways a landmark of film history, mostly because of its technical virtuosity. Its plot, part history and part fiction, follows two families—one pro-Union, the other pro-Confederacy—from the Civil War through Reconstruction. In this account, immoral and ignorant Blacks, aided by greedy White radical Republicans, take control of the government of South Carolina, their evil machinations thwarted only by the heroic Ku Klux Klan. The film was so popular that President Wilson screened it at the White House, calling it "history written in lightning." It remains controversial as probably the most racist film ever made in Hollywood.) Many Whites still feared the influx of European immigrants and southern Black migrants. And pseudoscientific studies claimed that the United States was committing race suicide, reinforcing notions of White supremacy and setting the stage for the congressional imposition of immigration restrictions.

Compounding matters was the labor unrest that besieged the nation. In 1919 alone, there were thirty-six hundred strikes mounted by workers seeking better wages and improved working conditions. The prevailing public perception was that the strikes were part of a Communist plot to overthrow the US government. (The Bolsheviks had overthrown the Russian provisional government in 1917, finally establishing the Soviet Union in 1923.) And this perception seemed to be confirmed when, over the period 1919–1920, President Wilson's attorney general, A. Mitchell Palmer, ordered some three hundred alien residents and six thousand foreign-born American citizens arrested as spies. The conviction in 1921 of the Italian-born anarchists Nicola Sacco and Bartolomeo Vanzetti for a murder committed during the course of an armed robbery only added fuel to the fire. The first Red Scare was off and running.

In the midst of this turmoil, the Black intellectual and cultural revival known as the Harlem Renaissance was born. The Harlem Renaissance reflected a renewed militancy among African Americans. It was unusual among such movements in its close relationship with civil rights organizations. Over the 1920s and 1930s, it inspired hundreds of Black artists of all stripes—writers, painters, actors, dancers—seeking to convey their own social and cultural perspective in their work. Most popular among the Harlem Renaissance voices, however, were the performers—the musicians, singers, and dancers—who ushered in the Jazz Age. During the height of Prohibition, Whites and Blacks alike flocked to Harlem to hear performers such as Edward K. "Duke" Ellington, Bill "Bojangles" Robinson, Earl "Snakehips" Tucker, and a young Louis Armstrong.

Probably the most extreme political response to the challenges of the 1920s was that of Marcus Garvey and the Universal Negro Improvement Association, which espoused a radical form of racial pride and self-help. Garvey attracted several million followers, creating the largest Black mass movement in the United States to date. Unlike most Black civil rights leaders at the time, Garvey believed that Black and White Americans needed to live separate lives, going so far as to advocate a return to Africa. His downfall came when he started selling shares for an envisioned Black Star Line, a Black-owned and -staffed passenger and shipping line that would travel between Africa and the Americas. He and three associates were indicted by the federal government on twelve counts of mail fraud. They were found guilty and sent to a federal penitentiary in Atlanta in 1925. President Calvin Coolidge later commuted Garvey's sentence and deported him in 1927.

Blacks did find a home in sports during the 1920s. Most notably, Andrew "Rube" Foster established the eight-team baseball Negro National League, the first stable Black American baseball league in the nation, with teams in Chicago, Dayton, Detroit, Indianapolis, Kansas City, New York, Philadelphia, and St. Louis. Black American baseball thrived, becoming for a time the third largest African American business venture in the nation.

African Americans, FDR, and the New Deal

The Roaring Twenties came to an abrupt end with the Wall Street Crash of 1929. By the time the crash was over, stocks had lost 90 percent of their value, bank failures had caused millions of Americans to lose their life savings, even more had lost their jobs, and, seemingly overnight, the United States found itself in the throes of the Great Depression. Not surprisingly, Black Americans were especially hard-hit. Receiving, not unexpectedly, little help from President Herbert Hoover's Republican government, they were left to their own devices.

Still, Black Americans continued tirelessly to pursue the quest for civil rights. During the 1930s, the NAACP became even more proactive, challenging institutional racism in government-sponsored relief programs, inequality in education, and the exclusion of Blacks from the voting process in the South. Its efforts eventually led to several important cases being brought to the US Supreme Court, the most prominent being *Brown v. Board of Education* (1954) (discussed below). Black women too continued their involvement with the civil rights movement; for example, some took part in NAACP fundraising and membership drives and campaigns, and others served as White House advisers after the election of Franklin Delano Roosevelt in 1932 as, during his first hundred days in office, the president devised and pushed through Congress the set of economic initiatives that became known as the *New Deal.* Indeed, so much progress had been made that Roosevelt assembled a group of twenty-seven prominent Black men and women who served as informal advisers to the president—the so-called Black Cabinet—who pushed for the color-blind adoption and implementation of public policy. Even relations between African Americans and labor unions improved. More precisely, local unions that were linked to the American Federation of Labor continued to bar Blacks from joining, but the fledgling Congress of Industrial Organizations welcomed interracial and multiethnic organizing efforts.

World War II and the Seeds of Revolution

As the world's economy worsened during the 1930s, the international order also began to collapse. In Europe, the rise of nationalism ushered in fascist governments in Germany and Italy that sought to take political and economic control of Europe, and, in Asia, Japan sought to establish a new order with itself at the center. When hostilities broke out, isolationism prevailed in the United States, and Roosevelt was at first reluctant to become involved. But that changed with the bombing of Pearl Harbor by the Japanese on December 7, 1941. War was declared on Japan on December 8 and on Germany, Japan's ally, on December 11.

Many African Americans responded to the emerging world crisis with increased activism. The initial spark was the invasion of Ethiopia by Italy in 1935, which prompted fundraising campaigns in Black communities across the nation. The conflict alerted many African Americans to the dangers of fascism, renewed an identification with Africa, and helped generate interest in the creation of a Black American international perspective.

Despite the fact that the United States was gearing up for all-out war, it was business as usual as far as racial discrimination was concerned. Particularly galling was the unwillingness to allow Blacks to participate in the civilian war effort. Hoping to create a spirit of activism, a young Black man wrote a letter to the African American *Pittsburgh Courier* suggesting a

"Double V campaign": victory over fascism abroad and victory over racism at home. Black America embraced this new slogan. Scattered protest movements became a unified, grassroots movement that focused its attention on the federal government and planned what would have been the first March on Washington, which was averted only when the president issued Executive Order 8802: "There shall be no discrimination in the employment of workers in the defense industry or government because of race, creed, color, or national origin." To ensure compliance, Roosevelt created the Fair Employment Practices Committee, which was given the power to investigate complaints of discrimination. Sadly, the order did not broach the topic of the desegregation of the military.

Indeed, demands that the armed forces be integrated met with intense resistance. Despite clear evidence to the contrary, Blacks were still considered naturally mentally inferior and physically unfit for combat. They remained restricted to segregated, noncombat units. Nevertheless, their wartime performance was outstanding. Especially noteworthy was that of the famous Tuskegee Airmen.

With victory in Europe in May 1945 and victory in the Pacific in August, the United States began the transition to peacetime. Unfortunately, with the dismantlement of the nation's wartime machinery came the dismantlement of many of the gains Black Americans had seen during the war years. They were almost back at square one, having to renegotiate access to quality public education, affordable housing, and fair working conditions, to name only a few. But they were not willing to give up without a fight. Interestingly, they were aided by the onset of the Cold War. In that tense East-West contest, the state of race relations in the United States gave the lie to America's claim to be a role model of democratic government that the rest of the world should follow, prompting a renewed urge to remediate the situation.

An Overview of the Modern Civil Rights Movement

Thanks to World War II, the United States came roaring back from the Great Depression, and, during the early 1950s, most White Americans experienced unparalleled prosperity. But, for Black Americans, not much had changed. Because of White flight and the decline in the number of factory jobs in urban centers, they suffered high rates of unemployment, and once-nice neighborhoods deteriorated, becoming increasingly dangerous. The scene was set for a political explosion.

The foundation of the coming social movement was the 1954 US Supreme Court decision in *Brown v. Board of Education of Topeka, Kansas.* That case changed the landscape of the nation forever, dismantling as it did the entire system of legal racial segregation that had prevailed since 1896 and *Plessy v. Ferguson.* In it, the Court concluded: "In the field of public education the doctrine of 'separate but equal' has no place. Separate educational facilities are inherently unequal." And it seemed just a matter of time before the entire structure of Jim Crow fell. That was not, however, the case.

In response to the *Brown* decision, White resistance campaigns were mounted to stop integration at all costs. But Black efforts were galvanized by the lynching in 1955 of fourteen-year-old Emmett Till and the acquittal of the two men who killed him. This tragedy triggered the 1955 Montgomery Bus Boycott, thereby setting in motion the first phase of the modern civil rights movement. Congresses and presidents were pressured to pass such civil rights legislation as the Civil Rights Acts of 1957 and 1964 and the Voting Rights Act of 1965. *Brown v. Board of Education* led to the integration of Central High School in Little Rock, Arkansas, in 1957. Grassroots organizers created the Southern Christian Leadership Conference in 1957 and the Student Nonviolent Coordinating Committee in 1960 and organized the sit-ins of the 1960s, the freedom rides of 1961, and the March on Washington for Jobs and Freedom of 1963. President Johnson launched the War on Poverty in 1964. This much progress had not been seen since the Reconstruction Era.

Still, the violence continued, White support began to fall away, and government-led social progress slowed, Johnson's attention turning from domestic policy to foreign policy as US involvement in the Vietnam War increased. Disillusionment set in, and younger African American activists were radicalized. Whereas the goal of older generations of activists had been integration brought about by peaceful civil disobedience, the younger generation championed separatism and, with it, the notions of Black nationalism and Black Power. The new role model was not Martin Luther King Jr. but Malcolm X, not the NAACP but the Black Panther Party. The second phase of the modern civil rights movement had begun.

With the rise of Black nationalism and Black Power came the rise of the Black Arts movement, which generated intense political and cultural

A young woman holding a banner at the March on Washington, August 28, 1963. (Courtesy of Rowland Scherman. https://creativecommons.org/licenses/by/2.0/legalcode.)

debate in the late 1960s and early 1970s. What role should Black art and Black artists play in the ongoing struggle for civil rights? What role (if any) should politics play in art? The Black Arts movement was never not controversial. Artists and authors tended to be racially exclusive and even homophobic, and the movement itself was male dominated. Nevertheless, it had a significant impact on the American arts scene, particularly in terms of poetry and the theater.

Black Americans made great strides politically during this period, a point made more forcefully by some sample statistics. By 1974, there were roughly fifteen hundred African American elected officials outside the South, and, by 1980, that number had increased to almost twenty-five hundred. While in 1972 there were thirteen Black members of Congress, there were forty by 1997. In 1993, there were roughly eighty-one hundred Black elected officials nationwide, a number that only increased during the presidency of Jimmy Carter and beyond.

Finally, three post–World War II developments stimulated immigration, especially from the Caribbean, and, thus, had a major impact on the lives of African Americans: global economic restructuring, the growth of transnational communities, and increased immigrant inclusion. Global economic restructuring remade industrial capital, leading to the concentration of managerial and specialized services in major urban centers and the relocation of other employment opportunities to the urban outskirts, and these changes stimulated an influx of immigrants seeking to fill the low-skill, low-wage service jobs that many Americans refused to take. This influx, in turn, restructured communities as immigrants settled in already-established communities. Initially, the new immigrant populations remained insular, reproducing the cultures they left behind to come to the United States, a sort of segregation by choice. Gradually, however, integration into the existing community occurred as, of necessity, children attended school, parents conducted essential business, families attended church, and so on. The result has often been social and political cooperation between Blacks and Latinos.

Conclusion

Speaking at the 1988 Democratic National Convention, Jesse Jackson asked: "Shall we expand, be inclusive, find unity and power or suffer division and impotence?" (p. 537). And Black Americans answered the call. The power that they now wield manifested itself most famously in the nomination of future president Barack Obama at the 2008 Democratic National Convention and the crafting of the most progressive platform in party history. Black American politics seems to have come of age, testifying to Black Americans' perseverance and validating the struggle that came before.

5

African Americans
and Education

Thomas O. Fuller—the youngest of fourteen children—was born on October 25, 1867, in Franklinton, North Carolina, to J. Henderson Fuller, a wheelwright and carpenter, and Mary Eliza, both formerly enslaved. He attended a local private school, enrolling at age five, then the State Normal School in Franklinton from 1882 to 1885, and then Shaw University, where he studied theology, obtaining a bachelor's degree in 1890 and a master's in 1893. In 1906, he earned a doctorate from the Agricultural and Mechanical College in Norman, Alabama; in 1910, he earned a second doctorate—this one in divinity—from Shaw University.

In this midst of all this, Fuller was ordained a Baptist minister in 1890. That same year, he took a job teaching in the Granville County, North Carolina, public school system. In 1892, he returned to Franklinton to serve as pastor of the local Baptist church. While in Franklinton he also helped establish the Colored Grade School and the Girls' Training School. In 1895, he was appointed principal of the Shiloh Institute in Warrenton, North Carolina. He also became the pastor of a local church as well as the recording secretary of the North Carolina State Sunday School Convention.

In the 1890s, African American Republicans controlled both the Warren County and the Eleventh District political machine, and party officials asked Fuller to run for the district's state senate seat in the 1998 elections. His opponent was a Democrat who ran on a White supremacy platform, and the campaign was a bitterly fought one. He won nevertheless, the first African American to serve in the state senate and the last until 1968.

Fuller held office at a time when racial tensions were running high. The Black community looked to him to push for racial equality, but instead he was a proponent of accommodation. This position gained him little support, either from Blacks or from Whites, and he was given no committee assignments and, for all intents and purposes, rendered impotent despite his best efforts to represent his constituents. During his term in office, the legislature passed a constitutional amendment that effectively disenfranchised Blacks, and his political career was at an end.

When his term ended in 1900, Fuller accepted a position as pastor of a Black Baptist church in Memphis, Tennessee. In 1901, he also began to teach a regular religion course to a group of ministers at Howe Institute, an elementary and secondary school owned by his church. In 1902, he became the principal of Howe, fortifying the curriculum, growing the student body, and raising academic standards. Fuller remained at Howe until 1931. During Fuller's tenure there, Howe became a model for African American education, not just in the South but nationally, owing to its focus on academic achievement, racial uplift, and self-help and the development of a nurturing environment.

Learning Objectives

▼ ▼ ▼

1. How important was literacy during the enslavement period?
2. How did African Americans influence the development of the nation's universal education system?
3. What were the various obstacles African Americans faced as they tried to access numerous formal and semiformal educational facilities?
4. How did African Americans respond to the development of a formally segregated public education system?
5. How did northern segregated public schools function differently than southern segregated public schools?
6. What was the lasting effect of *Brown v. Board of Education*?
7. Do integrated public schools really work?

▲ ▲ ▲

Literacy in the Age of Enslavement

African culture was traditionally oral, so, not surprisingly, illiterate enslaved African Americans employed the tactic of eavesdropping on their masters in order to pick up the news of the day and other useful information. For example, as Henry Bibb noted in his *Narrative of the Life and Adventures of Henry Bibb, an American Slave, Written by Himself*: "All that I heard about liberty and freedom to slaves, I never forgot" (p. 15). But some went beyond eavesdropping. Despite law and custom in the antebellum South that prohibited them from learning to read and write, some enslaved people did manage to become literate. One method employed was to pocket a discarded newspaper, convince a literate acquaintance to read it aloud, and follow each word and phrase carefully. Another was to pay White men and boys to teach them. Yet another was to take advantage of the classes offered by missionary associations. Some individuals even taught themselves.

Of course such activities took place in secret because, if they were discovered, the punishment was severe. Accordingly, those African Americans eager to educate themselves took advantage of the Sabbath, the one day of the week they were not required to work. Since most Whites attended church and socialized afterward, enslaved people were largely unsupervised on Sundays. They simply waited for their owners to leave, then pulled out reading material and writing implements.

Whites feared Black literacy because they recognized its potential to make populations of enslaved people unmanageable. But what was it that motivated Blacks so strongly? Literacy meant access to information and thus power. And it also had its practical aspects. The ability to read and write meant the ability to forge a travel pass and, thus, move freely around the South and even escape to the North.

The Rise of Universal Education in the South

Elite southerners had long believed that the government did not have the authority to mandate state-funded public education for all children. At root, they feared that such government interference would result in the dismantling of the existing social order. Thus, few challenged the status quo. But Black Americans felt differently. Flexing their newfound political muscle (such as it was) in the aftermath of the Confederate surrender at Appomattox, they campaigned for universal, state-supported public education. In this endeavor they were aided by the progressive wing of the Republican Party, the Freedmen's Bureau, northern missionary societies, former members of the Union Army, and a few progressive White southerners.

Initially, such endeavors were jump-started and maintained by both federal money (via the Freedmen's Bureau) and state money (via property taxes). But, when these sources of funding were cut off in the mid-1860s, Black Americans took sole responsibility for the maintenance and operation of their communities' schools. In fact, in 1865, several African American leaders in Georgia formed an education association to supervise the many Black American–sponsored schools throughout the state and establish policies and procedures for them.

In another important way, formerly enslaved people of color initiated and sustained schools without help from any outside financial entity. For instance, the little-known Sabbath school system was operated largely by formerly enslaved African Americans. Frequently, such schools were established before any free or public schools emerged in a local community. These facilities, normally sponsored by a local church, operated mainly in the evenings or on weekends and provided instruction in basic literacy.

The African American
Education System North and South

The years between 1820 and 1860 saw most northern public schools move toward a racially segregated education system. The impetus was usually the presence in a school district of a large number of African American children. The rationale given publicly was that the changes necessary to accommodate innately mentally inferior Black students would lower the quality of the education received by White students. The actual rationale was that an integrated school district would lead to integrated neighborhoods. Needless to say, segregation won out.

The result was a mixed bag. Some states did take on the responsibility of developing and funding separate schools for Blacks, but others refused to do so, leaving Black communities to create their own, private, schools. Furthermore, the education on offer in those Black schools that were created was not necessarily on a par with that on offer in White schools. There were several reasons for the difference. Curricula in Black schools tended to be neither as rigorous nor as comprehensive as those in White schools owing to preconceived notions of the students' limited capabilities. Black schools, public or private, also tended to be inadequately funded, most were overcrowded and dilapidated, and the teachers who worked in them,

EDUCATION

OF

COLORED CHILDREN.

CORRESPONDENCE BETWEEN

THE

BOARD OF EDUCATION OF SAVANNAH

AND THE

AMERICAN MISSIONARY ASSOCIATION OF NEW YORK,

RELATIVE TO THE

ESTABLISHMENT OF SCHOOLS FOR THE COLORED CHILDREN

In the City and County.

SAVANNAH:

MORNING NEWS STEAM-POWER PRESS.

1872.

Title page of a pamphlet outlining attempts to establish a school for African American children in Savannah, Georgia, during the Reconstruction period. (Printed by Morning News Steam-Power Press, 1872. Courtesy of African American Pamphlet Collection, Library of Congress: https: //lccn.loc.gov/91898971.)

White and Black both, were badly paid. At best Black students received a substandard education. At worst—where no schools had been created for them or those that had been created were closed—they received no education at all.

Somewhat surprisingly, some northern African American leaders and progressive Whites defended the system of segregated schools, claiming that such facilities would help students preserve their cultural identity. Not surprisingly, most parents accepted it, at least initially. Better a segregated education than no education at all. But, as the antebellum years drew to a close, more and more Black Americans—most notably Frederick Douglass—came to see the value of an integrated education and pressed persistently and passionately for such a system, to little avail. In the run-up to the Civil War, only Massachusetts ended the use of segregated schools altogether.

In the South, by comparison, many African American children received no formal education whatsoever. Public schools were segregated, and, even if they were not, enslaved children forced to serve as agricultural laborers would have had no access to them. What Black schools there were operated only sporadically—out of churches or people's homes—and generally had to do without books, chalkboards, desks, and writing implements.

There were, however, some notable exceptions. Progressive northerners and northern institutions funded facilities that regularly offered courses in English, composition, math, and religion. And African American voluntary associations (including mutual aid, benevolent, and self-improvement societies and fraternal organizations) regularly served as schools. (Mutual aid societies were particularly attractive in that they also offered health care and childcare.) African American men's literacy societies and Masonic lodges also took up the banner of literacy, seeking to reduce the illiteracy rate among African Americans as quickly and as quietly as possible. Such activities predated the Civil War and continued through it and into the antebellum years.

After the war, a small but important group of African American leaders emerged who, with the support of the Republican Party, eagerly pushed for statewide integrated public education systems. The task was difficult, unpopular, and, most importantly, expensive. Schools had to be built, teachers employed, textbooks provided. In the end, the results were very limited, primarily because most southern states were still in economic and social turmoil.

Such efforts were not aided by the fact that many Americans, Black and White, opposed compulsory public education, arguing that parents, not the state, should determine whether their children should attend school or work. In the end, the results of the push for integrated public education were uneven where they had any success at all. And higher education institutions serving Blacks had to wait for Reconstruction.

Quite a few African American Reconstruction leaders supported the development of higher education institutions. Atlanta University, founded in Atlanta, Georgia, in 1865—three months after the end of the Civil War—was the first of these. And others soon followed—for example, Claflin University, founded in Orangeburg, South Carolina, in 1869, and Alcorn A&M College, founded in Lorman, Mississippi, in 1871—many taking advantage of the 1862 Morrill Land-Grant Act, which provided federal funds for the creation of agricultural and mechanical colleges. By the mid-1880s, almost every southern state hosted a Black college or university.

Public Education and the "Race Problem" around the Turn of the Century and Beyond

African Americans who sought an education during the late nineteenth century and the early twentieth faced many obstacles. Chief among them was the poverty in which most lived during these years. Only a very few had the opportunity to acquire a quality formal education, no mean feat given that they had to work to help support their families and that rural schools rarely operated regularly. Even into the early years of the twentieth century, few public high schools for Blacks were to be found in the South, and those that did exist continued to be underfunded, despite *Cumming v. Richmond County Board of Education* (1899), which sought to bar the collection of taxes that were earmarked only for the support of White schools but was ultimately dismissed by the US Supreme Court. As a result, African Americans seeking a quality secondary or postsecondary education had to leave home to find it.

It was also generally held, even among African Americans, that the most appropriate type of formal education for Blacks was industrial or domestic training, which imparted the kinds of skills they needed to become productive members of society. Typical of such training was that provided at the Hampton Normal and Agricultural Institute, founded in 1868 in Virginia.

Led by Samuel Chapman Armstrong, a White missionary, Hampton trained thousands of African Americans (and Native Americans) in vocational skills, instilling the notions of hard work, disciplined behavior, and Christian morality in the process. Little emphasis was placed on critical thinking. Instead, students were taught to conform to middle-class values and advised to acquiesce to Jim Crow social norms.

Hampton's most famous graduate was Booker T. Washington, a formerly enslaved person who became the nation's leading advocate for industrial/vocational training. In 1881, Washington founded the Tuskegee Institute, developing there a curriculum modeled after his experience at Hampton that became the foundation for African American public education nationwide, especially in the South. Most notably, however, he was the architect of what became known as the Atlanta Compromise, an unwritten agreement with White leaders that, in return for receiving a rudimentary education, basic economic opportunities, and justice within the legal system, southern Blacks would not fight discrimination, segregation, and disenfranchisement. However, not all African Americans agreed with him.

Washington's most vocal opponent was probably W. E. B. Du Bois. A graduate of Harvard University (from which he obtained a doctorate in 1895), Du Bois was convinced that a different approach to African American education and race relations was sorely needed. In 1903, while serving as a professor of economics, history, and sociology at Atlanta University, he published *The Souls of Black Folk,* an effort to portray the genius and humanity of Blacks. In it, he called for the growth of a cadre of African American male intellectuals to lead the race toward better lives, academically, politically, and economically. While Du Bois's ideas were embraced by African American elites, the debate over the kind of education most appropriate for Blacks continued into the 1930s.

Unfortunately, despite the best efforts of African American public figures like Du Bois, race relations in almost every American city—especially northern urban centers—deteriorated in the early years of the twentieth century. Any gains that African Americans had made during Reconstruction had all but vanished. Not even northern White Republicans were ready to support full social and political equality for Blacks, who therefore found themselves in a particularly precarious position. Harmony between the races was maintained as long as Blacks did not get above themselves and interacted with Whites only when absolutely necessary. But with the First

This 1916 political cartoon depicts the specter of Abraham Lincoln looming disapprovingly over a man who is cracking the whip of "Negro Segregation." (Wood engraving by Jack Smith, 1916. Courtesy of the Missouri History Museum: http: //collections.mohistory.org/resource/148270.)

Great Migration—the movement of large numbers of African Americans from the rural South to the urban North beginning in 1916 and motivated largely by the economic upturn triggered by the entrance of the United States into World War I in 1914—race relations turned positively toxic. Blacks were effectively locked out of the very opportunities—educational and otherwise—they sought in fleeing north. Developments in Chicago are exemplary of the situation in which they found themselves.

By 1890, Chicago was an industrial powerhouse with a population of roughly 1 million, and, of that 1 million, about 1.3 percent was Black. By 1900, the Black proportion of the population had grown a bit, to 1.9 percent, but then it exploded to 4.1 percent by 1920 and 6.9 percent by 1930. These new in-migrants, who were forced to settle on the city's South Side, found themselves hemmed in by hostile middle-class White neighborhoods to the west and the south whose residents viewed their new neighbors as potential competition in the labor market and a threat to the quality of the public education system. Despite organized efforts by Black activists—and, in fact, in response to them—White public officials closed ranks and refused to allow African Americans to play any role whatsoever in the city's schools, not even the segregated schools to which their children were relegated. The situation stayed this way into the 1950s.

The Road to *Brown* and Its Impact

Only with the 1954 ruling in *Brown v. Board of Education of Topeka* was segregation in American public schools finally put to rest. But that ruling was but the last step in a journey that the Legal Defense and Educational Fund (LDEF) of the National Association for the Advancement of Colored People (NAACP) began in the 1940s. Of course, the LDEF program was not narrowly focused on ending segregation in education. It took on segregation across the broad spectrum of American life.

Spearheading this venture were Constance Baker Motley, a 1903 graduate of Yale Law School, and Charles Hamilton Houston, a 1923 graduate of Harvard Law School. Under their direction, the LDEF won unexpected victories in *Smith v. Allwright* (1944), which declared the use of segregated voting procedures unconstitutional, *Morgan v. Virginia* (1946), which declared unconstitutional a state statute requiring segregation on interstate train travel, and *Shelley v. Kraemer* (1948), which outlawed the use of restrictive residential covenants prohibiting Blacks from owning or renting property. Having established these precedents, the LDEF set its sights on segregation in public schools.

In arguing *Brown* before the Supreme Court, the LDEF team, spearheaded by Motley and Thurgood Marshall (who took over for Houston after his death in 1950), contended that the current education system, which still rested on the 1896 decision in *Plessy v. Ferguson*, was unconstitutional even if the separate education provided in Black schools were equal in quality to that provided in White schools. The Court agreed, ruling unanimously that a classification based solely on race was a violation of the Fourteenth Amendment. In laying out the Court's opinion, Chief Justice Earl Warren proclaimed: "We conclude that in the field of public education the doctrine of separate but equal has no place. Separate educational facilities are inherently unequal."

The *Brown* decision meant the end of the Jim Crow system nationwide. But the process of dismantling that system was neither easy nor simple, school desegregation being a case in point. In 1955, in a case that came to be known as *Brown II*, arguments were brought before the Supreme Court by a number of school districts requesting relief from the task presented by immediate desegregation. The Court's decision gave oversight power to the district courts and ordered that desegregation take place "with all deliberate speed," language that was seen by critics as too ambiguous to ensure timely compliance. (In fact, many states took advantage of the *Brown II* decision to delay integration for years.) It did not help matters that President Dwight D. Eisenhower was strongly opposed to the integration of public schools.

Importantly, the Civil Rights Act of 1964 came to the aid of the desegregation process. This landmark piece of legislation outlawed discrimination based on race, color, religion, sex, and national origin and prohibited the unequal application of voter registration requirements, racial segregation in schools and public accommodations, and employment discrimination. Title VI of the act was especially pertinent to the desegregation of public schools in that it outlawed discrimination by programs receiving federal funds and mandated the immediate withholding of such funds from noncompliant institutions. The power that the Civil Rights Act gave federal authorities was bolstered by the Elementary and Secondary Education Act of 1965, which provided federal funding for primary and secondary education and emphasized equal access. (The act was part of President Lyndon B. Johnson's War on Poverty program.) Nevertheless, by the mid-1960s, only about 15 percent of school districts in the South had been integrated.

Not surprisingly, the desegregation process saw setbacks. For example, in the late 1960s, lower courts began to rule that the *Brown* decision applied only if it could be proved that segregation was intentional and not the result of natural settlement patterns or other factors. Also, resistance to segregation was so fierce in places that some governors—most famously George Wallace of Mississippi—refused to allow Black students to enroll in their states' flagship institution (in Wallace's case, the University of Mississippi). It took the federal government's mobilization of the national guard to ensure compliance with the law.

After the 1971 Supreme Court ruling in *Swann v. Charlotte-Mecklenburg Board of Education* (which upheld busing as an appropriate remedy for racial imbalance), busing became the sole means of desegregation employed nationwide. But busing was never popular with the American public. (Even President Richard M. Nixon opposed it.) Forced integration through busing prompted urban unrest, the worst instance being in Boston, which saw at least forty antibusing riots from autumn 1974 through autumn 1976. But it also triggered White flight from large and small urban centers nationwide, a last-ditch, desperate end run. Obviously, new strategies were in order.

One such strategy was the development of the *magnet* and *alternative* school movements. Magnet schools are public schools offering specialized courses or curricula. Alternative schools are private educational establishments that employ nontraditional curricula and methods and are meant to appeal to students for whom mainstream institutions are not a good fit. Both are designed to draw students from different school districts, thus achieving de facto and voluntary desegregation.

Unfortunately, by the 1990s, the tide had turned against desegregation, and, thanks to state supreme court rulings that it was meant to be only a temporary redressing of historical wrongs, school districts across the nation began the process of resegregation. And, despite the continuing presence of magnet and alternative schools, all available evidence shows a pattern of growing segregation. The current state of affairs is, fortunately, not a case of one step forward, two steps back, but it is still disheartening.

6

African Americans at Home and Abroad

Racial Construction and Resistance

Born on April 9, 1898, in Princeton, New Jersey, Paul LeRoy Robeson was the youngest of the five children of William Drew Robeson, a runaway enslaved African American who went on to become an ordained minister, and Maria Louisa Bustill, a biracial Quaker who came from a Pennsylvania abolitionist family. In 1910, the Robesons moved to Somerville, New Jersey, where William served as pastor of the St. Thomas African Methodist Episcopal Zion Church until his untimely death in 1918. After graduating from high school, young Paul attended Rutgers University on a four-year academic scholarship. While at Rutgers, he was inducted into Phi Beta Kappa and the National Honor Society, was elected his class's valedictorian, and earned fifteen varsity letters in a number of sports. He was, however, inducted into the College Football Hall of Fame only posthumously.

Robeson went on to receive a law degree from Columbia University, meeting and marrying Eslanda Cardoza Goode while he was still in school. After graduating in 1922, he worked at a prominent New York law firm for a while, but his true passion was acting. And Essie—a pathologist—supported them while he launched a career in the theater. Success came quickly when, in 1925, he was cast as the lead in a revival of Eugene O'Neill's *The Emperor Jones* and his powerful performance catapulted him to fame. His credits ultimately included memorable productions of *Show Boat* (1928) and *Othello* (1930) in London and such films as *Body and Soul* (1924), *Jericho* (1937), and *Proud Valley* (1939).

During his travels abroad, Robeson had noticed that racial prejudice was not as ingrained in Europe as it was in the United States. And, during the 1930s and 1940s, while he continued to perform, he also became politically active, speaking out against racism, and also supporting organized labor and antiwar campaigns worldwide. It was because of this outspokenness that he ran afoul of the House Un-American Activities Committee (HUAC) during the height of the Red Scare. Accused of being a Communist, he saw his acting and singing engagements dry up after his 1956 HUAC testimony. He performed only sporadically thereafter but remained politically active until his retirement in 1963, after which he spent the remainder of his life in seclusion, dying in 1976 after a stroke.

Learning Objectives

▼ ▼ ▼

1. What factors have led to the creation of an African or African American foreign policy consciousness?
2. How did the ideology of Black nationalism originate and develop in the United States?
3. What are some of the differences between Black nationalism and Pan-Africanism?
4. What was the Ethiopian movement?
5. How was the modern civil rights movement affected by the emerging international conflicts during the 1950s and 1960s?
6. How did some leaders in the African American community respond to the crisis in South Africa?
7. How are the origins and development of the field of Afrocentricity viewed from an international perspective?

▲ ▲ ▲

African American/African Consciousness, Connections, and Concerns

There is in the United States a long tradition of immigrants organizing for the purpose of lobbying the federal government. When their target has been domestic policy, the aim has usually been an increase in migrant quotas—to their own ethnic group's advantage. When their target has been foreign policy, the aim has usually been US involvement in their home country's affairs. The success or failure of these groups' efforts aside, it is noteworthy that African Americans have rarely taken such collective action. Only in the last sixty or seventy years have they become interested in the international relations and internal affairs of African nations.

Until the early years of the twentieth century, few African Americans had the time or any reason to concern themselves with the affairs of foreign nationals, African or otherwise. But, more insidiously, negative stereotypes about the continent of Africa and its inhabitants dating at least to the earliest years of the slave trade were so powerful that they colored the views of even African Americans. Africanness was to be a source of shame and thus avoided at all costs. Still, there have always been some African Americans who have taken an interest in their cultural heritage. During the colonial period, for example, many enslaved people tried to maintain a connection to their homelands through religion, music, clothing, food, and so on. During the eighteenth century, most Blacks in the United States preferred *African* over any other racial signifier, such as the Spanish- and Portuguese-rooted *Negro,* which was imposed on enslaved people of color by their European captors. In fact, the frequent use of *African* in the naming of organizations and businesses—for example, the Free African Society, the African Methodist Episcopal Church, the African Lodge of Prince Hall Masons, and the Free African Mutual Aid Society—was, in part, designed to instill pride in African Americans North and South.

During the New Nation period (1790–1828), proponents of maintaining an African identity created programs and initiatives to promote the welfare of Africa through emigration, evangelization, and business ventures. As we have seen, in the early nineteenth century, Paul Cuffe promoted emigration to Africa with an eye toward converting the inhabitants and ending the slave trade—until his untimely death in 1817. But others followed in his footsteps. Daniel Coker, an African Methodist Episcopal bishop from Baltimore, and Lott Carey, a Baptist minister and lay physician from Richmond, Virginia, aligned themselves with the mostly White American Colonization Society and, as we have seen in chapter 3, organized the emigration of thousands of African Americans to what became known as Liberia. (Carey himself served as the first governor of Liberia.) The Black nationalist movement, however, had different ideas.

Black Nationalism

Black nationalism is based on the belief that people of African descent share a common ethnic and cultural background, heritage, identity, worldview, and historical experience or perspective. Nationalism has led to and inspired many great social and political movements throughout the history of civilization. Although objectives and tactics may differ, nationalist movements generally espouse certain universal ideas, the most prominent being freedom and equality. However, many historical events and other factors can shape such ideas. Thus, nationalism occasionally aims to create a more inclusive environment within existing institutions.

Racial or ethnic solidarity is an important element of Black nationalism, and it can be created in different ways: the geographic isolation of one society from another, the geographic proximity of similar societies, or the isolation of one group within the larger society. From a transatlantic vantage point, the emergence of a Black nationalist consciousness is both a reaction to and a reflection of Western society's dehumanization of a group of people solely on the basis of their skin color, a form of resistance designed to affirm the unique cultural identity of people of African descent. And, interestingly, Black nationalism has taken many forms: for example, attempts at assimilation into a larger society, isolation within that society, and emigration to escape that society entirely.

Black nationalism in the United States was originally engendered by the transatlantic slave trade, and some of its earliest manifestations were slave revolts and the participation of free Black Americans in the northern abolitionist movement. By the mid-nineteenth century, the Black nationalist consciousness led to the assertion of a distinct African American identity and the demand for full and equal participation in society. However, continued enslavement in the South and unequal treatment in the North led many African Americans to espouse emigration and the creation of a new national identity somewhere else, whether that be back in Africa or in the Caribbean.

The outbreak of the American Civil War in 1861 led to a temporary halt of the pursuit of both emigration and separation owing to the expectation that the successful resolution of the conflict would not just end slavery but, equally as important, allow people of African descent to know real freedom as true participants in the American national identity. This expectation was, however, only temporarily realized, the end of the Reconstruction

Era bringing with it a new and even amplified round of racially based violence and political oppression and, concomitantly, the resurgence of Black
nationalism.

Pan-Africanism

By the early years of the twentieth century, Black nationalism had been
absorbed into a stronger, more vigorous movement known as Pan-Africanism.
Pan-African ideas—which can be boiled down to the notion that all people
of African descent share not just a history but a worldview and a destiny
and, thus, a sense of interconnectedness—first began to circulate around the
middle of the nineteenth century. They were espoused by a variety of groups
but did not truly come of age until 1900, when Alexander Walters, a bishop
of the African Methodist Episcopal Zion Church, joined the Trinidadian
Sylvester Williams, Anna Julia Cooper, and W. E. B. Du Bois to organize a
Pan-African conference in London. The outcome of the conference, which
attracted over thirty delegates from Africa, the United States, the Caribbean,
and various parts of Europe, was the creation of the Pan-African Association. The association took as its mission securing civil and political rights
for and improving the living conditions of African people everywhere and
promoting friendly relations between races, and it hoped to do this by
establishing branches throughout Africa, the Caribbean, and the United
States and sponsoring an international conference every other year. Unfortunately, the association drew little interest outside the Caribbean and was
underfunded and plagued with internal disagreements and, thus, survived
for only a year or so.

Nevertheless, the Pan-African movement continued to live on. For
example, drawing on their experience as members of Alexander Crummell's
American Negro Academy, founded in Washington, DC, by Alexander
Crummell in 1897 to support African American academic scholarship,
in 1911 John E. Bruce and the Puerto Rican native Arturo Schomburg
established a research institute in Harlem promoting the study of the works
and views of people of African descent throughout the Americas. Originally
known as the Negro Society for Historical Research, the institute eventually became the basis for the establishment of the Schomburg Center for
Research in Black Culture. Also influential in the United States was the
work of Edward Wilmot Blyden, a Liberian scholar born in the Danish West

Indies in 1832 who introduced to the Pan-African movement such ideas as vindicationism, or the detailed examination of the importance in world history of African nations, and Ethiopianism, or the belief that Ethiopia is the birthplace of humankind and the cradle of Christianity. Blyden was also, however, very much a product of his time, viewing as he did African civilization as primitive, barbaric even, and needing to be brought into the modern era.

By the 1920s, a variety of forms of Pan-Africanism had developed. Particularly important, as we saw in chapter 4, was Marcus Garvey and the Universal Negro Improvement Association. Another enterprise, small but potent, was the African Blood Brotherhood, founded in 1919 by Cyril Briggs, which sought to link its Pan-African politics to African liberation, various independence movements in the Caribbean, and the struggle against racism in the United States. The 1920s and 1930s saw a revival of the Pan-African Conference by means of a series of Pan-African congresses led by such prominent figures as W. E. B. Du Bois, William Walling, and Blaise Diagne of Senegal. The congresses pushed for the independence of African nations, but it would take the Second World War for Europe to loosen its grip on its colonies on the continent.

The Ethiopian Movement

In November 1934, an Anglo-Ethiopian commission accompanied by an escort of approximately six hundred Ethiopian soldiers was surveying the border between Ethiopia and Italian Somaliland when it encountered an Italian military force. Hostilities ensued, both sides suffering high casualties. The conflict was referred to the League of Nations, which declined to blame either side. But the stage was set for the Second Italo-Ethopian War, which began in October 1935 with the invasion of Ethiopia by the Italian army.

Despite dealing themselves with rampant racism and the continuing economic depression, African Americans took the Italian fascists' threat to heart and came out in support of Ethiopia, mounting small- and large-scale public demonstrations. Prominent public figures, including Walter White, Adam Clayton Powell Jr., Mary Church Terrell, W. E. B. Du Bois, Carter G. Woodson, and Charles Wesley, and organizations, including the National Association for the Advancement of Colored People, the Urban League, and the National Association of Colored Women, became involved, pledging support for Ethiopia and its people, largely on racial grounds. The African American press also became involved, such publications as the *Baltimore Afro-American,* the *Chicago Defender,* and the *Pittsburgh Courier* providing extensive coverage of the conflict.

The feeling was that African Americans deserved a voice in their nation's foreign policy, especially when African countries were involved, and activists kept applying pressure wherever they could. Money was raised for Ethiopia's defense, the White House was lobbied to abandon its official position of neutrality, and the Vatican was asked to intervene in the conflict. The newly formed Provisional Committee for the Defense of Ethiopia, led by Garvey-ites and Communists in New York, and International Council of Friends of Ethiopia, led by the historian Willis Huggins in London, organized a cadre of community activists, leftist intellectuals, and civil rights leaders to formally push the League of Nations to come to Ethiopia's aid.

In the end, the effort to aid Ethiopia failed, and the country fell in the spring of 1936, occupied by the Italians until their defeat in World War II. And the question remains as to why, at this time, African Americans felt a greater sense of racial identity with Ethiopia than they did with the rest of the continent. The takeaway for us, however, is that, though it was unsuc-cessful, this first flexing of African American political muscle emboldened activists in their attempts to organize their political base, whether the issues were foreign or domestic.

The Civil Rights Movement and International Politics

During the 1940s and early 1950s, activists continued the push to develop among African Americans an identification with others of African descent elsewhere in the diaspora and link the struggle against racial violence and political oppression in the United States with the emerging international anticolonial movement. One organization that figured prominently in this effort was the Council on African Affairs (CAA), founded in Harlem in 1937 by Black American socialists with ties to both the Communist Party and the African National Congress. The council published a regular newsletter, *Spotlight on Africa,* and a monthly bulletin, *New Africa,* and remained active until the mid-1950s, when the politics of the McCarthy era caught up with it as it had with other, similar organizations.

Thereafter, activists retrenched for a while, focusing on the differences between Black Americans and Africans rather than on the bonds that had been so forcefully articulated during and after World War II. However, during the later years of the modern civil rights movement, interest in US foreign policy not just toward Africa but also globally began to revive among some African American nationalists. For example, during the mid-1960s, whereas some civil rights leaders had severed ties with the American labor movement, others began aligning themselves with the international labor movement, most prominently in the cases of the South African and the Brazilian freedom movements. Still others split the difference between American affairs and international affairs, supporting nonviolent direct-action campaigns at home and the African decolonization movement abroad. Such African-centered and internationalist views had, however, very little influence among African Americans generally, most likely because the idea of the inferiority of Africa and Africans had over the years become so ingrained. Only twice were activists able to organize across class lines and influence US foreign policy: first, as we have seen, in the 1930s in support of an Ethiopia facing invasion by the Italians and, later, in the 1990s in support of the South African antiapartheid movement, to which we now turn.

The Free South Africa Movement

When, at the end of the Second Boer War (1899–1902), Great Britain seized control of the South African Republic and the Orange Free State (which were originally Dutch colonies) and the region was reorganized as the Republic of South Africa, the majority Black population—which had historically been discriminated against—expected to receive full economic, political, and social rights. Instead, the system of racial segregation—which came to be known as *apartheid*—continued and, in fact, became legally institutionalized with the Nationalist Party's electoral triumph in 1948. Not surprisingly, over the course of the twentieth century unrest grew, and, in 1984, violence erupted when the majority of Black South African citizens were denied the right to vote in the newly created tricameral parliament.

Up through the first half of the twentieth century, most African Americans still maintained a romanticized view of the continent of Africa and viewed South Africa in particular as too remote and isolated to be in any way linked to the struggle for civil rights in the United States. Even during the Eisenhower and Kennedy administrations, apartheid was an issue of concern mainly for the predominantly White American Committee on Africa, a private think tank established in 1953. However, as more and more African nations began fighting for their independence, increasing numbers of African American activists began to see the important connection these movements had with the US civil rights movement. For example, in 1962, Martin Luther King Jr., A. Philip Randolph, and several other civil rights leaders formed the American Negro Leadership Conference, a grassroots organization that, among other things, lobbied the Kennedy and Johnson administrations to help all Africans in the fight for freedom and justice.

In the 1970s, during the second phase of the modern civil rights movement, as Black Power, separatist, and nationalist ideas took hold among activists, a powerful Pan-African ethos called for African Americans to identify with the global African world (Africa and the African diaspora). Leading this charge were organizations such as the Congress of African Peoples, the National Black Political Convention, the TransAfrica Forum, and the Congressional Black Caucus. However, it would take until the 1980s and the Regan administration for apartheid to become a central concern among African Americans—and even then only because the brutality employed by the ruling South African regime in quelling dissent could not be ignored by the international community. Even the US government pursued a policy of constructive engagement with the government of P. W. Botha.

During the 1980s, the African American–led antiapartheid movement became more prominent. In the early 1980s, the TransAfrica Forum initiated a series of sit-ins at the South African embassy in Washington, DC, to protest the arrest and imprisonment of Black South African dissidents, chief among them Nelson Mandela. In 1986, the Congressional Black Caucus persuaded the US Congress to enact a trade embargo against South Africa, overriding President Ronald Reagan's veto of the legislation. The pressure continued, and, during the early 1990s, the South African government ended the ban on the African National Congress, released Nelson Mandela from prison after twenty-seven years, granted universal suffrage, and arranged for free elections.

Afrocentricity

Through the early 1980s, the notion of *Afrocentricity* was little known outside Black studies departments. However, it came to prominence beginning in the late 1980s with three books published by the Temple University professor Molefi K. Asante—*Afrocentricity* (1980), *Kemet, Afrocentricity, and Knowledge* (1990), and *The Afrocentric Idea* (1998). Asante's argument was that people of African descent must move beyond the Eurocentrism that had been imposed on them for centuries to develop a new perspective, one arising from their own history and experience.

At the core of Afrocentrism is the notion that the culture into which African Americans are expected to assimilate was designed and has developed historically specifically to keep them marginalized in relation to the dominant White society. In response, people of African descent must reject the notion of assimilation into that great melting pot that is American society—which means the rejection of European cultural traditions and heritage—and reclaim a positive and empowering African American identity. Only in this way can people of African descent become independent actors in their own right and true agents of human history going forward.

But not everyone agrees. Some scholars have argued that Afrocentricity is regressive, fostering self-segregation and heightening current racial conflict. They also see it as naive, positing an imagined West as a symbol of all that is bad in the world and an imagined Africa as a symbol of all that is good. Things are not so black and white, they argue.

Conclusion

Owing largely to global economic crisis, the number of migrants arriving in the United States each year has increased exponentially since the 1970s, and many of these migrants are Latin Americans of African descent. But some members of these newly arriving groups have not thought deeply about the concept of race, particularly what it means to be Black in the United States, and are unprepared for the discrimination they face even if they are granted a path to full citizenship. As a result, many have created their own voluntarily segregated communities in such major urban centers as New York, Chicago, Los Angeles, and Houston.

Despite continued progress, the African American community still does not speak with one voice when it comes to race relations abroad. Yes, a consensus of sorts was reached about the evils of apartheid and the need for intervention in the South African situation. But, at the same time, most African Americans, along with most of the international community, ignored the violence of the Rwandan genocide (1994). African Americans still seem more concerned with race relations at home.

7

African American Religious Traditions

The Origin and Development of a Black Liberation Theology from the Colonial Era to Reconstruction

Born into slavery on February 14, 1760, Richard Allen was as a young man influenced by the political rhetoric of individual and natural rights surrounding the American Revolution, the religious revivalism of the First Great Awakening, the creation of numerous church denominations, the gradual end of slavery in the North, the increasing manumission of enslaved African Americans in the Upper South, and the emerging free Black American community in the North. Purchasing his freedom for about $2,000 in 1780 and converting to Methodism, he quickly distinguished himself as an orator despite the fact that he possessed no formal training, beginning a six-year tour as a lecturer and prophetic minister that took him to Delaware, Maryland, New Jersey, and Pennsylvania.

In 1786, Allen joined the staff of Philadelphia's St. George Methodist Church as a lay preacher. For many years, the White church trustees had restricted the number of services at which the African American members of the congregation were allowed. And, during these supposedly integrated church services, strict segregationist practices were adhered to, such as relegating African Americans to the gallery and restricting Black preachers to early morning services. Partly in response to their experience at St. George, Allen and Absalom Jones, another Black lay preacher, proposed creating an all-Black church, but at the time the idea received very little support among both Blacks and Whites.

Nevertheless, Allen persevered. In 1787, along with Jones, he established the Free African Society, an organization dedicated to the elimination of slavery and racial prejudice everywhere. Then, in 1794, he founded the St. George Mother Bethel African Methodist Episcopal Church. Dedicated to the expression of African and African American religious traditions, practices, and theology, Mother Bethel quickly became the largest African American church in Philadelphia. Allen was ordained in 1799 and became the pastor of Mother Bethel. However, he still was subjected to the authority and power of the White leadership of the Methodist Church. It was only in 1816 that the Pennsylvania Supreme Court granted Mother Bethel independent status, marking the beginning of the independent Black American church movement in the United States.

Learning Objectives

▼ ▼ ▼

1. What are some of the distinguishing characteristics of African American religion?
2. What are some of the main themes or core concepts of African American religion?
3. How did the cultural heritage of people of African descent affect evolving notions of their faith during the colonial period?
4. How did enslaved African people respond to the Christian faith of their captors?
5. What are some of the foundational principles of African American religion?
6. What were the origins of the first African American churches?
7. How did African American churches emerge in the North?
8. What factors led to the growth of African American churches during the antebellum years, the Civil War, and Reconstruction?

▲ ▲ ▲

African American Religious Traditions

From the time they first arrived in the Western Hemisphere, people of African descent brought with them their own religious/philosophical heritage, one rooted in such traditions and customs as protective charms, herbal medicine, a belief in an afterlife, and the protection afforded by sacred ground. They were, naturally, introduced to the Western Christian religious heritage and often embraced it, but they also held on to their African-centered worldview and, ultimately, created a synthesis of the two that addressed their particular concerns and experiences. And that synthesis is at the heart of the Black American religious experience even today. But that synthesis cannot be understood without basic knowledge of the traditional African religious experience.

African religious traditions and practices are complex and diverse, but some general themes appear. First, there is a belief in one supreme god. Mostly this god is a father, but sometimes it is a mother, and occasionally it takes on both male and female characteristics, representing a type of universal spiritual being. Second, in African religious traditions, God is both near and far. Africans engage with him or her as well as his or her assistants daily. Third, deceased ancestors are regarded as intermediaries or intercessors between the living and their creator. This arrangement reinforces the respect accorded a family's elders. Fourth, the importance of balance between individual identity and responsibility and collective identity and responsibility is emphasized, whether that collective unit is a family, a village, or a country, the emphasis here being living up to high moral standards. Fifth is respect for nature, the natural and the human worlds seen as being interconnected. Finally, there is a belief in some form of life after death as a stage of human development that reflects the natural pattern of death and rebirth.

Complicating matters are external influences that varied by region. For example, when the slave trade took hold, Islam dominated North Africa, Eastern Christianity dominated West and East Africa, and Western Christianity could be found in North Africa as a result of the influence of Rome. Unfortunately, however, given the limited amount of information available, reconstructing the religious life of enslaved Africans is difficult. Some scholars contend that enslavement and the introduction of Western Christianity destroyed all traces of African cultural traditions, and some scholars contend that those traditions survived intact. The truth most likely lies somewhere in between.

The Core Themes or Concepts of African American Religion

Religion has played a critical role in the lives of people of color since they first arrived in the Western Hemisphere. The character of this religious experience reflects the precarious status that Black Americans hold within the larger society. Their religious institutions may contain some of the same basic elements as those of White Protestants, but other elements are distinctive to the African American religious experience.

The term *religion* does not necessarily apply to the beliefs of people of African descent because it is culturally grounded. It loses its meaning when it is translated from a Eurocentric to an African or African American frame of reference. The African religious scholar John S. Mbiti, for example, holds that, from an African perspective, religion is a natural, organic philosophy that links the physical and spiritual worlds, especially through music. Thus, because of their African heritage, African Americans have a natural and instinctive conceptualization of God, a conceptualization that can be traced back to the first African indentured servants, who arrived in Jamestown, Virginia, in 1619. And, over time, it has been theorized, this conceptualization was manifested in the concepts of survival, preservation, and liberation.

Survival—which describes the use of religion as a tool to stay alive, that is, to maintain one's sanity, to nourish one's soul, and to navigate the intricacies of life as an enslaved person—came first. *Preservation*—which describes the process of preserving the cultural, educational, and religious institutions that grew up in response to racism—followed. *Liberation*—which describes direct action to free enslaved people of color and combat racial discrimination—burst forth with the end of the Civil War and continues today. This neat classification does not, however, necessarily hold up. It cannot, for example, account for antebellum insurrections or the long history of the African American church. And the modern civil rights movement can be seen as firmly rooted in all three notions.

The Christianization of Enslaved African Americans

Crucial to any exploration of the origin and development of African American religion are two issues: the attitude of Whites toward the Christianization of enslaved Africans and the abolition of slavery. From the founding of the thirteen colonies to the War of Independence, the relation between race and religion had been ambiguous and came down to the question, Did the fact that Africans or Native Americans had adopted the Christian religion make a difference? (The first case of an African being baptized in the British North American mainland colonies was recorded in Virginia in 1624.) The answer was a resounding no. In fact, in 1667, Virginia enacted a law declaring that religious conversion did not release enslaved people from bondage. That is, skin color—not the heathen nature of an individual's religious beliefs—justified bondage, and Christian belief was used to justify continued obedience to their masters. In a sermon delivered in 1743 to a group of enslaved Africans in Maryland, for example, the Reverend Thomas Bacon proclaimed: "I tell you, that your masters and mistresses are God's overseers, and that if you are faulty towards them, God himself will punish you severely for it in the next world" (quoted in Higginbotham, 1978, p. 37). Echoing this sentiment, Maryland passed legislation in 1667 making it official that baptism would not alter the status of any enslaved person and in 1670 dividing non-Christian servants into two groups: those who were shipped to the colony and would be enslaved for the rest of their lives and those who willingly came to the territory and would be held in bondage for thirty years. This latter distinction remained in place until 1682, when all non-Christian laborers were judged to be enslaved for life.

Virginia and Maryland were not alone. In New York, the 1665 Duke of York Laws made great changes in the enslavement laws of the region that regulated the number of enslaved Africans that could be brought to the colony, the role that the institution itself would play in the area, and the number of indentured servants who could come to the colony. Several years later, in 1706, the colony clarified its position further when it declared that the act of baptism did not grant freedom.

Nevertheless, efforts to convert enslaved Africans to Christianity continued. A Reverend Thomas taught the gospel to enslaved people in his South Carolina parish, and by 1705 he had about twenty African American converts. By 1713, two White women were instructing enslaved Black Americans on the ways of Christianity at St. Andrew's Church, also in South Carolina. By 1724, a group of Anglican clergymen in Virginia and Maryland had convinced several Africans to convert to their brand of Christianity. The largest conversion episode in the region took place in Bruton Parish in Williamsburg, Virginia, where, in 1732, about two hundred African Americans were baptized at one time by the Reverend William Black. The overall results were, at best, mixed. Few enslaved African Americans regularly attended public worship services.

The question then becomes, What motivated Whites' conversion efforts? Perhaps they assuaged guilty consciences. With the possible exception of the Quakers, most White churches accepted the institution of slavery until Emancipation. While, as we have seen, some progressive Whites did join with Black Americans in pushing for abolition, most Whites accepted the status quo.

The Origin of Southern Black American Christianity

While White churches dithered over the issues of slavery and conversion, southern African Americans secretly pursued their own distinctive forms of worship blending remembered African traditions and newfound Christian practices. It will mostly likely never be known precisely when this process began, but the available evidence traces back to the early seventeenth century and reports compiled by Christian missionaries attesting to enslaved Africans continuing to employ traditional practices—conjuring, protective charms, herbal medicine, and rhythmic drumming and dancing—in their religious ceremonies even after conversion. For example, in 1665, after arriving at Marston Parish in York County, Virginia, the Reverend Morgan Godwin noted in his journal the continuous presence of African traditions within the culture of the local enslaved population. This was not just a southern phenomenon. In Philadelphia, for example, a passing observer named John Watson complained to a colleague about the style of music preferred by Black revivalists at a Philadelphia conference: "In the blacks' quarter, the coloured people get together, and sing for hours together, short scraps of disjointed affirmations, pledges, or prayers, lengthened out with long repetitious choruses." Further, he noted: "With every word so sung, they have a sinking of one or other leg of the body alternately; producing an audible sound of the feet at every step, and as manifest as the steps of actual negro dancing in Virginia" (quoted in Southern, 1983, p. 62). Not surprisingly, the religious dance most frequently described was the "ring shout" of the enslaved in the Sea Islands. The ring shout involved a leading individual singing a phrase that the audience would then repeat, then singing another phrase that would then be repeated, and so on. Worship dancing was also usually involved. Most scholars agree that the ring shout is one of the strongest examples of African-influenced religious dance present in the United States. Additionally, such activities almost always included a great amount of worship dancing and shouting.

As for the first African American church in the colonies, some scholars believe it was established in 1758 on the plantation of William Byrd III in Virginia. However, according to the documentary record, the first African American church was founded during the 1770s in Silver Bluff, South Carolina, along the Savannah River (discussed below), the first instantiation of a Baptist missionary movement launched throughout the region, a movement that led eventually to the establishment of African American churches in Georgia and Louisiana as well as Nova Scotia, Sierra Leone, and Jamaica. Regardless of denomination, a distinctive form of African American Christianity emerged and gradually took hold across the South during the Revolution and its aftermath.

Not all Whites were in favor of conversion, however. Many southern Whites began to fear that it would lead not to acquiescence and obedience but to rebellion, whether writ small or large. For example, a 1767 advertisement in the *Virginia Gazette* seeking the return of an enslaved person, Hannah, blamed her religious faith for inspiring her escape, and a similar 1793 advertisement placed by a Thomas Jones in the *Maryland Journal and Baltimore Advertiser* sought the return of a runaway who had been raised in a religious family. And some of the best-known slave rebellions were led by men who had been radicalized by their religion. Influenced by northern abolitionists and his own interpretation of the Bible, Denmark Vesey—a leader in a Charleston, South Carolina, African Methodist Episcopal church and a free man since 1800—planned a slave insurrection to coincide with Bastille Day in 1822. (Details of the plot were leaked before it could be implemented, and Vesey was captured and executed.) Similarly, the religious visionary Nat Turner saw himself as called by God to free all enslaved African Americans and in 1831 led a group of approximately seventy rebels who went house to house in Virginia freeing any enslaved persons they found and killing at least sixty Whites. (The rebellion was soon quashed by the state militia and Turner eventually captured, tried, and executed.)

Religious faith did not of course always lead to rebellion. The same tradition that inspired runaways and armed rebels also fostered a number of Black American preachers, who centered their messages mostly on the New Testament call to help the poor and the wretched. One notable example was David George. Born in 1742 to the enslaved African Americans John and Judith George, young David labored in the fields before escaping at age nineteen to North Carolina. He eventually returned to and settled in South Carolina, where in 1770 he married and, with his wife, Phyllis, began attending a loosely organized religious prayer meeting led by a person known only as Cyrus. Influenced by the sermons of George Liele, another important African American Baptist minister who led worship services on many plantations along the Savannah River, David and Phyllis were baptized and converted to the Baptist faith. With the help of Wait Palmer, a radical White Baptist preacher who was a member of the Separate Baptist movement, David George went on to found a Baptist church on George Galphin's Silver Bluff plantation that by 1778 boasted a congregation of thirty.

Another African American Baptist convert was Andrew Bryan. Born into slavery in 1737 in Goose Creek, South Carolina, Bryan was also influenced by Liele. He began his religious mission by holding informal services for enslaved people, but in 1788 he was ordained by Abraham Marshall, a White Baptist clergyman who helped him organize the Ethiopian Church of Jesus Christ. By 1790, the church had over five hundred members. As for George Liele—the first African American Baptist minister ordained in Georgia, though born in Virginia in 1752—he was himself converted and baptized by Matthew Moore, a White ordained Baptist minister, and encouraged by his owner, Henry Sharp, a Baptist deacon and a Loyalist during the American Revolution who freed Liele sometime before the Revolution. After he was ordained, Liele preached in slave quarters on plantations around Savannah, influencing many more people than just David George and Andrew Bryan. In 1784, Liele and his family moved to Jamaica and started a church in Kingston. By 1791, that church had about four hundred members.

The Emergence of Northern Black Churches

A different religious tradition developed among African Americans in the North, one most strongly influenced by the First and Second Great Awakenings and their message of spiritual equality (see chapter 3). This pragmatic tradition especially appealed to African Americans who were beginning to

CHAPTER IX.

Rev. Andrew Bryan and His Pastorate.

Andrew Bryan was the minister and founder of the Bryan Street African Baptist Church, Savannah, Georgia, 1788. (Engraving originally printed in *History of the First African Baptist Church, from Its Organization, January 20th, 1788 to July 1st, 1888* [Savannah, GA: The Morning News Print, 1888].)

enjoy greater freedom and access to economic and educational opportunities. A sense of racial pride and cultural identity led, as we saw in chapter 6, to the founding of mutual aid and other race-based societies in major cities throughout the North. It also led to the founding of churches that served as centers of civic activity for Black Americans seeking religious and socioeconomic autonomy.

Among the most prominent Black American churches to emerge in the North were the Union Church of African Members, founded by Peter Spencer in Wilmington, Delaware, in 1813; the African Methodist Episcopal

Zion Church in New York, led by James Varick; the First African Presbyterian Church of Philadelphia, organized by John Gloucester; and the First African Baptist Church of New York, founded by Thomas Paul. All were led by strong and progressive African American preachers who promoted quality education and the betterment of Black communities, programs largely forbidden in the South.

While most leaders of the developing independent African American church movement were men, some African American women did press to be included. Most notable was Jarena Lee, who in 1809 petitioned for the right to preach in the soon-to-be-built African Methodist Episcopal Church in Philadelphia. Although her petition was refused, she was granted the right to hold daily prayer meetings in her home. For a time, these meetings satisfied her, but the call to service eventually grew so strong that she became an itinerant preacher, traveling thousands of miles each year on foot.

Still, a "womanist" or Black feminist perspective did not really take hold in the African American church until the 1880s and 1890s. This movement was both an affirmation and a critique of the emerging theology of liberation, discussed in the next section. Black American women largely distanced themselves from White feminist theologians—who tended to discount the effects of racism—and joined Black American men in the struggle against White supremacy in the church as well as the larger society. They insisted that they had the right to name their own experience and to develop a theological framework that accounted for it. And they claimed that the right to follow their calling to preach came not from the male-dominated church but directly from God.

The Growth of Northern Black Churches

While the northern African American church movement initially concentrated on the survival and preservation of Black communities, as it grew and strengthened it came to focus more and more on their liberation. David Walker and Martin R. Delany are good examples of this orientation. Walker's *An Appeal in Four Articles,* as we have seen in chapter 2, urged Black Americans to use whatever tactics were available to them, including violence if necessary, to gain their freedom as quickly as possible. In 1852, Delany, born in 1812 to a free mother and an enslaved father, published *The Condition, Elevation, Emigration, and Destiny of the Colored People of*

BISHOP BENJAMIN W. ARNETT, D.D.

This engraving depicts Bishop Benjamin W. Arnett giving an address before the International Sunday School Convention, 1896. (Courtesy of African American Perspectives, Rare Book and Special Collections Division, Library of Congress: https://lccn.loc.gov/91898108.)

the United States, Politically Considered, one of the most important books ever written on the condition of free Americans in the nineteenth century. In it, he contended, as we have seen in chapter 2, that education, self-help, and the quest for equality and racial justice were goals ordained by God.

The notion of liberation and the attendant notion of elevation in many ways dominated the African American church during and especially after the Civil War, when it became the most powerful and important institution in Black American communities—after, of course, the family. Not only did the church fill a spiritual and emotional need; it offered an explanation of as well as a means to overcome the hardships of daily life. Whereas in the early years of the nineteenth century church attendance was not common, congregations began to grow after the Civil War, especially among Baptist and Methodist churches, some congregations doubling in size from the late 1860s to the 1880s. And African American churches would play a crucial role in the politics of the Reconstruction Era, as we will see in the next chapter.

Conclusion

The religious life and experience of African Americans has always been strongly influenced by their life experiences. Moving from a mind-set that prioritized survival to one that prioritized preservation to one that prioritized liberation, the African American church borrowed from the traditions it had to hand, fully coming of age in the Reconstruction Era, when its message finally crystallized.

8

African American Religious Traditions

Reconstruction to the Present

Nannie Helen Burroughs was born on May 2, 1879, in Orange, Virginia, to John and Jennie (Poindexter) Burroughs. John Burroughs attended the Richmond Institute (later Virginia Union University) and eventually became a part-time preacher. Her mother was an independent woman who in 1884, then a widow, moved to Washington, DC, to obtain full-time employment and better educational opportunities for her children. Eventually, young Nannie attended M Street High (later Dunbar High), the colored high school, where she was taught by such noteworthy African American women as Mary Church Terrell and Anna Julia Cooper.

On graduating from high school, Burroughs initially sought to be hired as a domestic science teacher, but her skin color and social position thwarted that ambition. So, in 1896, she moved to Philadelphia, where she took a job as a clerical worker at the *Christian Banner*. While in Philadelphia, she met the Reverend Lewis G. Jordan, the pastor of the Union Baptist Church and a National Baptist Convention (NBC) board member. In 1898, she followed Jordan to Louisville, where she worked as an editorial secretary and a bookkeeper for the Foreign Mission Board of the NDC. She also became involved with the Women's Convention (WC) of the NDC, first serving as corresponding secretary and then, from 1900, president.

In her first year as corresponding secretary—1899—Burroughs worked 365 days, traveled some 22,125 miles, and delivered 215 speeches. Her youthful energy and resourcefulness were such that the WC membership had increased to 1 million by 1903, and to 1.2 million by 1907. But it was a brief speech that she delivered at the 1900 annual NBC convention in Richmond, Virginia—"How the Sisters Are Hindered from Helping"

Nannie Helen Burroughs, an African American educator, orator, religious leader, and businesswoman, 1900. (Courtesy of Prints and Photographs Division, Library of Congress: LC-USZ62-79903.)

Educator and activist Nannie Helen Burroughs holding a Woman's National Baptist Convention banner during the early 1900s. (Courtesy of Prints and Photographs Division, Library of Congress: LC-DIG-ds-13272.)

(1900)—that truly brought her to prominence, igniting a firestorm with a passionate call for the Black Baptist church movement to utilize the passion and energy of African American women.

Never married, Burroughs devoted her life to the religious and educational mission of the WC. Under her leadership, the WC provided Black American women in the NBC a venue in which to articulate their religious, social, and political views freely. She also challenged all Black American churches to educate their female members about their political rights and responsibilities as American citizens.

Learning Objectives

▼ ▼ ▼

1. How was the African American church transformed during the Reconstruction Era?

2. What role did the African American church and Black American religion play in the lives of people of color during the post-Reconstruction period?
3. What was the Holiness Christian movement?
4. How did African Americans fare in the Episcopalian Roman Catholic Church?
5. What effect did nationalism and the Nation of Islam have on African Americans?
6. How did African American Christianity and the Black church become an integral part of the modern civil rights movement?
7. What is the current state of African American religion and the Black church?

▲ ▲ ▲

Overview

A conceptualization of God that was manifested in the concepts of survival, preservation, and liberation was still present in the African American religious experience during the post–Civil War period. As we have seen, in the years leading up to the Civil War, the church, along with the family, had become the primary focus of the lives of most Black Americans. Its position in the community became even stronger in the postwar years. More and more churches representing more denominations were founded, providing an ever stronger shield in the face of increasingly institutionalized racism in the form of Jim Crow laws.

The Black American Baptist church experienced the greatest growth, boasting about one million members by 1890. This dramatic increase occurred mostly because Baptist congregations enjoyed more autonomy than did congregations of other denominations, such as the African Methodist Episcopal, the African Methodist Episcopal Zion, the Methodist, and the Presbyterian Churches. But, whatever the denomination, this growth enabled African Americans to continue practicing their traditional religious beliefs and customs. Ministers became the most influential people in the African American community, and their churches helped train a cadre of activists and political leaders.

The African American church did not just fill its members' spiritual needs. It also empowered them. As we have seen, it helped them preserve

Gertrude Emily Hicks Bustill Mossell published several books under the pen-name Mrs. N. F. Mossell, including *Little Dansie's One Day at Sabbath School* (1902), a children's book used to illustrate patience, sacrifice, and other religious values. (Frontispiece photo from edition by the Penn Printing and Publishing Company. Courtesy of the Daniel Murray Pamphlet Collection, Library of Congress: https://lccn.loc.gov/91898186.)

their culture and traditions, and, despite limited funding, it sponsored mutual aid societies and offered programs that would help thousands learn to read and write. And it offered African American women an opportunity to thrive through participation in church-related activities.

Church services themselves were especially important aspects of the African American religious experience. Whereas Blacks generally found White religious services too sedate, too lifeless, Black services were anything but. The minister was in attendance not simply to deliver a sermon but to capture hearts, minds, and souls. He was an active participant, and his words would be punctuated continuously by shouts of *Amen!* Members of the congregation would also testify, shout, laugh, cry, and faint, and they would stay on at the church for hours just to be with God. Consequently, many more traditionally trained ministers were forced to abandon their ingrained formality and adopt a passionate sermon style and culturally conscious dress.

In many cases, African American ministers had little or no formal education. They learned their craft by mimicking available models and honed it by trial and error. A few Black leaders disapproved of this trend. For example, Booker T. Washington claimed that more than half of all African American Baptist and Methodist preachers were unfit, incapable of conveying the message of the gospel, and W. E. B. Du Bois wanted African American churches to be led by more formally trained ministers. But they were in the minority.

The African American Religious Experience as a Refuge

For many African Americans, immersion in religious services offered a means of escape from the oppressive experience of life in the post–Civil War United States. And the most important part of those services was always the sermon. Sometimes it addressed the journey to heaven broadly, sometimes it focused on specific texts, and sometimes it highlighted the events of the day. But always its message was that oppression could be overcome, even if only in death and subsequent salvation in Christ.

Few Black American preachers were, however, willing to challenge White supremacy openly. All Black clergymen in the South were keenly aware that even the slightest slip of the tongue could provoke a lynching, something visiting northern Black ministers had to be reminded of. Despite this reluctance to challenge the status quo, many White Americans still viewed African American religious gatherings as a threat. As a result, during the late nineteenth century, hundreds of Black churches were burned down, and numerous ministers were assaulted or killed, especially in the South.

The role of the African American church during these decades must, however, be examined in its social, political, and economic context. For example, like their White colleagues, Black American ministers often stressed the positive attributes of middle-class values, noting that African Americans found themselves in their current state because of their sinful ways. In other words, they needed to change their behavior and foster a better relationship with God. But it is also necessary to consider the bigger picture.

The racial caste system that developed immediately after the Civil War excluded African Americans from almost all occupations except agrarian labor and domestic service. It also severely limited their educational opportunities and stripped away the political gains they had made with the ratification of the Thirteenth, Fourteenth, and Fifteenth Amendments. The end in the 1890s of the Populist movement, with its fragile alliance between African American and White tenant farmers, also heightened the divisions between the races and ushered in and extended Jim Crow laws and practices throughout the nation, especially in the South. As a result, while White Americans were only a little better off than were their African American counterparts, the emerging racial caste system gave the former a sense of superiority. White workers began to leave the agricultural sector for more skilled and semiskilled jobs, while Blacks had trouble finding jobs outside the agricultural and domestic service sectors. Admittedly, some African Americans found jobs in the lumber industry, coal mines, textile mills, and tobacco factories and with the railroads, but these were menial positions that offered no opportunity of advancement.

Given the social, economic, and political climate, the African American church as it developed became a multifaceted and paradoxical entity.

The Holiness Movement and the Establishment of Pentecostal Churches

The Holiness movement emerged in the mid-nineteenth century in response to the legalism of traditional mainstream denominations but especially the Methodist Church, and Pentecostalism emerged in the early years of the twentieth century among the more radical adherents of the Holiness movement. Both took a more personal approach to religious belief and, thus, held a particular appeal for African Americans, taking hold very rapidly in the South. That appeal should not be surprising. The biblical accounts of healings, miracles, spiritual power, speaking in tongues, and the presence of the Holy Spirit that both emphasized resonated with the traditional cultural heritage of African Americans. Both preached a direct, personal relationship between God and the individual believer. And, importantly, both were more willing to ordain women, who figured prominently in the spread of this new style of religion.

From a denominational perspective, the Church of God in Christ (COGIC) took the lead in the spread of the Holiness movement in most African American communities. In 1907, two Black ministers, the Reverend Charles Harrison Mason and the Reverend C. P. Jones, formed the first COGIC churches after two successful revivals in Mississippi and Tennessee. However, Mason was soon removed from his position as pastor because he practiced speaking in tongues, also known as glossolalia—that is, speaking a language that only God could understand—which frightened many people. More specifically, he went on to found the Pentecostal General Assembly of the Church of God in Christ in Lexington, Mississippi. He quickly became a bishop and began to elevate many other African American men to COGIC bishoprics in the South and the West.

Simultaneously, a formerly enslaved person named William J. Seymour helped establish the Holiness movement in the western United States. Born in 1870 in Centerville, Louisiana, Seymour slowly began to embrace the tenets of the Holiness movement as he attended a church and a school sponsored by Charles Fox Parham, a White preacher and evangelist. However, owing to the racism he experienced almost daily at both church and school—schools especially were still strictly segregated—when a friend invited him to move to Los Angeles, he jumped at the chance. In 1906, soon after his arrival in Los Angeles, he delivered his first sermon at the Santa Fe Street Mission—on the baptism of the Holy Ghost and speaking in tongues as the third work of God's grace. He was never allowed to preach at the mission again. But he was invited to conduct a service and preach at the home of Richard and Ruth Asbury, who had, at one time, stayed at the mission.

The resulting revival initially lasted several days. When it was over, seven individuals had been baptized, filled with the Holy Spirit, and able to speak in tongues. But then large crowds began to arrive at the Asburys' home almost daily to participate in services. Those crowds grew so large, in fact, that the services had to be moved from the Asburys' home to a former stable that had been refurbished as a large hall. At this new location, revival services took place three to nine times per day, attracting people not just from Los Angeles but from across the nation and around the globe. Significantly, this religious movement that grew out of the efforts of Jones and Stewart and similarly inspired other revivals became the first noteworthy religious crusade to cross racial barriers in the United States.

Episcopalians and Roman Catholics

During the post–Civil War era in the United States, most religious Blacks were members of the main Protestant denominations: Baptist, Methodist, or Holiness/Pentecostal. However, by 1890, there were about 200,000 African American Catholics nationwide. Black Americans who practiced Catholicism were not fully accepted by the established churches or the Catholic Church itself, especially in the South. However, in the 1890s, they increased their efforts to improve race relations nationwide. For instance, Daniel Rudd, the publisher and editor of the *American Catholic Tribune,* the only national newspaper published by a Catholic of African descent in the United States during the nineteenth century, called for a national meeting to examine race relations in the Catholic Church. As a result, in 1889, about one hundred Black delegates, along with some progressive Whites, met in Washington, DC—to little avail. The position of African Americans within the Catholic Church continued to mirror their position within the larger society. Unlike the Baptist and Methodist Churches, the Catholic Church did not split over the question of slavery and racial equality. In fact, it upheld local cultural norms.

Nevertheless, some African American Catholics did manage to make their way in the world very successfully despite the racial climate. Two of the most important came from the Healy family. Eliza Clark was an enslaved African American who bore nine children to her White owner, Michael Healy, a prominent White Irish Catholic plantation owner from Georgia. Unusually when it came to a relationship between a White man and a Black woman, Healy seemed to care deeply for all his children. Some even had the opportunity to attend school in the North. James A. Healy graduated from the College of the Holy Cross in Massachusetts and was ordained as a priest in 1854, later becoming the bishop of Portland, Maine. Patrick Healy, who also attended Holy Cross, served for eight years as the president of Georgetown University in Washington, DC, and is known as the first African American Jesuit priest. It should be noted, however, that most White Americans were unaware of the biracial background of the Healy family and that members of the family itself acknowledged it only decades later.

Another important Black American Catholic during the nineteenth century was Augustus (Augustine) Tolton. Born into slavery on April 1, 1854, in Rolls County, Missouri, Tolton was the second son of Peter Paul and Martha Jane Tolton, who had three other children. After Peter was killed during the Civil War fighting for the Union, Martha moved the family to Quincy, Illinois, seeking a new start. There, young Augustus began working at a local tobacco plant and met a White, Irish American priest named Father Peter McGiff, who arranged for him to attend a parochial school in the winter months when the tobacco plant was closed. On his graduation, however, despite the support of Father McGiff, he could not obtain admission to any American seminary. So, after graduating from St. Francis Solanus College in Quincy, Illinois, he went to Rome and trained as a priest at the Pontifical Urbaniana University. He was ordained in Rome in 1886 at the age of thirty-one. Soon after, he returned to the United States and served for two years as the pastor of St. Joseph's Church in Quincy, Illinois. Next, he was transferred to Chicago, where he became the first African American priest in the diocese and the chaplain of St. Monica's Catholic Church, a position he held until his sudden death in 1897 at the age of forty-three.

A broader movement among African American Catholics was not attempted again until the second decade of the twentieth century. Dr. Thomas Wyatt Turner, a Black Catholic educator, helped form the Committee against the Extension of Race Prejudice in the Church—later the Committee for the Advancement of Colored Catholics. The committee's goal was an ambitious one—to end discriminatory practices against African

Americans, especially in the church. However, little progress was made, and Turner left the organization after a ten-year association.

The Episcopal Church attracted fewer Black Americans than did the Catholic Church, associated as it was with wealth, privilege, and elitism. By 1903, there were only about fifteen thousand African American Episcopalians in the United States.

Black American Religious Nationalism and the Islamic Movement

During the latter part of the nineteenth century, African American clergymen and lay preachers had laid down a strong foundation on which to base an argument for a permanent separation between White and Black Americans. This nationalist sentiment was reinforced by the reopening of the western frontier and various colonial ventures abroad. Another, crucial factor was the increase of racial violence and political oppression throughout the nation, especially in the South, during the World War I years. The overall effect was that a great many Black Americans began to look to their ancestral African culture for comfort and direction.

During the early years of the twentieth century, nationalism was an extremely attractive ideological and political position for many African Americans. On the strength of that fact, Marcus M. Garvey's Universal Negro Improvement Association (UNIA) and the Nation of Islam—as well as, in later decades, some Black American Hebrew groups—began to build organizations and institutions and, thus, some degree of sociopolitical autonomy that insulated Blacks from Jim Crow America. Garvey's goal was to have his followers (who numbered in the millions during the 1920s) return to Africa and liberate it from colonial rule. The Nation of Islam was unabashedly separatist from its inception, especially when it came to the Black religious experience. Its goal was to spark in its members a spiritual conversion focused on a kind of Black self-awareness, racial uplift, and racial solidarity that could be achieved within the confines of the United States.

The exact origins of the Nation of Islam remain ambiguous. They seem to lie with one Timothy Drew, who at some point changed his name to Noble Drew Ali and founded the Moorish Science Temple of America, which flourished in Chicago, Detroit, and other midwestern cities during the early 1920s. After Drew's death in 1929, an odd door-to-door salesman known as Wallace D. Fard, Master Farad Muhammad, or Wali Farad took over the leadership of the Detroit temple. He attracted hundreds of African Americans to the temple, where he taught a mixture of Qur'anic principles, Christianity, and the nationalist philosophy of Marcus Garvey.

In 1934, Fard mysteriously disappeared. An associate, Elijah Pool, whom Fard had renamed Elijah Muhammad, became the leader of the temple and established a second temple in Chicago. During World War II, the Nation of Islam attracted the attention of the federal government, especially the FBI, when its members refused military service. In 1942, Muhammad was arrested and charged with instructing his followers to resist the draft. On his release in 1946, he moved to Chicago permanently and began expanding the movement.

In short, the Nation of Islam taught its followers that Blacks were the original human inhabitants of the earth, a technologically superior race that originally lived in Africa, free from any type of oppression. Gradually, deca-dent races emerged: first Brown, then Red, then Yellow, and then White, the most debased. Around six thousand years ago, all non-Blacks were banished from Africa, but the White race regrouped and eventually became ascendant. Muhammad proclaimed, however, that its supremacy would soon come to an end and that Black Americans should prepare for their reemergence as national and international leaders. One Black American who took that message to heart was Malcolm Little, who began to embrace the beliefs of the Nation of Islam while serving a prison term for larceny and breaking and entering. While incarcerated, he read the Qur'an regularly, renounced his "slave name," and reinvented himself as Malcolm X, becoming on his release from prison after being paroled in 1952 one of the Nation of Islam's most influential leaders.

Under the leadership of Elijah Muhammad, the Nation of Islam boasted roughly 50,000–100,000 members and developed a financial empire worth roughly $46 million. After Muhammad's sudden death in 1974 and the organization's almost total collapse, Warith Deen Muhammad, Muham-mad's son, took over. However, within a few years, he left and founded the Muslim American Society, which became the largest group of African American Muslims, with a membership of approximately 500,000. Minister Louis Farrakhan then took over the Nation of Islam. Under his tutelage, the organization rebounded quickly, increasing its membership by about 20,000 and in 1995 sponsoring the Million Man March in Washington, DC.

The African American religious nationalists who founded the Moorish Science Temple, UNIA, the Nation of Islam, and similar groups redefined Black American identity along the lines of a mostly African cultural context and an Islamic belief system. In doing so, they targeted a strain of racial prejudice in American Christianity that could be traced back to the colonial period. Hence the thousands of African Americans who found themselves gravitating toward these nationalist groups during the late nineteenth century and the early twentieth.

The Black Church and the Civil Rights Movement

In the post–World War II era, activist individuals and organizations began attempting to reinfuse in the freedom struggle the three core African American religious concepts of survival, preservation, and liberation, which had been demonstrated in previous centuries to be integral to real social, political, and economic progress. Progress was slow at first despite the efforts of a key cadre of Black ministers and the expanding influence of Pentecostalism within Black communities, but then the Reverend Martin Luther King Jr., a brilliant young Baptist minister from Atlanta, Georgia, became involved with the 1955 Montgomery bus boycott, bringing to the campaign his prophetic ministry, deep spirituality, and unique leadership skills. This combination captured the hearts and minds of (progressive) Whites and Blacks alike. More importantly, it inspired alienated and impoverished Blacks in both rural and urban America to organize and fight for true freedom, justice, and equality.

The African American church and Black American religion continued to evolve after the assassinations of Malcolm X and Dr. King. The scholar James H. Cone chronicled this in his *Black Theology and Black Power*, which traces the history of African American religion in the United States from the colonial period to the late 1960s. Most importantly, Cone contended that, by the 1960s, a new type of African American theology linked to the Black Power philosophy of the modern civil rights movement—something he called *Black liberation theology*—had emerged within the African American religious community. One example of this is the establishment in 1975 of the Ninth Congregation of the Pan-African Orthodox Christian Church, also known as the Shrine of the Black Madonna. This denomination was originally established during the 1950s by the Holy Patriarch Jaramogi Abebe

Agyeman, who was born Albert B. Cleage Jr. (the father of the writer Pearl Cleage) in Detroit, Michigan. During the 1960s and 1970s, the church's main theological framework was rooted in the belief that God supported the freedom of African Americans from all forms of oppression, that Jesus was Black and would come to be known as the "Black Messiah," and that the Hebrew nation in the Bible was, in fact, a Black nation.

Ultimately, Black liberation theology rested on five main principles. Black American churches must transcend denominational divisions. They must be fully committed to helping the poor. They must be focused on uplifting their communities. They must be places of economic, political, cultural, and theological education. And they must rise above petty internal divisions.

The African American Church and Black American Identity Today

Given the problems facing the African American community today and the changing demographics of the nation as a whole, African American churches have emphasized outreach, using both traditional and nontraditional strategies to protect and aid the most vulnerable members of their communities. Collectively, they remain the largest Black-controlled institution in the nation, claiming more than 30 million members. They also remain one of the most potent forces in their communities, places not only to worship but also to meet and organize and continue the struggle. The major denominations continue to be those founded during the nineteenth century: the African American National Baptist Convention, the Progressive National Baptist Convention, the African Methodist Episcopal Church, the National Missionary Baptist Church, the Churches of Christ, the United Church of Christ, and the African Methodist Episcopal Zion Church. And, in recent decades, these dominations have made inroads in Africa and Latin America.

African Americans have also not only joined but become leaders in predominantly White churches. For example, in 1966, Harold R. Perry was ordained as the first Black Roman Catholic bishop. In 1970, John M. Burgess became the first African American bishop to head an Episcopal diocese in the United States. And, in 2002, Wilton Gregory became the first African American to head the US Conference of Catholic Bishops. African

American churches have also become more and more politically active, tackling such problems faced by the African American community as crime, drugs, and underdeveloped education facilities, developing community outreach programs in major cities such Chicago, New York, Philadelphia, Houston, and Los Angeles.

An internal problem for the African American church that remains to be confronted is that it still tends to be socially conservative when it comes to gender and, thus, patriarchal in structure. For example, although most Black American congregants are women, very few Black women have obtained leadership positions in their churches. It was not until 2005 that the first African American female bishop, Pastor Vashti M. McKenzie, was elected to the national African Methodist Episcopal Church board. An external problem is the growth of the Black Muslim faith, which has over the years steadily gained converts. There are an estimated 1.5 million Black Muslims in the United States, and, with increasing immigration from Islamic countries, that number is likely to grow.

Conclusion

During the post–Civil War era and beyond, African Americans began to organize, develop, and lead their own churches and denominations. In addition, the existing Black American theological framework began to evolve. One result was a new theology—Black liberation theology—that changed the experience of some African American churchgoers forever.

9

Black Feminism

The Construction and Development of Black Feminist Thought

Born into slavery in Edenton, North Carolina, in 1813, Harriet Ann Jacobs was the daughter of Delilah (the daughter of an enslaved African American woman named Molly Horniblow) and Daniel Jacobs, a White local carpenter. In 1819, when Harriet was six years old, her mother died unexpectedly. Soon after, she was sold to a local plantation, where she was taught how to read and sew, two skills that would prove crucial later in life. Several years after, in 1825, Jacobs was sold again, but this time to Dr. James Norcom. Once Jacobs became an adolescent, the now middle-aged Norcom began to harass her sexually. In her *Incidents in the Life of a Slave Girl* Jacobs proclaimed: "[Norcom] peopled my young mind with unclean images, such as only a vile monster could think of. I turned to him with disgust and hatred" (p. 19). To escape his advances, she became sexually involved with the attorney Samuel Tredwell Sawyer, and the relationship produced two children: Joseph (called "Benny") and Louisa Matilda (called "Little Ellen").

When Harriet turned twenty-one, Norcom ordered her to be his mistress, threatening to sell her two children if she did not comply. She once again resisted, escaping in 1835 and hiding some distance away at a friend's house. Shortly thereafter, Joseph and Louisa Matilda were purchased by their father and sent to live with Molly Horniblow, their great-grandmother. Despite the fact that Norcom had offered a $300 reward for her capture, Jacobs decided to return and live at her grandmother's home as well. However, because she was still considered a fugitive, she was hidden away in a small crawlspace above the porch that measured only seven feet wide, nine feet long, and three feet high at its tallest point. As she described it in *Incidents*: "There was no admission for either light or air" (p. 89). This is where she stayed for nearly seven years.

Abolitionist Harriet Jacobs. (Photo by Gilbert Studio, 1894. Courtesy of Wiki-media Commons and the *Journal of the Civil War Era*.)

During her self-imposed captivity, Jacobs could not help but focus on her horrible living conditions. As she slept, she heard rats and mice run over her bed. But she could also hear the voices of her children, which brought some consolation. In *Incidents* she recalled: "It seemed horrible to sit or lie in a cramped position day after day . . . yet I would have chosen this, rather than my lot as a slave" (p. 90).

Finally, in 1842, Jacobs left her grandmother's house and headed north to reunite with her children, who had been sent there several years earlier. She obtained employment as a domestic worker with the Willis family in New York City but in 1849 headed farther north to Rochester to join her brother, John S. Jacobs, a member of a famous abolitionist group that included Frederick Douglass. After the enactment of the 1850 Fugitive Slave Act, she left Rochester and returned to New York City, where Norcom almost captured her, so she fled to Massachusetts. In 1852, the Willis family purchased Harriet from Norcom and freed her.

Determined to assist in the ongoing abolition movement, and stirred by her new freedom, Jacobs decided to make public her own personal story of sexual abuse under enslavement. She was aided by the Quaker abolitionist (and feminist) Amy Post, the African American abolitionist William C. Nell, and the White abolitionist Lydia Maria Child, and, in early 1861, her *Incidents in the Life of a Slave Girl* appeared pseudony-mously. The book made her an instant celebrity, but it was assumed to be a fictional tale, not an attempt to spur Black women to political action, and gradually fell out of favor until it was rediscovered during the civil rights movement of the 1960s.

Learning Objectives

▼ ▼ ▼

1. What are the foundational principles of Black feminism?
2. What are some core themes or concepts of Black feminism?
3. Who were some of the early Black feminists?
4. How are the concepts of racial and gender equality linked to Black feminism?
5. Why were Black women's clubs so important to the development of Black feminism?

6. What major changes took place in the field of Black feminism from the 1920s to the 1950s?
7. What is the current state of the field of Black feminism?

▲ ▲ ▲

The Core Themes or Concepts of Black Feminism

Since its origins, Black feminist thought has been based on the resistance of African American women to oppression. It has attempted to articulate how to be a Black woman in a nation that denigrates, objectifies, and oppresses women of African descent. And its primary themes can be classified as falling into four main categories. First is the relationship among racism, sexism, and classism, which highlights the differences, not the commonalities, in the experiences of Black women in America in an attempt to transcend normal classifications. Second is the search for an authentic voice by challenging traditional, negative stereotypes and replacing them with images of the true condition of Black women in America. Third is the relationship between intellectual inquiry and political action as activists attempt to realize their goals. Fourth is the empowerment of Black women in their everyday lives, linking individual struggles to a broader, collective enterprise.

Of course these ideas have been expressed differently in different historical periods. What follows is a historical overview.

Early Black Feminists

Any consideration of the development of Black feminism must of course begin with an exploration of the ideas and experiences of African and African American women in the antebellum United States. During these years, they struggled against racial, gender, and political oppression. More practically, they suffered the violence associated with the state of enslavement, most commonly regular beatings and sexual assault. Their families were separated, they were force to live in appalling conditions, and they were treated like subhumans. And their resistance took many forms.

Consider Phillis Wheatley. Born in Senegal around 1753 and brought to the British North American mainland colonies at the age of eight, she was forced to learn a new language, practice a new religion, and generally lead a very different way of life. She did, however, adapt, going on to become the first African American poet to be published in the United States.

Wheatley was fascinated by the idea of self-identify, discussing, for example, how she missed her African culture and lifestyle, but also expressing pride that she had survived the terrible transatlantic voyage. She also took an interest in politics and political themes, commenting on the Boston Massacre and its aftermath, dedicating a poem to George Washington, and discussing the 1783 Treaty of Paris. Although she did not specifically address the concepts of race and gender, her focus on identity and community created a foundation on which other African American women, including Harriet Jacobs, could build subsequently.

Many of the Black American women who articulated the intellectual and activist tradition from which Black feminist thought emerged centered their work on the African American churches that had grown up during the late eighteenth century and the early nineteenth. Some even managed to become important leaders in that largely patriarchal environment. Jarena Lee was one. Born on February 11, 1783, in Cape May, New Jersey, she became the first known African American woman to petition the African Methodist Episcopal (AME) Church for the authority to preach (this 1809 request was denied).

Jarena married Reverend Joseph Lee, an AME minister, in 1811. The couple soon left Philadelphia and moved to Snow Hill, New Jersey. However, on their sixth anniversary, Joseph died, and Jarena was left to raise two children alone. She returned to Philadelphia and asked Richard Allen, the recently elected bishop of the African Methodist Episcopal Church, for permission to preach. This time she was successful, and she went on to preach throughout the Northeast. In her sermons, she primarily stressed the importance of African Americans having both the right and the ability to preach the gospel in any church.

Rebecca Cox Jackson was also an evangelist, a religious visionary, and a trailblazer in the early African American church movement. Born a free Black American in Horntown, Pennsylvania, in 1795, her youth was divided between the homes of her mother and her maternal grandmother. Soon after her 1830 marriage to Samuel S. Jackson she experienced a powerful religious conversion, became an active member of the Holiness movement, and started to preach publicly, generating controversy not only because of her gender and race but also because she espoused the notion that celibacy was the only way to reach heaven. Jackson's devotion to her spiritual calling led her to leave her husband and her church.

After several years of preaching on her own, Jackson joined the United Society of Believers in Christ's Second Appearing—popularly known as the Shakers—attracted by the group's emphasis on pure spirituality and concept of a dual-gendered God. But, when the predominantly White Shakers refused to take their message to the local African American community, she once again struck out on her own, ultimately leaving a legacy of belief in prophetic dreams and supernatural gifts that provided a spiritual path that other African American women would later follow.

Beyond the church, Black American women played crucial roles in the reform and humanitarian movements of the early nineteenth century. Consider Maria W. Stewart, a free Black woman from Connecticut with strong abolitionist, feminist, and religious impulses. She was probably the first Black American woman to speak in public about the civil and political rights of women, but she is best known today as the first woman in America to lecture in front of a mixed-race audience. During a lecture series delivered in 1832 in Boston, Stewart discussed issues relevant to the African American community such as education, economic empowerment, racial solidarity, and self-help, but her most powerful words came when she encouraged Black women to acquire formal educations and seek careers and community leadership roles outside the home as a means of reaching their full potential. She also advocated for voluntarily segregated schools organized by and for Black women, a response to the highly patriarchal nature of African American society.

The Abolition and Women's Rights Movements

While women were not given the right to vote in the United States until 1920, the movement for female suffrage began to gain strength in the 1840s. Most of the women involved in this movement, such as Elizabeth Cady Stanton and Lucretia Mott, were White, but they still felt the obvious connection between the emerging women's rights movement and the abolition movement. Although Frederick Douglass, the most prominent African American involved in both the abolition and the women's rights movements, argued that the antislavery cause was doing much to bring the predicament of women to the forefront of the nation's consciousness, he fully believed that what was really needed was an independent movement organized and led by women, both Black and White. And many Black women took up the cause of women's rights.

Sojourner Truth was born probably in 1799 in Ulster County, New York, some eighty miles north of New York City, near the Hudson River. She was the second youngest of the twelve children of James and Elizabeth Baumfree, who named her Isabella. Young Isabella was owned by several people before she was emancipated by an 1827 New York state law. As a free African American woman, she worked as a domestic for several years, attended both the White John Street Methodist Church and the Black African American Methodist Episcopal Zion Church, and began to preach at local revival meetings around the city. On June 1, 1843, she changed her name to Sojourner Truth, which meant "itinerant preacher." From this point until her death, she continued her ministry, but she also became one of the most powerful and important African American women involved in the women's rights movement during the nineteenth century.

For example, Truth attended the second women's rights convention in Salem, Ohio, in 1850 and spoke at the third women's rights convention in Worcester, Massachusetts, the following year. But her most powerful and eloquent words came at the women's rights convention in Akron, Ohio, in 1851, where she declared: "A'n't I a woman? Look at my arm! I have ploughed, and planted, and gathered into barns, and no man could head me! And a'n't I a woman? I could work as much and eat as much as a man—when I could get it—and bear de lash as well! And a'n't I a woman" (p. 67). She was not always welcome. Apparently, there was some concern that White abolitionists would object to her presence. But she nevertheless prevailed.

Sarah Mapps Douglass was another African American woman who contributed to the emerging Black feminist vision. Born a free African American in Philadelphia on September 9, 1806, she was exposed to the abolition movement as a child. As a young woman, she joined the Philadelphia Female Anti-Slavery Society, which her mother had founded years earlier. Her closest associates in the society were the Forten sisters, the daughters of the wealthy African American shipbuilder, James Forten, and the Quakers Lucretia Mott and the Grimke sisters, Sarah and Angelina, all three White. Her lifelong friendship with the latter helped challenge the culture of racial and gender discrimination within local Philadelphia Quaker society. In 1853, Mapps Douglass became a teacher and administrator at the Institute for Colored

Youth, a Quaker-sponsored teacher-training educational facility, but she continued to attend women's rights and abolitionist meetings.

A journey similar to Mapps Douglass's was that of Sarah Parker Remond. Remond was born in Salem, Massachusetts, on June 6, 1826, to a family that included many abolitionists. From childhood she learned about the horrors of slavery and the power of the Underground Railroad. As a result, early in life she was determined to fight against racial and gender discrimination. This consciousness crystallized in May 1853 when she was denied a seat at an opera to which she had purchased a ticket at the Howard Athenaeum in Boston. Several years later, in 1856, she accompanied her brother Charles on his antislavery lecture tour of New York State. Although at first she spoke only briefly, she gained confidence each time and, by 1858, was ready to begin her own antislavery tour, delivering over forty-five lectures in England, Scotland, and Ireland between 1859 and 1861. Her work continued throughout her life.

Another window into Black feminism during this period is Mary Ann Shadd Cary. Born in Wilmington, Delaware, on October 9, 1823, Shadd Cary became the first Black American female newspaper editor in North America. Her father was a leader in the Underground Railroad movement and subscribed to William Lloyd Garrison's abolitionist newspaper the *Liberator*. She herself became known for her advocacy of African American political and economic autonomy.

After the passage of the 1850 Fugitive Slave Act, Shadd Cary and her brother Isaac moved to Canada, and in 1852 she published *A Plea for Emigration; or, Notes of Canada West*, a forty-page pamphlet that encouraged the immigration of Black Americans to Canada in which were compiled myriad statistics to illustrate the positive aspects of an integrated society. A year after the passage of the act, with the assistance of Samuel Ringgold Ward, an abolitionist and fugitive slave, Shadd Cary began publishing the *Provincial Freeman,* a weekly newspaper in which she first criticized such African American leaders as Henry Bibb, Josiah Henson, and John Scoble, who were advocating for the development of a Black American separatist and nationalist movement in Canada. She also accused these individuals of being sexist.

After the death of her husband, Thomas F. Cary, Shadd Cary moved back to the United States in 1863, started a school for African American children in Washington, DC, wrote regular articles for Frederick Douglass's newspaper the *New National Era,* and became a full-time abolitionist lecturer. In 1870, she graduated from Howard Law School to become the first African American female lawyer in the United States. Soon thereafter, she won a case before the US House of Representatives Judiciary Committee arguing the right of women to vote. She thus became one of the few women to vote in a federal election during the Reconstruction Era. She also fought for the right of all women to vote through the Colored Women's Progressive Franchise Association, which she founded in 1880.

The Women's Club Movement

As discussed briefly in chapter 4, in the last few decades of the nineteenth century, many years before the more widely recognized civil rights organizations such as the National Association for the Advancement of Colored People and the Urban League were founded, Black women's clubs began to emerge. Initially, their members—mostly middle class—were concerned mainly with cultural and religious matters, but they soon began to focus their attention on their communities' social problems.

During the late 1890s, the national women's club movement was spurred to tackle larger political problems by an 1895 incident in which the White journalist John W. Jacks sent a letter to Florence Belgarnie, a member of the London Antislavery Committee, in which he referred to Black women as, at best, lower-class citizens. He was especially outraged by the writer and activist Ida B. Wells-Barnett, who had recently delivered a fiery antilynching speech in Europe. A copy of the letter soon made its way into the hands of Josephine St. Pierre Ruffin, a member of the White New England Women's Club and the founder of the African American Woman's Era Club. In late 1895, Ruffin called a meeting at Boston's Charles Street AME Church that was attended by over one hundred Black women. The result was the formation of the National Federation of African American Women, which eventually boasted thirty-six chapter clubs in twelve states. At the same time, at its 1895 meeting the Colored Women's League of Washington, DC, reinvented itself as the National Colored Women's League. One year later, the National Federation of Afro-American Women (led by Margaret Murray Washington, Booker T. Washington's second wife) and the National Colored Women's Association (headed by Mary Church Terrell) merged, establishing the National Association of Colored Women (NACW).

Activist and women's suffrage advocate Mary Church Terrell during the early 1900s. (Courtesy of Prints and Photographs Division, Library of Congress: LC-DIG-ppmsca-68742.)

With Terrell as its first president and "Lifting as We Climb" as its slogan, the NACW was prepared to mobilize, and, by the early years of the twentieth century, it had about fifty thousand members in roughly one thousand clubs nationwide. There were, of course, internal conflicts over the years involving personalities, leadership styles, skin complexions, and ideological frameworks. Still, the organization's focus remained on eliminating poverty, ending racial discrimination, promoting quality education, and uplifting the race, laying the foundation for the construction of a coherent Black feminist perspective.

During the same years, Black American women also developed several other types of clubs. For instance, Phillis Wheatley clubs and homes arose across the nation. These facilities provided living quarters for single Black American women in several cities, especially in those whose Young Women's Christian Association refused to serve African Americans. Some of these clubs also provided classes in domestic skills and nursing. In Indianapolis, the local Phillis Wheatley Club continued to function even during the Great Depression.

Another pivotal development in the emerging African American women's club movement was the articulation of Black women's views through various local, regional, and national publications. One of the first periodicals in this area was *Woman's Era,* launched by Josephine St. Pierre Ruffin and designed as the official publication of the NACW. The first issue appeared on March 24, 1894, and, from the beginning, it was apparent that the editors were determined to stress the importance of the right to vote. Also strongly advocated in *Woman's Era* was the need for African Americans to enter the political arena if the race was ever to make progress.

Two other important figures in African American women's publishing history were Ida B. Wells-Barnett, best known as the publisher of the periodical *Free Speech,* and Anna Julia Cooper, whose 1892 collection of essays *A Voice from the South* represented the first foray into African American feminist thought. Both are discussed at some length in chapter 2.

A Change in the Environment, 1920s–1950s

Black feminist thought largely disappeared from the national stage during the period from the 1920s to the 1950s, an era that brought great changes to the African American community, both structurally and politically. The primary reason for these changes was the presence of de jure segregation in the South and de facto segregation in the North. During this period, most African American women were domestic workers, employed by affluent Whites. Also important was the decline of Black women's clubs during the 1920s, which left African American women with very few political opportunities until the emergence of the early years of the civil rights movement in the 1950s and 1960s. Still, important work was being done.

Prominent among that work was the feminist writing of Amy Jacques Garvey, Marcus Garvey's second wife, which targeted working-class, urban African Americans who were involved with the Universal Negro Improvement Association (see chapter 4). As the editor of the women's page of *Negro World*, the official weekly newspaper of the organization, Amy Garvey wrote about the evils of capitalism, imperialism, and racism and those institutions' connection to the gender oppression that African and African American women faced in the United States and globally. As she noted in a 1925 editorial: "Who is more deserving of admiration than the Black woman, she who has borne the rigors of slavery, the deprivations consequent on a pauperized race, and the indignities heaped upon a weak and defenseless people? Yet she . . . stands ever ready to help in the onward march to freedom and power" (p. 252).

Also on the Black feminist agenda during these years was the issue of birth control. Some activists considered it a form of African American genocide. Yet, under slavery, attempts to take control of their reproductive rights were considered empowering by African and African American women because of their potential to limit their number of children and thus prevent their owners from maximizing their labor force. By the early years of the twentieth century, limiting family size became a way of gaining more economic power and improving a family's standard of living. And reproductive rights became a major political issue in the years leading up to the 1973 *Roe v. Wade* decision, which legalized the right of women to terminate a pregnancy (until a reversal in 2022).

Their family and social responsibilities, combined with the reality of racial segregation, meant that few Black women had the time to devote themselves to the agendas of women's clubs. So they began to work through such existing organizations as Black churches. Some helped create a Black feminist theology that reflected a more welcoming, humanistic, and spiritual orientation. Some focused on empowering family members and friends, encouraging self-reliance and thereby enhancing self-esteem. But then Black women had been unrecognized leaders in their churches for decades.

Many African American women became noted combatants in the literary arena during this period. Writers such as Zora Neale Hurston, Lorraine Hansberry, and Gwendolyn Brooks featured the daily experiences of African American women prominently in their works. Especially noteworthy is Hurston's *Their Eyes Were Watching God* (1937), which encouraged African American women to find their own voice and thus liberate themselves, thereby ushering in a new era in Black feminist thought.

Perhaps the best representative of the transition in the Black feminist movement during its early years is Mary McLeod Bethune. Born on July 10, 1875, near Mayesville, South Carolina, Bethune enrolled first in the Trinity Presbyterian Mission School at the age of ten and then in the Scotia Seminary in North Carolina three years later. After teaching for several years at Dwight Moody's Institute for Home and Foreign Missions in Chicago, she moved to Daytona, Florida, and founded the Daytona Educational and Instructional Institute for Training Negro Girls. At this point, she began to see her life's mission as working for the advancement of African American women everywhere. So, for example, while she continued to fight to improve the condition of Black American women, she also supported the emerging international women's suffrage movement. In 1923, she established the coeducational Bethune-Cookman College, and in 1935, she founded the National Council of Negro Women. She also held an administrative position at the Office of Minority Affairs in the National Youth Administration during the presidency of Franklin D. Roosevelt.

Second-Wave and Contemporary Black Feminism

The struggle for Black women's liberation emerged, in part, as a result of the successes associated with the African American freedom struggle of the 1960s and 1970s. Also significant, however, was the second wave of feminism that emerged in the United States during the same period, energized by the passage of the Civil Rights Act of 1964, which outlawed both racial and gender discrimination in the workplace, creating an opening for those who opposed gender oppression whatever their race to move forward with their own agenda. The inclusion of many non–African American women in the Congress of Racial Equality and other civil rights organizations and especially their rise to positions of leadership provided a venue in which they could explore their power and potential as future organizers.

One of the most important legal successes for this second wave of feminism was the passage of Title IX of the Education Amendments Act of 1972, which required colleges and universities to end gender discrimination across the board. The previously mentioned *Roe v. Wade* decision was also important, despite the backlash from conservative groups it prompted.

There is no question that African American women were directly involved in the development of the modern feminist movement from its inception. Over the years, many Black female activists have contended that a critique of America's patriarchal society is incomplete without the inclusion of a race and class analysis. But they have faced opposition. Many White feminists have been silent on issues of race and class discrimination within their own movement as well as within the larger society, and many African American male leaders have proclaimed that the elimination of racial oppression must initially at least be the primary focus of any civil rights struggle, fearing that the embrace of gender and class equality would undermine their efforts. Still, African American feminists have continued to attempt to carve out a place for Black feminism within the civil rights movement.

The primary factor that today distinguishes Black feminism from its earlier manifestations is its change in perspective. That is, Black feminists had come to the conclusion that what was needed were organizations that focused solely on the needs and concerns of African American women and did so from a more humanistic and inclusive perspective. Two things led to this shift. The first was the increasing class stratification among African Americans in general but especially among Black American women. The second was a confluence of factors: the continuing racism within the mainstream women's movement, the continuing sexism within the African American–led civil rights struggle, and the omnipresence of the Black nationalist perspective that had emerged during the late 1960s and early 1970s. No one was speaking solely for African American women.

One effort to address the problem was the founding, in 1973, of the National Black Feminist Organization to lead a new African American women's liberation movement. Another was the founding, in 1975, of the more radical Combahee River Collective, so-called after Harriet Tubman's 1863 campaign in South Carolina that freed almost eight hundred enslaved

African Americans. Of course these groups were not created out of thin air. They were outgrowths of the work of a group of trailblazing African American women who took it on themselves to speak out about the concerns of Black American women at every opportunity. Most prominent among their publications were Shirley Chisholm's autobiography *Unbought and Unbossed* (1970), Toni Morrison's *The Bluest Eye* (1970), and Audre Lorde's *Cables to Rage* (1970). (See also Toni Cade Bambara's *The Black Woman: An Anthology* [2005].) But academic historians such as Elsa Barkley Brown, Sharon Harley, Darlene Hine Clark, and Rosalyn Terborg-Penn also advanced the Black feminist agenda by centering their research on the lives and experiences of African American women. The movement continued into the 1980s, a decade that saw the publication of some of the most important works on Black feminist thought to date, such as Angela Y. Davis's *Women, Race, and Class* (1981), bell hooks's *Ain't I a Woman* (1981), Alice Walker's *In Search of Our Mothers' Gardens* (1983), and Barbara Smith's *Home Girls* (1983). And the trend continued into the 1990s. That decade saw the emergence of Black women's studies as a major field of inquiry at most colleges and universities and the publication of such important works as Patricia Hill Collins's *Black Feminist Thought* (1990), Michele Wallace's *Invisibility Blues* (1990), Johnnetta B. Cole's *Conversations: Straight Talk with America's Sister President* (1994), Beverly Guy-Sheftall's anthology *Words of Fire* (1995), and Deborah Gray White's *Ar'n't I a Woman?* (1999).

Today, Black feminist thought—in particular the connection it makes between class, race, and gender—has began to influence such national women's organizations as the National Organization for Women and the National Women's Studies Association as well as such mainstream groups, both academic and otherwise, as the Organization of American Historians, the American Historical Association, the Children's Defense Fund, and the Smithsonian Institution whose missions are not necessarily focused on a feminist agenda, Black or otherwise. Today, Black feminist thought is both an ever-changing political movement and a valued field of study.

Conclusion

The evolution of Black feminism is a testament to the fact that race or gender alone cannot fully explain the complex experiences of African American women. And Black feminist thought continues to change with the times and provide useful insights regarding both the situation of women of color and the state of the larger society. Most importantly, however, women of African descent who today subscribe to a Black feminist ethos continue to fight against gender and sexual oppression not just for their own sake but also for that of the next generation.

10

The African American Experience from a Sociological Perspective

Black American Identity and Culture

William Edward Burghardt (W. E. B.) Du Bois was born in Great Barrington, Massachusetts, on February 23, 1868, the only child of Alfred and Mary Silvina Du Bois. Mary, who was of Dutch, African, and English ancestry, was part of a very small but important free Black American community in Great Barrington and for years had owned several acres of land in the region. Alfred left the family in 1870, and Mary, who was forced to work several jobs simultaneously thereafter, died in 1885.

The Du Bois family lived in a predominantly White community, so young William inevitably experienced some degree of racism. Still, he attended a local integrated public school and played regularly with his White classmates, and his teachers encouraged him to pursue his academic dreams. After graduating from high school in 1884, he enrolled in Nashville's Fisk University, graduating in 1888. He then attended Harvard University, receiving his second bachelor's in 1890 and a doctorate in sociology in 1895. While in college and graduate school he traveled widely, throughout the American South while he was at Fisk, and throughout Europe while he was at Harvard, having received a John F. Slater Fund for the Education of Freedmen Fellowship to attend the University of Berlin. It was during his travels that he learned how sheltered from overt racism he had been in Great Barrington, at Fisk, and at Harvard.

On receiving his doctorate, Du Bois accepted a teaching position at Wilberforce University in Ohio. Two years later, he accepted a one-year research appointment at the University of Pennsylvania, during which time he studied several African American neighborhoods in Philadelphia, the fieldwork that was the basis for his landmark *The Philadelphia Negro* (1899), which laid the foundation for the development of the field of Black

Scholar and activist William Edward Burghardt Du Bois. (Photo by Addison N. Scurlock, 1928. From Photographs of Prominent African Americans, James Weldon Johnson Collection in the Yale Collection of American Literature; Beinecke Rare Book and Manuscript Library.)

sociology. In 1897, he took a professorship in history and economics at Atlanta University and remained active as a scholar for the rest of his life.

As we have seen in chapter 4, Du Bois was politically active throughout his life. Importantly, he expanded his scope to include international affairs, cochairing the Council on African Affairs and later chairing the Peace Information Center. Politically, he first gravitated to socialism, but then, after traveling widely throughout Russia and China, in 1961 he joined the Communist Party of the United States. Ultimately, he took up residence in Ghana, and he died there in 1963.

Learning Objectives

▼ ▼ ▼

1. What are some of the fundamental principles of Black sociology?
2. What are some of the core concepts or main themes of Black sociology?
3. Who were some of the early Black sociologists?
4. What factors led to the development of the field of Black sociology?
5. How did the concepts of race, color, and culture affect the growth of the field of Black sociology?
6. How was the field of Black sociology integrated in various institutions of higher education?

▲ ▲ ▲

The discipline of sociology—the supposedly objective, value-neutral study of the values, beliefs, relationships, and structures of a given social group—originated in Europe during the eighteenth and nineteenth centuries. The earliest sociologists—for example, Auguste Comte (who coined the term *sociology*), Herbert Spencer, Émile Durkheim, and Max Weber—saw their role as guarding an orderly and well-functioning society. Importantly, sociological theory was preoccupied with the concept of race and race relations. Unfortunately, in its early stages that preoccupation took the form of elevating Western, White societies over African, Black societies, thus providing a justification for the institution of slavery. Also unfortunately, such notions of racial superiority/inferiority held sway into the 1950s and

1960s. The field of Black sociology was the inevitable result. And the scholars who developed it conceived of it as the study of the specific structural forces and foundational principles shaping African American communities, negatively or otherwise.

The Core Themes or Concepts of Black Sociology

Certain core concepts have shaped the development of Black sociology, most prominently that the field itself must be led by African American scholars, that the research published must be centered on the plight of people of color, that the approach must be interdisciplinary, and that the findings produced must be generalizable—that is, they must have positive public/social policy implications. In other words, the discipline of Black sociology is based on the premise of racial difference—that people of African descent have distinct historical experiences, cultural heritages, and worldviews that are different from those of Whites and make their outlook on life unique.

The notion of a specifically Black sociology does, however, raise certain questions. How valid are sociological studies of African Americans conducted by White/European scholars? Should the norms considered standard for Whites/Europeans be used to evaluate African Americans? Should African American scholars be able to create methodologies and theoretical frameworks based on their own historical and cultural experiences when studying fellow African Americans? Can a group's cultural and behavioral patterns be conveyed more accurately by a member of that group than they can be by a supposedly disinterested outsider? Which features of social relationships are common to all human beings, and which, if any, are race specific? Is race a genetic or a social construct?

Before the 1960s, African and African American culture and behavior had been characterized by White Europeans as having little, if any, value. Consequently, the pioneering generation of Black sociologists envisioned the field of Black sociology as bolstering the self-image of people of African descent. They also viewed it as a vehicle for guiding the various strands of the Black liberation movement toward the goal of achieving true social, political, and economic equality for African Americans. In other words, their sociology was not value neutral. They meant it to function more like an applied science. And to do so it had to develop its own approaches and methodologies.

Pioneering Black Sociologists

Although the field of Black sociology did not formally emerge until the 1960s, the foundation for it had begun to be laid as early as the 1890s. The first formulation was attempted by the preeminent scholar W. E. B. Du Bois, whose groundbreaking *The Philadelphia Negro* (1899)—one of the earliest examples of a statistically based social science—was the first case study of a Black community ever conducted in the United States. The University of Chicago–trained Charles S. Johnson followed Du Bois's lead some twenty years later with *The Negro in Chicago* (1922), a study of race relations prompted by the race riots that had broken out across the nation in 1919.

Among the many other examples of African American scholars who articulated the intellectual and activist traditions that formed the foundation for the emerging field of Black sociology during the 1940s and 1950s, St. Clair Drake stands out prominently. In 1946, in collaboration with Horace R. Cayton, he published *Black Metropolis,* a study of the African American ghetto in Chicago that appeared to great acclaim. This massive volume—based on an enormous amount of research conducted by Works Progress Administration field-workers—aimed to identify the factors that led to the highly segregated and economically disadvantaged conditions in which African American residents of Chicago's South Side found themselves living during the Depression and the war years.

It is important to note a common thread in the work of all these researchers. The conditions of African American life might be harsh, but, with careful study, they could be changed.

The Emergence of Black Sociology as a Field of Inquiry

Through at least the 1930s, mainstream sociology accepted as a given the notion that Blacks constituted a biologically and intellectually inferior race and were hardly worth serious scholarly attention. The result was that unbiased studies were few and far between. And this lack of interest left a void that Black sociologists were more than willing to fill.

The earliest attempt to fill the void—long before Black sociology was recognized as a discipline per se—can be found in the Atlanta Conference of Negro Problems. This discussion series—held annually at Atlanta University from 1896 to 1914—was instigated by several university alumni who saw the need for the unbiased, scientific investigation of the social, economic, and physical condition of African Americans, particularly those living in urban areas. Topics considered included the transition of African Americans from enslavement to freedom after the Civil War, their migration from the South to the North, the differences between de jure segregation and de facto segregation, the state of the African American church, crime in Black neighborhoods, and the continuing episodes of violence toward people of color in the United States. Importantly, the Atlanta Sociological Laboratory—a separate university department—was created to oversee and coordinate the research to be presented at the conferences.

The findings that emerged from these conferences were regularly published as journal articles, presented to larger audiences at national conferences, and turned into books. They were also shared with colleges and universities across the nation as well as government officials and private citizens who represented entities such as the US Bureau of Labor, the US Census Office, the Insurance Press of London, and the General Assembly of the state of Georgia. Overall, the sociological studies produced by the Atlanta Sociological Laboratory had a wide impact on both academic and nonacademic communities located far beyond the city of Atlanta or even the state of Georgia.

Race, Racism, Color, and Culture in the African American Community

The emergence of the field of Black sociology has, not surprisingly, been affected by the evolving concepts of race, racism, color, and culture, all key factors determining the nature and influence of the sociological relationships of people of African descent.

The notion of race as we recognize it today was first developed in the fifteenth century when European explorers began classifying the populations they encountered into three distinct groups: Negroid or Black, Mongoloid or Yellow, and Caucasian or White. While there is still no universally accepted definition of the term *race,* certain biological components have generally been recognized. That is, certain physical characteristics have been used to classify individuals or populations: for example, skin color, eye color, hair

Advertisement for the 1900 Pan-African Conference at Westminster Town Hall, London, England. (Henry Sylvester Williams, 1900. Courtesy of the W. E. B. Du Bois Papers, Robert S. Cox Special Collections and University Archives Research Center, UMass Amherst Libraries.)

texture, and body type. Classification based solely on physical appearance can, however, be problematic since historically migration and assimilation have led to the intermingling of members of different populations. It can also be disingenuous in that it can be used to conceal the kind of ethnocentrism behind colonization.

The notion of racism—at core the belief that racial difference, however conceived, produces inherent superiority or inferiority—is more straightforward. The real issue is, however, not one of definition but one of demonstration. When acted on, racism is an enforceable practice that actively discriminates against individuals or populations.

Color is more problematic. It is not a reliable indicator of race because skin tone varies from light to dark even among members of a so-called race. Historically, lighter skin tones have been more highly prized (white being considered the ideal) and have translated into greater privilege and can afford individuals as much advantage as race can, if not more. (Lighter-skinned African Americans have often passed for White, and, even among populations of enslaved people, biracial individuals were often accorded more privileges.) Darker-skinned African Americans have, of course, suffered the greatest disadvantage, but clearly they have not been alone when it comes to color-based discrimination.

The notion of culture is equally problematic. Culture is the set of beliefs, social forms, and material traits shared by a social group. To understand a group's culture, one must understand its worldview. But is culture linked to race? The debate is still ongoing, but, from an Afrocentric perspective, the answer is yes. Consider the experience of Africans and people of African descent in the United States. Their experience has been one of enslavement, segregation, and social and economic inequality, an experience that results largely, if not wholly, from others' perception of and attitude toward their race. They might share certain experiences—for example, income inequality—with other groups, but for different reasons. And thus it is hard to see how their culture could not be raced based.

Black Sociology in the
Twentieth Century and Beyond

Especially during the first half of the twentieth century, sociology was, as we have seen, dominated by the work and ideas of White Europeans who sought to maintain the status quo. While African Americans who became sociologists at this time were schooled in European thought, they were more influenced by the work of the Chicago-school sociologists. Led by the University of Chicago professor Robert Park, the school conducted urban field studies that sought to understand African Americans—and migrant groups generally—on their own terms. It also trained a small but important group of African American sociologists who went on to collect and present an enormous amount of data on the social conditions of African Americans in both urban and rural America. These and other African American scholars coming out of the historically Black colleges and universities began to critique the existing social, economic, and political structures that continued to oppress African Americans.

One of the main foci of African American sociologists was the origins, development, and impact of Black social institutions, especially Black

American theology and the African American church. While religion in its various forms may be a universal given, it does have cultural dimensions that must be taken into consideration. As we have seen, the general understanding today is that African American religion is drawn partly from enslaved persons' memories of African culture and partly from their experiences of American culture. However, some African American sociologists, like E. Franklin Frazier, claim that African religious practices and beliefs were wholly lost during the enslavement period and that the African American church that we see today is completely White or Eurocentric in its nature and practices. Disagreements in this and other areas continue, but so does progress toward a distinctively Black sociology.

Conclusion

In short, Black sociology rests on the notion of racial difference. The premise is that the history, culture, and worldview of Africans and African Americans are distinct from those of White Europeans. These distinct elements helped create a unique psyche that enables Black American scholars—and especially sociologists—to develop approaches and methodologies better suited to an examination of the norms, values, and behaviors of people of African descent than those offered by traditional models.

11

The African American Experience from a Sociological Perspective

The Black Family

Edward Franklin Frazier was born in Baltimore, Maryland, on September 24, 1894, the son of James Edward Frazier, a bank messenger, and Mary E. Clark. Frazier's father taught himself how to read and write, and he always stressed the critical importance of formal education as a means to escape poverty. After he graduated from Baltimore Colored High School in 1912, young Edward attended Howard University in Washington, DC, graduating with honors in 1916. At Howard, along with nurturing an interest in sociology, Frazier demonstrated a mastery of languages, literature, and mathematics, subjects he would teach at a variety of institutions until entering the graduate program in sociology at Clark University in Worcester, Massachusetts, in 1919, graduating with a master's degree in 1920. He then spent a year as a research assistant at the New York School of Social Work, followed by a year at the University of Copenhagen in Denmark, where he was a research fellow for the American Scandinavian Foundation.

Returning to the United States in 1922, Frazier held a combined appointment as the director of the summer program at Livingstone College in Salisbury, North Carolina, the director of the Atlanta University School of Social Work, and an instructor in the Sociology Department at Morehouse College in Atlanta, Georgia. In 1927, he became a research fellow in the Department of Sociology at the University of Chicago, and in 1929, he accepted a position as a lecturer in the Department of Sociology at Fisk University in Nashville. After earning his doctorate in 1931, he remained at Fisk, soon becoming a research professor of sociology in the Department of Social Science. In 1934, he became a professor in and the chair of the Department of Sociology at Howard University. He retired

Illustrated fact sheet on the pioneering African American sociologist E. Franklin Frazier. (By Charles Henry Alston, 1943. Courtesy of Office for Emergency Management, Office of War Information. Domestic Operations Branch. News Bureau, National Archives at College Park.)

in 1959 but continued to do some teaching, both at Howard and in the School of Advanced International Studies at Johns Hopkins University.

Throughout his career Frazier published on a number of topics—for example, the activities of African American business leaders and the development of the African American middle class—but his major research interests were race relations and the African American family. Two of his early books—*The Negro Family in Chicago* (1932) and *The Negro in the United States* (1949)—established him as one of the most important sociologists in the United States. But his 1957 *Black Bourgeoisie* was his most controversial work. In it, he explored the economic, political, and social behavior of the African American middle class as it was shaped by the enslavement period and the forces of racial prejudice and discrimination that followed. Specifically, he argued that the African American middle class had developed as a hybrid group. On the one hand, lacking a secure economic base and, like the African American population generally, facing social isolation and marginalization, it adopted many of the same moral values as middle-class Whites. On the other hand, when it came to material consumption/savings behavior, it tended to behave like lower-class Whites did.

Learning Objectives

▼ ▼ ▼

1. Why is the field of Black sociology important to people of color?
2. Why is researching the Black American family so important to Black sociologists?
3. What are the differences between the weak and the strong family theories?
4. How has the African American middle class changed over time?
5. How have class divisions within the African American community increased?
6. What is the African American underclass?
7. How has the health gap changed within the African American community?

▲ ▲ ▲

Chapter 10 discussed the rise of Black sociology generally. The current chapter tackles one specific focus of Black sociology: the African American family.

The African American Family and Black Sociology

For sociologists, the family in general is the most important social institution governing the development of behavior within the family and the strength of the surrounding community. Not surprisingly, then, the African American family has traditionally been at the heart of much of the literature produced by Black American sociologists, many of whom have stressed the uniqueness of the Black American experience—particularly the retention of African cultural traits—and whether that experience makes Black American families different from White American families. The question remains open, but an examination of the debate offers a good illustration of the continuing value of the field of Black sociology.

Traditional African family structures were in many ways very different from traditional European family structures. They were based on kinship networks and descent systems significantly different from European forms. Both matrilineal and patrilineal family structures existed, and monogamy (where both men and women have only a single spouse), polygamy (where men have more than one spouse), and polyandry (where women have more than one spouse) were all practiced. Families tended to be extended, and those extended families could include several nuclear families as well as immediate blood relatives, more distant relatives, adopted kin, and family friends who eventually assumed the family name.

Many, if not most, of these traits have disappeared from African American family structures. Time and distance may have played a role in this, but so too may the imposition of European notions of family structure on enslaved Africans and African Americans. Nevertheless, some African traits have survived, and the result is the hybrid nature of the African American family structure. Also entering into the mix are the conscious attempts by African Americans to rediscover their cultural heritage evident in the resurgence of vibrant African prints and colors in clothing, the inclusion of more African musical beats in rap music, and the celebration of Kwanzaa, a practice that originated during the Black Power phase of the modern civil rights movement.

Over the years, several perspectives on the history and development of the African American family among Black sociologists have emerged. One—espoused by scholars such as John W. Blassingame and Herbert G. Gutman—is that the forced adoption of Christianity encouraged the acceptance of the two-parent household and the abandonment of traditional African practices. Another points to evidence that some traditional African practices persist, especially in the forms taken by extended African American families. Interestingly, both these perspectives see continuing strength in the African American family.

However, most non-Black American sociologists are less concerned with the effects of the loss or retention of cultural traditions on African American families than they are with the effects of social and economic conditions on those families, which they see as weakening them. This type of analysis has a long history. And, over the years, two major schools of sociological theories on the origin and development of the African American family have emerged from it: the weak family theory and the strong family theory.

The Weak Family Theory vs. the Strong Family Theory

A characteristic example of the weak family theory is *The Negro Family* (1965), in which Daniel P. Moynihan claimed that the enslavement period had a highly detrimental effect on the African American family, leaving it vulnerable to the economic, social, and political manifestations of racism and resulting in ramifications that we see to this day: educational underachievement, high rates of unemployment, entrenched poverty, a preponderance of female-headed households, high rates of illegitimacy, and an environment characterized by violence and crime. As Moynihan put it: "The family structure of the lower class Negroes is highly unstable, and in many urban centers is approaching complete breakdown" (p. 21).

In some ways, Moynihan's claims mirrored those of *The Negro in the United States* (1949), in which E. Franklin Frazier contended that the rapid increase in various social problems that emerged in the African American community during the late nineteenth century and into the twentieth rested on the unique history of the Black American family, which left it ill prepared to cope with the complex and consistently changing nature of modern American society. He specifically noted the ongoing impact of racism on African American men, who, faced with few employment opportunities, turned to crime to support their families or simply abandoned them. He concluded that the situation would be rectified only when African Americans had the same opportunities as middle-class Whites.

Prominent White scholars such as the sociologists Nathan Glazer and David A. Schulz agreed. The weak family theory was, however, uniformly rejected by such strong family theory proponents as the Black sociologists Andrew Billingsley, Robert B. Hill, and Robert Staples. Strong family theorists contend that the African American family must be evaluated within the context of its own social and economic reality. They also contend that the research focus must be extended beyond the lower socioeconomic stratum of the African American population if we are truly to understand the great progress that the Black American family has made throughout the history of the United States.

For example, in his pathbreaking 1994 study *Climbing Jacob's Ladder*, Andrew Billingsley noted that the Black family—as well as the overall African American community—is directly dependent on and simultaneously subordinate to the economic structures of the larger, White society. Thus, if low-income African American families are to be properly understood, they should be compared not to White families but to middle- and upper-middle-class African American families, all of which have, because of the severe limitations on their resources, had to make adjustments in the face of the volatility of the marketplace economy. To demonstrate this point, Billingsley conducted a case study of middle-class African Americans that highlighted how their adoption of conventional patterns of organization was a response to economic instability.

The African American Middle Class

It continues to be debated whether sociologists' focus should be on the middle or the lower classes of African American communities. Those who champion the former position point out that fundamental changes to national economic structures and social systems have led to a transformation of the African American middle class since the 1950s and that scholarship has not kept up with these developments.

For example, much of the literature has produced race-based analyses focused on Black American politicians, intellectuals, business owners, and other community leaders with direct ties to such organizations as the National Association for the Advancement of Colored People, the Urban League, Black American churches and fraternal institutions, and the historically Black colleges and universities, but class-based analyses rarely appear. (African American union leaders and domestic workers have received scant attention.) As a result, the African American middle class has been presented as monolithic and static, with no internal divisions or conflict. (Characteristic of this approach is Frazier's 1957 *Black Bourgeoisie.*) Admittedly, until the 1930s this depiction was relatively accurate. However, then a new

African American middle class started to emerge. Initially, it was still able to speak for the entire African American community and was, thus, able to make a significant contribution to the developing modern civil rights movement. Gradually, however, it became too economically and culturally different and too focused on communities outside the African American to continue to do so.

This new African American middle class began to grow rapidly during the 1950s, partly because of the changes in the American job market—notably the armed forces, the civil service, and industrial labor—changes prompted by the Truman administration's pursuit after World War II of affirmative action policies meant to combat discrimination and segregation in the workplace. Further changes came with the 1954 *Brown* decision, which opened up colleges and universities nationwide to African Americans.

Some critics have argued that this new African American middle class is an artificial construct, the product of handouts, and that hundreds of thousands of non-Black immigrants have made it to the middle class without any help from the government. Such a position fails, however, to acknowledge that, despite blatant racism and discrimination, there was already a large pool of highly trained and educated African American professionals ready to fill the positions that were being opened to them, and this new population of African American professionals helped create the African American middle class as we know it today.

Class Divisions Expand Inside the African American Community

Through the 1970s, the African American middle class expanded rapidly. Between 1960 and 1965, roughly 380,000 African Americans annually were able to secure white-collar jobs, which helped enlarge the Black American middle class to about 4 million, at the time roughly one-fifth of the entire African American population. By 1980, the number of African Americans working in white-collar jobs had increased by about 40 percent. Still, the growth of the Black American middle class had begun to slow. Regardless of whether it was racially motivated, the call for smaller government during the presidencies of Ronald Reagan and George H. Bush had an immediate impact on the African American middle class because of the numbers of government civil service jobs that had begun to disappear. Deregulation and privatization had a similar impact because of the shifting of employment opportunities from one sector of the economy, where equal hiring practices were legally guaranteed, to another section, where they were not. Furthermore, as deindustrialization progressed, the economy took on a service orientation that left many skilled and semiskilled laborers fewer ways to earn a living wage. Finally, the end of the Cold War, the subsequent closing of military bases, and the elimination of thousands of military contracts also meant significantly fewer job opportunities for African Americans.

The Black American middle class began to contract. By the end of the 1980s, about a third of African American families earned only between $25,000 and $50,000 annually. They were now not middle class but lower middle class, uncomfortably close to the expanding African American underclass. They were, however, not alone. During the 1980s, the overall number of poverty-level workforce participants increased from 25.7 percent to 31.5 percent.

What remained of the African American middle class began to entrench itself socially, politically, and culturally, many of its members distancing themselves from the Black American lower class and underclass. Still, some alliances remained. The spirit of Black solidarity previously found mostly in the lower- and underclass populations of the African American community from which historically nationalists such as Marcus Garvey and Malcolm X drew their supporters began to percolate upward into the African American middle class. A detailed examination of the current state of class divisions within the African American community can be found in the writings of the Black sociologist William Julius Wilson.

African Americans and the Underclass

Invisible to most American eyes during the 1950s and only occasionally discussed by scholars during the 1960s, the nation's underclass population exploded during the 1980s. By the 1990s and the first decade of the twenty-first century, African Americans living in poverty made up a great majority of the underclass, and they were under assault. Both political parties had turned away from the needs of poor people, colluding in the dismantling of Lyndon Johnson's War on Poverty programs. The media were filled with images of the violence and immorality of underclass life. Other than the occasional newspaper article and the 1982 *The Underclass*, in which Ken

Auletta coined the term *underclass,* the situation went largely unnoticed until William Julius Wilson's 1987 *The Truly Disadvantaged* was published.

According to Wilson, more than racism or the dominant political policies of the 1960s, the nation's massive, post–World War II reconstruction of the economy and, later, Lyndon Johnson's Great Society program were responsible for the creation of the African American underclass. For example, between 1945 and 1975, almost two-thirds of the nation's manufacturing jobs disappeared, disproportionately affecting African Americans. The resulting social and economic decline in African American communities in urban areas was dramatic. Like Frazier and Moynihan before him, Wilson saw African American men turning to crime to support their families or simply abandoning them and African American communities being populated largely by female-led households, those families often reduced to living in high-risk areas and federal housing projects. In other words, he saw the underclass as populated by families that were socially and geographically outside the mainstream of the nation's economic system. The situation could be changed, he concluded, only through a massive government works project like that the nation had seen in the 1930s.

Health Care and African Americans

Another area of concern for Black sociologists has been the health care industry. As the income and education of African Americans increased, so too did their access to health care, which was accompanied by a decline in mortality rates. For example, in 1970, the life expectancy of African American men was 60 years of age and of African American women 68.3. By 2009, those numbers had increased to 69.5 and 76.5, respectively. In comparison, during the same decade, the life expectancy for Whites, both women and men, is approximately 80–85.

Hypertension, heart disease, cancer, and HIV/AIDs remain among the most severe health problems affecting African Americans today. For example, African American men are more likely than White men to die from cancer within five years of diagnosis. African American women are less likely than White women to contract cancer, but, when they do, they die at higher rates. And the risk factors of smoking, heavy drinking, and obesity are found more often in African American populations than they are in White populations. A lack of access to quality health care for the lower classes within the African American community also exacerbates the problem. And many African Americans continue to harbor a mistrust of the health-care system, mostly for historical and cultural reasons.

Many Black sociologists argue that the best way to combat these health-care issues is to bring more people of color into the medical field. And their numbers have increased over the past seventy years. In 1950, for example, only 2.1 percent of medical doctors in the United States were African American. By 1989, that figure had increased to 3.7 percent. The number of African American physicians historically has determined both the availability and the quality of medical care for the Black American population because minority health professionals have tended to practice more in low-income, inner-city areas.

The situation is, however, improving. For example, during the 1960s, following a national call from the American Medical Association as well as many African American physicians for more physicians, the number of medical schools in the United States increased from 86 in 1960–1961 to 103 in 1970–1971. This led to an increase in the number of African Americans enrolling in medical school and eventually becoming doctors. Most Black sociologists saw this increase as only a start. Of course, more work needs to be done in this area.

Conclusion

Nearly fifty years ago, Daniel Moynihan issued a national call to action to respond to the real threats to the African American family. Citing a number of social problems within the Black American community, fairly or unfairly he laid both the problem and the solution at the door of the Black American family. He concluded that, if the federal government did not intervene, the African American family would eventually be destroyed. Many of the trends that Moynihan identified can still be found today. The problem of single-parent African American households still exists. The problem of African American families living below the poverty line still exists. And the problem of African American children lagging behind their White counterparts educationally still exists. Still, progress has been made. And it remains the mission of Black sociology to examine why in the furtherance of that progress.

12

Black Psychology

The Origin, Nature, and Development of an African-Centered Worldview

Kenneth Clark was born in 1914, in the Panama Canal region, to Arthur B. Clark and Miriam H. Clark. His father worked for many years for the United Fruit Company. When he was five, his parents divorced, and his mother took him and his younger sister, Beulah, to the United States to live in Harlem. His mother worked as a seamstress for a local sweatshop for many years, organizing a union and becoming a shop steward for the International Ladies Garment Workers Union. Clark attended Howard University, obtaining his master's degree in psychology in 1935. While working on his doctorate at Columbia University (which he received in 1940), he became a researcher on a study of race relations for the Nobel Prize–winning Swedish economist and sociologist Gunnar Myrdal. In 1942, he became the first African American to be promoted to a tenured full professor at the City College of New York (CCNY). Several decades later, in 1966, he became the first African American appointee to the state of New York's Board of Regents. Following the 1967 race riots, President Lyndon B. Johnson appointed him to the National Advisory Commission on Civil Disorders (also known as the Kerner Commission). In 1970, he became the president of the American Psychological Association. Even after retiring from CCNY in 1975, he remained an advocate for the civil rights movement.

His wife, Mamie Phipps Clark, was born on October 18, 1917, in Hot Springs, Arkansas, to Harold H. Phipps, a physician and native of the British West Indies, and Kate Florence Phipps, who assisted in his practice. Young Mamie attended a public, segregated elementary school and the segregated Langston Hughes High School. She then attended Howard University in Washington, DC, where she met Kenneth Clark, whom she married in 1937. At Howard, she completed a bachelor's in psychology in 1938 and a master's in psychology in 1939 and then went on to earn a doctorate in psychology from Columbia University in 1943.

The Clarks' research together was focused on the impact of racism on African American children. They are best known for their 1947 article "Racial Identification and Preference in Negro Children." The study on which they reported—which used four dolls that were identical except for skin color—involved asking children questions about the dolls designed to determine racial perception and preference. Most of the children preferred the white dolls, and, when asked to color an outline of a child the same color that they were, many of the Black subjects chose to use white or yellow. The Clarks' conclusion was that segregation caused personal and psychological damage to children of all races.

When Thurgood Marshall, the recently appointed executive director of the Legal Defense and Education Fund of the National Association for the Advancement of Colored People (NAACP), argued *Brown v. Board of Education* before the Supreme Court, he used the Clarks' study to support his contention that, in racially segregated schools, the children discriminated against developed feelings of inferiority and the privileged children feelings of superiority. This evidence, combined with arguments based on the Equal Protection Clause of the Constitution, led the Court to conclude: "Whatever may have been the extent of psychological knowledge at the time of *Plessy v. Ferguson* [1896], this finding is amply supported by modern authority. . . . We conclude that in the field of public education the doctrine of 'separate but equal' has no place."

Learning Objectives

▼ ▼ ▼

1. What are some of the foundational principles of Black psychology?
2. What are some core themes or concepts of Black psychology?
3. Who were some of the early Black psychologists?
4. What are some of the foundational traditions of Black psychology from the post-Reconstruction period to the 1930s?
5. How did the field of Black psychology emerge as a discipline?
6. What are some of the most important Black psychology groups and organizations?

7. How have Black psychologists influenced the larger field of psychology?
8. What is the link between Black psychology and African centeredness?

▲ ▲ ▲

Like sociology, the discipline of psychology—the study of behavior and the mind—has its roots in eighteenth- and nineteenth-century European thought. Some of the earliest philosophers who contributed to the development of psychology saw a link between psychology, race, and culture and relied on testing techniques meant to measure racial superiority, people of African descent inevitably being determined to be intellectually inferior. Although clearly methodologically and conceptually flawed, such studies—which continued into the 1950s and 1960s—fueled the fire of White supremacy in the United States. Obviously, a new approach—a specifically Black psychology—was called for.

The early proponents of Black psychology considered people of African descent and people of European descent to have had distinct cultural experiences and were, therefore, concerned with the psychological consequences of being a person of African descent in the West. They were also reacting to early psychological studies of people of African descent that were more anthropological than psychological in nature and, thus, focused on the physical and cultural characteristics of what were considered to be nonliterate racial or ethnic groups. For example, during the early twentieth century, many such studies were based on tests designed to measure the difference in intelligence between Whites and other races. In most of these studies, the non-White groups or races were defined as the most unintelligent and undesirable. The pioneering Black psychologists challenged this methodology and the underlying assumptions.

A number of approaches have been taken to Black psychology. Two, however, are currently dominant. The first holds that psychological constructs are universal and, thus, can be used to evaluate both African and European Americans. The second holds that psychological constructs specific to people of African descent must be developed if they are to be evaluated appropriately. And this second approach is itself divided into two camps, one centered on the experience of African Americans specifically and one centered on the experience of people of African descent generally.

The Development of Black Psychology as a Profession

As we have seen in chapter 5, after the Civil War, educational opportunities for African Americans opened up only gradually, so, not surprisingly, they entered the field of psychology slowly. And, by and large, the first few generations of African American psychologists saw their mission as educating their fellow African Americans about the importance of maintaining good mental health. A few obtained academic positions, but most had to find other employment, working, for example, as teachers or counselors (on the counseling profession, see below). As their numbers increased over the years, Black psychologists began forming their own professional organizations (e.g., the Association of Black Psychologists [ABPsi]) and taking leadership roles in established professional organizations (e.g., the American Psychological Association [APA], the American Counseling Association [ACA], and the Society for Research in Child Development [SRCD]).

A relative newcomer to the scene, the Association of Black Psychologists (ABPsi) was formed in 1968 after a group of Black psychologists attended a meeting of the predominantly White APA and came away feeling that the group as a whole lacked any real understanding of the concepts of diversity and inclusion and realized that they were African Americans first and psychologists second. But ABPsi members also worked within the APA, demanding, for example, that the organization make a greater effort to integrate its membership, purge its journal of racist material, and establish a venue in which minority concerns could be voiced. Nearly all other ethnic minority psychological associations point to the establishment of ABPsi as their inspiration.

ABPsi proved to be a positive force for change. In 1969, it successfully called for an end to the use of biased mental health tests that placed African American children disproportionately in developmental courses. In 1970, it developed a plan on how to recruit and retain Black doctoral students that roughly one-third of graduate psychology programs in the country adopted. In the same year, in partnership with the APA it inaugurated a three-year visiting professor program allowing African American social scientists to work at thirty historically Black colleges and universities. In 1971, it sponsored its first national conference. And, in 1974, it launched its own academic, peer-reviewed journal, the *Journal of Black Psychology*.

Simultaneously, the field of counseling and specifically its professional organization—known in the 1950s as the American Personnel and Guidance Association (APGA), becoming the ACA only in the 1990s—was similarly being challenged because of its lack of diversity. Owing to a lack of other professional opportunities, most Black psychologists were traditionally trained initially as counselors and, thus, were involved with APGA. But, frustratingly for them, the organization's conferences offered few forums for the presentation of African American perspectives and research by African American scholars, leading a group of Black psychologists to present a resolution at the organization's 1969 conference that the organization establish what is now known as the Office of Non-White Concerns. More importantly, in 1973, the African American counseling psychologists Thomas Gunnings and Gloria Smith organized a national conference on the counseling of minority students. Conducted in Hampton, Virginia, the conference focused on the testing of people of color not just in educational settings but also in government and industrial settings, and its success led the National Institute of Mental Health to sponsor a conference in Vail later that same year exploring how counselors and psychologists were trained to evaluate people of color and encouraging the adoption of a "scholar-practitioner" model of counseling education.

The journey to diversity and inclusion in the field of child development was not nearly as successful. Partly inspired by the establishment of ABPsi, the Black Caucus of the SRCD was founded in 1973. The caucus sought to change the profession by developing methodologies specifically designed to assess the mental health of Black children and giving African Americans more of a voice in the organization. And, in 1977, at the urging of the Black Caucus, the SRCD did establish its Committee on Minority Representation, which in 1978 proposed a strategy for increasing minority participation in the SRCD, but the committee's proposal went largely unheeded.

Still, such efforts to challenge the status quo did result in many professional organizations reevaluating their governance structures and expanding the role that African Americans played in them. This sea change, as tentative as it may have been initially, encouraged many Black psychologists to continue to promote the development of a multicultural perspective in the field of psychology.

African American Intellectual Contributions
to the Field of Psychology

The efforts of African American psychologists to become full participants in scientific and professional associations ultimately led to the creation of some important revisionist research traditions within the discipline, including the social contextual/multidisciplinary research tradition, the empirical social science research tradition, the Black scholar/activist research tradition, and the Afrocentric/African-centered research tradition.

The social contextual/multidisciplinary tradition is linked to the University of Chicago, which by the 1930s was providing training for a relatively large number of Black scholars, particularly in the social sciences. The university influenced the viewpoint of many of these scholars because of its focus on African American issues and communities and its use of a class/caste paradigm that included the concept of race. More specifically, the use of multidisciplinary and social contextual research methodologies and newly uncovered data, linked to patterns of social relations and community characteristics and processes, helped create concepts and tools useful in better understanding the plight of African American communities.

The empirical social science research tradition is associated with the University of Michigan, which promoted an empirical approach to social issues. That is, the university emphasized the use of powerful sampling techniques, the collection and examination of large amounts of data, and the use of complex and rigorous statistical data analyses. It was only in the late 1960s that the university began aggressively to recruit Black students. But at the same time it created research programs and sponsored conferences focusing on various aspects of the lives and experiences of people of color that provided research and networking opportunities for several generations of African American graduate students and faculty, especially those interested in psychology.

The Black scholar/activist research tradition is associated with Howard University, a private university governed by an independent board but funded by the federal government and foremost among the historically Black colleges and universities. Historically, Howard has attracted the best and the brightest of African Americans and has emphasized using research to support social change and empower Black communities. This tradition involved the interconnection of research, scholarship, training, community leadership, and advocacy and produced a great number of community activists.

The Afrocentric/African-centered tradition is rooted in the long history of Black nationalist, Pan-African, culture-centered traditions within communities of people of African descent throughout the diaspora. In the United States, such approaches—which emerged in response to a need to validate the integrity of the African American experience and can be traced back to several individuals discussed in earlier chapters, such as Paul Cuffe, Marcus Garvey, and Elijah Muhammad—are based on the link between the psychology of African Americans and their experience of oppression. A number of Afrocentric/African-centered perspectives have been articulated over the years, and their broad scope makes them difficult to pigeonhole. But they do all focus on the behaviors, thoughts, feelings, beliefs, attitudes, and ways of interacting and being of members of African American communities and emphasize the importance of self-determination and a positive self-identity.

Conclusion

The field of African American psychology as an organized discipline developed in the late 1960s, almost simultaneously with the field of Black sociology and the demand for the development of Black studies programs, the Black Power movement of the 1960s having created a social, political, and educational environment ripe for the development of racially and culturally unique fields of academic inquiry. Thus, it was no surprise that the African American–led freedom struggle also included an African American intellectual liberation campaign.

13

Black Psychology

Current Psychological Approaches

Joseph White was born on December 19, 1932, in Lincoln, Nebraska, to Dorothy Lee and Joseph L. White Sr. and moved with his family to Minneapolis, where he attended several Catholic schools. After his parents divorced, he moved to San Francisco with his mother, eventually enrolling in San Francisco State University, from which he graduated in 1964 with a bachelor's in psychology. After graduation, he spent two years in the military and then worked odd jobs for a few more years until returning to San Francisco State, from which he received a master's in 1954. He then moved on to Michigan State University, from which he received a doctorate in clinical and developmental psychology in 1961.

Early on in his professional career, White concentrated on developing curricula that eschewed the use of White, middle-class norms as the standard. And, while he was at California State University, Long Beach, he helped establish the school's Educational Opportunity Program, which assisted in the enrollment of thousands of under- and unrepresented student populations and was soon adopted by all California State University campuses. He was also instrumental in the foundation of the Association of Black Psychologists in 1968. By this time he had moved to San Francisco State University, where, in response to the 1968 student strike at the university, he was instrumental in establishing a Black studies program, the first of its kind in the United States. More importantly, in 1970 he published "Toward a Black Psychology"—a seminal document in the formation of Black psychology—in which he argued that a strictly Black psychology was necessary because any psychology created by Whites would always be inadequate to the needs of Blacks. In other words, he realized that a truly Black psychology needed to recognize the experiences and ethos that all people of African descent shared. Although this insight was not in itself original, reintroduced in the early 1970s it inspired a new generation of Black psychologists.

Learning Objectives

―――――――――――――――― ▼ ▼ ▼ ――――――――――――

1. What are some of the main themes that link the modern civil rights movement with the development of Black psychology?
2. What notions have defined Black psychology as an activist discipline?
3. What are the differences between mainstream psychology and African-centered psychology?
4. What are some of the main concepts in the field of Black psychology?
5. How would you define the term *psychological oppression?*
6. Why are the notions of identity and self-concept critical to the field of Black psychology?

―――――――――――――――― ▲ ▲ ▲ ――――――――――――

At least since the 1970s, the field of Black psychology has been an important part of the effort to create a larger African philosophy. Its proponents make, as we have seen, no concessions to mainstream White, Eurocentric positions, holding that African Americans must find their own ways to transform themselves psychologically in order to function within a society that dismisses their culture and history.

Crucial to the link between Black psychology and the creation of an African philosophy is Black activism, whether that takes the form of research and publishing, training, program organization, or community leadership. Also crucial, however, have been the many colleges and universities—and especially the historically Black colleges and universities—that have increasingly employed Black scholars and encouraged their activism. Not surprisingly, Howard University positioned itself on the front lines when, in the 1970s, it reinvented itself as a research institution. Not only did it support faculty members' scholarly endeavors; it also established a variety of cultural and scientific institutions to further such endeavors—for example, the Institute for Urban Affairs and Research (1972–1992), which focused on social problems afflicting underserved, poor, urban communities, and (in collaboration with Johns Hopkins University) the Center for Research on the Education of Students Placed at Risk (1994–2004), which sought to

In the early 2000s, the Southern Christian Leadership Council (SCLC) sponsored a protest at the criminal court building in New Orleans. (Photo by Bart Everson, 2007: https://creativecommons.org/licenses/by/2.0/legalcode.)

create a basic research agenda, develop intervention programs, and establish evaluation procedures aimed at the transformation of high-risk elementary and secondary schools.

The African-Centered/Afrocentric School of Black Psychology

During the early 1970s and into the 1980s, a group of radical psychologists of African descent proclaimed that a truly authentic field of Black psychology needed to broaden its scope beyond the Western Hemisphere to discover—or, more properly, rediscover—the African roots of people of color. As Wade Nobles put it in his "African Philosophy: Foundation for Black Psychology" (1972), an early contribution to the field: "Black psychology . . . is something more than the psychology of the so-called underprivileged peoples. . . . Its unique status is derived not from the negative aspects of being black in America, but rather from the positive features of basic African philosophy that dictate the values, customs, attitudes, and behaviors of Africans in Africa and the New World" (p. 18).

Particularly influential has been Na'im Akbar (born Luther Benjamin Weems Jr.). While attending the University of Michigan—from which he earned a bachelor's, a master's, and a doctorate in psychology—Akbar became involved with the emerging Black student activist movement. And his work on his dissertation, "Power Themes among Negro and White Paranoid and Non-Paranoid Schizophrenics," led him to question the assumptions of mainstream psychology about the mental health of African Americans. His first teaching job was at Morehouse College in Atlanta, where he designed and taught the first Black psychology courses ever offered there and, ultimately, the Black psychology program. After three years at Morehouse, he moved to Chicago to work for the Nation of Islam (during which time he changed his name). He eventually returned to the academy—first Norfolk State University and then Florida State University—where he continued to develope and teach Black psychology. He also became active with the Association of Black Psychologists soon after its founding, and he served on the editorial boards of the *Journal of Black Studies* and the *Journal of Black Psychology* for a number of years. Akbar has published extensively over the years, but his most influential book is *Light from Ancient Africa* (1994), in which he examined the African origins of psychology and contemporary applications of African psychology.

Linda James Myers, a professor emeriti at the Ohio State University, takes a similar approach, arguing that the African worldview—and the foundation it provides for not just an African philosophical framework but also a Black psychology—has the historical capacity to unite all humanity. That is to say, because humanity first emerged in Africa, and since cultural traditions and physiological and psychological characteristics develop in response to environment, the African worldview is the optimal perspective from which to evaluate not just African Americans but all racial and ethnic groups, since all human beings alive today can be considered people of African descent.

African-centered/Afrocentric psychologists did not all necessarily march in lockstep. Some, for example, began to emphasize the critical role of developing a positive ethnic/racial self-identity. Three important examples are William Cross, Thomas Parham, and Janet Helms, who explored the concept of Nigrescence—that is, the Negro-to-Black conversion experience, the process of developing a Black racial identity.

Some of the key concepts that guided this new African-centered/Afrocentric focus and helped link traditional African philosophy with more contemporary concerns within the field of Black psychology include a focus on the concepts of Ma'at, or how thought, emotion, behavior, and spiritual energy align; Maafa, or how the horrors of enslavement continue to affect people of African descent; and Sankofa, or recovering the past and bringing it into the present in order to make positive progress. For example, Kobi Kazembe Kambon (born Joseph Baldwin) focused on the functional definitions of liberation and oppression. Baldwin noted that individuals' definitional systems are determined by their cultural reality. Definitional systems that are determined by the oppressive conditions of White supremacy can, for people of African descent, result in cultural misorientation—that is, the internalization of European cultural traditions.

In the mid-1980s, Wade Nobles expanded on his earlier position, proposing that people of African descent have a common consciousness that is survivalist in nature. That is, in the face of the oppressive environments in which they have historically found themselves, African Americans have selectively adapted and fused elements of both African and European culture (a phenomenon known as *biculturalism*) to survive. This perspective has also been adopted by scholars such as Adelbert Jenkins and Anderson J. Franklin.

The late Amos Wilson developed a psychosocial analysis that seeks not just to understand the reality of the African American experience but, ultimately, to change it. As the scholar Bobby Wright noted in *The Psychopathic Racial Personality:* "Black Social Theory will not only tell us where we are going, but will also explain what to expect once we achieve our goal" (p. 1). Wilson similarly concluded in *The Developmental Psychology of the Black Child:* "At the center of African-centered psychology . . . is a psychology of power. It does not merely describe the traditional nature of African people, or the orientations of African people based on traditional African culture. It is psychology that is prescriptive as well as descriptive. It is a psychology of liberation" (p. 10). A related approach is that of Cheryl Tawede Grills, who conceives of African-centered/Afrocentric psychology as linking an African way of life, the world, and one's self and, thus, as being rooted in the cultural heritage of people of African descent throughout the diaspora. Yet another is that of Marimba Ani, who emphasized that African-centered/

Afrocentric psychology is a healing profession. She sees her work as elevating an individual's sense of self. In Ani's hands, Black psychology becomes a therapeutic exercise meant to reinforce one's compassion.

The Psychological Nature of Oppression

Another aspect of Black psychology is the study of the psychological effects of oppression. The fact of slavery was dehumanizing and debasing in itself, but enslaved persons were also conditioned both to fear and to be dependent on their owners. Slavery may have been abolished, but oppression persists, as does this relationship pattern.

There is, however, little agreement on what, if any, effect historical experience has on African American life today. African American clinical psychologists such as Na'im Akbar contend that the legacy of the enslavement period is ongoing, that the behavioral patterns of African Americans continue to be influenced by it. Evidence for the negative effects includes continuing color consciousness, family instability, and feelings of personal inferiority. But there have, according to Akbar, been some positive effects, including ambivalence about owning property and acquiring needlessly expensive material possessions. Frantz Fanon articulated a similar position in his classic 1963 *The Wretched of the Earth,* in which he discusses the relationship between the colonizer and the colonized in Africa. In short, both Akbar and Fanon, along with other African American psychologists, contend that both enslavement and colonization caused their victims to internalize negative attitudes and destructive behaviors that persist today.

Another psychological effect of slavery was the loss of a pure African identity, a pure African culture. Despite ongoing efforts by African Americans to reassert their racial identity and cultural heritage, the process has been impeded by psychological difficulties and ideological conflicts. That is, African Americans must wrestle not only with the perceptions of the larger White society but also with their own self-perceptions.

The development of identity is a psychological process of asserting both one's own worth and the worth of one's community. The dilemma for African Americans has been and continues to be what kind of identity to develop: one that adheres to the norms of the larger White society or one that acknowledges what it means to be an African American. The options have always been historically limited: Colored, Negro, Black, Afro-American,

African American. And the identity chosen depends partly on the prevailing cultural, economic, political, and social conditions. But it also depends on self-concept, one's feeling of self-worth, and how one perceives oneself in relation to others.

Conclusion

The contributions of the first and second generations of Black psychologists—sparked by the modern civil rights movement—demonstrate that, throughout the history of people of African descent in the United States, individual achievements have provided the foundation for a discipline in which the construction of abstract theories has benefited an entire group of people through a sense of collective affirmation. Over the years, various schools of thought have emerged, but all have been based in the realization that, as a professional discipline, Black psychology must rest on an African philosophical framework. Also critical to the field of Black psychology has been Black scholarly activism. The result has been a vibrant discipline that continues to make important progress to this day.

14

African Americans and Politics
From the Colonial Period to the 1930s

Frederick Augustus Bailey Washington was born into slavery near Tuckahoe, Maryland, in 1818. His father was a White man he never met, and his mother was part Native American, part African American. Young Frederick spent his early years with his grandparents and his aunt, seeing his mother on only four or five occasions before her death when he was seven years old. When he was eight, he was given to Lucretia Auld, the wife of Thomas Auld, and then sent to Baltimore to live with Thomas's brother Hugh. It was while he was living in Baltimore that he taught himself how to read. In 1833, Thomas took him back from Hugh and hired him out to the notoriously brutal Edward Covey, who whipped him frequently. He endured Covey's treatment for five years and then, on September 3, 1838, finally managed to escape, heading by train to New York and then settling in New Bedford, Massachusetts.

In New Bedford, Frederick Douglass (as he was now known) joined a local African American church and attended abolitionist meetings, becoming acquainted at some point with William Lloyd Garrison, the publisher of the weekly abolitionist newspaper the *Liberator*, with whom he worked closely thereafter. In 1841, he began his speaking career on the abolitionist circuit. In 1845, he published *Narrative of the Life of Frederick Douglass, an American Slave* and then embarked on a speaking tour of England, Ireland, and Scotland. The tour earned him enough money to purchase his freedom on his return to the United States in 1847.

Douglass then began a very active publishing career, working first with his fellow African American activist Martin Delany, with whom he cofounded the abolitionist periodical *North Star*, and then on his own. He continued to denounce the system of slavery, but he also took up other causes, including the integration of White churches, public schools, and other institutions and, notably, women's rights. In 1855, he published *My Bondage and My Freedom,* a revised and expanded version of his autobiography.

During the Civil War, Douglass continued to be a leading voice calling for the end of slavery, advising Abraham Lincoln, and helping recruit African Americans for the Union Army. After the war, he continued to speak out about racial equality and women's rights. He also held several government positions, such as assistant secretary to the Santo Domingo Commission, marshal of the District of Columbia, and US ambassador to Haiti. He is considered today the foremost architect and promoter of the African American political ideology of racial integration, the dominant perspective of most people of color in the United States during his lifetime and well past his death in 1895.

Learning Objectives

▼ ▼ ▼

1. Why is the field of Black American politics important to people of color?
2. What were some of the main concepts that formed early African American political thought?
3. What were some of the major trends of African American political thought during and soon after the American Revolution?
4. How did African American political views change after the American Civil War ended?
5. What were some of the major political views of most African American leaders from the end of the Reconstruction Era to the 1930s?

▲ ▲ ▲

Early African American Political Thought and Politics

Politics is the art of gaining, maintaining, and using power, whether the actor in question is an individual, a group, or an institution. Political science, by contrast, is the study of politics—or, more precisely, the description and analysis of government institutions.

Traditionally, political science has studied Western institutions. But political institutions are culturally specific, those arising in the West tending to be markedly different from those arising in Africa, based as they are on different values, ideologies, and experiences. Consider the kingdoms of Ghana, Mali, and Songhai discussed in chapter 3.

The political ideology of African Americans is a good case in point. People of color residing in the United States have historically been excluded from the political process, becoming full participants in the American political system only during the later stages of the modern civil rights movement. Therefore, traditional notions of Western political science cannot be applied to the African American political experience before the late 1960s because Blacks' political activity has of necessity taken such forms as labor strikes, economic boycotts, mass demonstrations, and other methods of civil disobedience rather than orderly participation in the electoral process and government institutions. People of color had to struggle simply to be heard.

African American Political Ideology during the War of Independence

An identifiable African American political ideology can be traced back to the American Revolution. The Founding Fathers were by no means abolitionists. So convinced were they that African Americans could never claim the same rights as White Europeans that, when Thomas Jefferson drafted the Declaration of Independence, he felt no need to justify or qualify his language proclaiming universal liberty: "We hold these truths to be self-evident, that all men are created equal, that they are endowed by their Creator with certain unalienable Rights, that among these are Life, Liberty and the pursuit of Happiness." Still, African Americans took heart, hoping that the Patriots would come to recognize that their claims of the equality of men applied just as much to Blacks as they did to Whites and that the Revolution would, in fact, lead to the destruction of the institution of slavery.

Some Patriots did, in fact, recognize those claims, most prominently James Otis and Thomas Paine, encouraging many people of color to take matters into their own hands. Their political efforts took many forms. The most violent form was the slave revolts in the South. But, in the North, African Americans began to use the court system, bringing *freedom suits* based on the principle of universal liberty. Not all these cases were successful, but those that were set a precedent. Other enslaved northerners petitioned first colonial and then state legislatures for gradual emancipation, their petitions employing the same kind of revolutionary rhetoric the Patriots had articulated in the face of English authoritarianism. For example, even before the Revolution, in 1773, a group of African American petitioners from Boston told a delegation of the Massachusetts colonial assembly: "We expect great things from men who have made such a noble stand against the designs of their fellow-men to enslave them . . . the divine spirit of freedom" (quoted in Nash, 1990, p. 173). In 1775, African American minutemen stood with their White counterparts at Lexington and Concord, both inspired by the same political rhetoric, a rhetoric that formed the basis of an African American integrationist political ideology.

African American Political Ideology in the Antebellum United States

Sadly, the egalitarian impulse sparked by the Revolution died out soon after. The dawning of the Romantic Age brought with it the belief that all ethnic and racial groups had their own inherent spiritual and cultural norms that distinguished them from one another. White Americans began to view themselves as self-reliant, intellectually curious, and uniquely capable of self-governance, qualities lacking in other groups. Even White northerners came to fear that contact with African Americans would have a degrading effect on their race. As a result, states set about restricting the in-migration of African Americans. African American suffrage was also limited where it was not withdrawn. Segregation became the norm, even in the North.

It was under these conditions that African American political ideologies first took the general shape that they retain today. Broadly classified, activists fell into three, often overlapping, camps: the integrationists, the separatists, and the nationalists.

Frederick Douglass, for example, became the primary architect and proponent of racial integration. The moral and ethical imperative for the desegregation of American society is one of the primary concerns of his life and work. This concern would be echoed years later by the National Association for the Advancement of Colored People and the Urban League when they were founded in the early years of the twentieth century.

Segregated transportation in the US South during the 1940s. (Courtesy of the Prints and Photographs Division, Library of Congress: LC-DIG-ppmsc-00199.)

A contrasting position is that of nationalism. As we have seen in chapter 3, in response to increasing racism and racial violence during the 1840s and 1850s, a small but influential group of African American leaders such as Henry Highland Garnet and Martin R. Delany, Prince Hall and Paul Cuffe, favored nationalism—whether through migration to Africa or separatism within the United States—as the best means for people of color to realize their objectives. But, as we have seen in chapter 4, it was only in the 1960s that, with the rise of such organizations as the Nation of Islam and the Black Panther Party, nationalism became a true political force.

African American Political Ideology after the Civil War

It was, however, only with the Freedom Generation (the first generation of formerly enslaved African Americans) and Black suffrage that the struggle for equal rights produced African American leaders who were recognizably politicians. After all, as we have seen, the Thirteenth Amendment had freed enslaved African Americans, the Fourteen Amendment had made them US

Segregated water fountain on the lawn of the county courthouse in Halifax, North Carolina, 1940s or 1950s. (Courtesy of Prints and Photographs Division, Library of Congress: LC-DIG-fsa-8a03228.)

citizens and granted them equal protection under the law, and the Fifteenth Amendment had granted them voting rights. And, during the early years of Reconstruction, African Americans availed themselves of those rights, seeking and attaining elective office. In fact, hundreds were voted into city, state, and national offices. Sadly, White Republicans still dominated the political arena, and, as we have seen, the backlash was severe and segregationist policies soon back in place, foremost the separate-but-equal doctrine embodied in the *Plessy v. Ferguson* (1896) decision.

Still, African American political leaders continued to emerge. As we have seen in chapter 4, Booker T. Washington encouraged African Americans to pursue economic success, believing that their political progress would be best assured by establishing a solid economic base, a form of class separatism. But, according to Ida B. Wells-Barnett, one of Washington's harshest critics, life was not so simple. Wells, a prominent advocate of African American civil rights, women's rights, and economic rights (see chapter 2), argued that the status of African Americans had little do with their ability to attain economic success, noting in particular the lynching of three African American businessmen in Memphis whose only crime had been to establish successful grocery stores along a popular streetcar route. She saw these lynchings, as well as thousands of others, as political and economic terrorism pure and simple, something against which Washington's doctrine of economic uplift was powerless.

It was also during this time that, as we have seen in chapter 6, Black nationalism in its nineteenth-century form had been superseded by the Pan-African or back-to-Africa movement. All these schools of thought waxed and waned, achieving little, until the mid-1930s, when most Black American leaders overwhelmingly began to support the notion of integrationism.

Conclusion

From the Revolution to the 1930s, African American political ideologies have been more affected by race and race relations than political ideas themselves. In the end, the politics of integration won. However, the journey contained many ups and downs as African Americans continuously tried to define their destiny on their own terms, which was no easy task, especially before World War II.

15

African Americans and Politics

From Black Empowerment
to the Criminal Justice System

Shirley Chisholm was born in 1924 in the Bedford-Stuyvesant section of Brooklyn as Shirley Anita Sainte Hill. She excelled academically and, after high school, attended Brooklyn College, receiving her undergraduate degree in 1946, and then Columbia University, earning a master's in early childhood education in 1951. She then held a series of teaching jobs.

In the 1950s, Chisholm became involved with the local Democratic Party, and it gradually became evident to her that women held no power in the party and that her majority-Black district had no Black elected officials. Spurred by the disinterest of the regular Democratic Party in issues affecting the everyday lives of African Americans, she joined a new political organization, the Unity Democratic Club (UDC), which was integrated and boasted women in leadership positions. The UDC's main purpose was challenging the regular local Democratic Party by running African American candidates for any open political offices, and Chisholm was inspired to run for the New York State General Assembly in 1964, winning handily.

For the next four years, Chisholm was the only woman in the state's general assembly and one of only eight African Americans to hold government office in New York State. In 1968, she became the first African American woman elected to Congress, keeping her seat until she retired in 1982. During her fourteen-year tenure in the House of Representatives, she was a staunch advocate of an expanded civil rights agenda and women's rights. She was also an early member of the National Organization for Women, a founding member of the National Women's Political Caucus, and a key spokesperson for the National Abortion Rights Action League. In 1972, she became the first African American to seek a major political party's nomination to run for president. In short, she was an outspoken

Shirley Chisholm, the first African American woman to serve in Congress, announcing her entry into the Democratic presidential primary, 1972. Chisholm was the first Black candidate to run for a major-party nomination for the office of president. (Courtesy of the Prints and Photographs Division, Library of Congress: LC-DIG-ppmsc-01264.)

supporter of liberal policies during the 1960s, 1970s, and 1980s who sought to break down established racial and gender barriers, an integrationist who worked within the traditional two-party system.

After retiring from the House, Chisholm resumed her teaching career, beginning with a faculty position at Mount Holyoke College. In 1991, she moved from New York to Ormond Beach, Florida, where she lived until her death in 2005 at the age of eighty.

Learning Objectives

▼ ▼ ▼

1. What were the major political themes during the civil rights era?
2. What was the Black Power political movement?
3. How did the Black Power movement affect northern states?
4. What were the positive aspects of Black American politics during the 1970s?
5. How did African American politicians fare after the 1970s?

▲ ▲ ▲

Black Intellectual and Political Thought during the Civil Rights Era

Between the mid-1930s and the early 1960s, most African American leaders were committed to achieving social, political, and economic integration. For example, as we have seen in chapter 12, Thurgood Marshall worked within the established legal system when arguing *Brown v. Board of Education* before the Supreme Court.

The Reverend Martin Luther King Jr.—whose participation in the 1955 Montgomery bus boycott first brought him to national attention—took a somewhat different approach. Focusing on mass action, he encouraged African Americans to become active participants in the struggle against segregation and espoused a form of nonviolent resistance modeled on Mahatma Gandhi's successful 1915–1947 campaign for Indian independence from British rule. Rejecting separatism, he looked forward to the day when unity across racial, gender, and class lines would be the norm, a vision he articulated most forcefully in his address to the participants of the March on Washington for Jobs and Freedom in 1963—his deservedly famous "I Have a Dream" speech.

Ella "Jo" Baker was another community activist who built on a philosophical framework that would be echoed by King in later decades, but she also took it in another direction, preferring a more grassroots, democratic, non-leader-centered orientation. For example, in the 1930s, she worked with the Young Negroes Cooperative League to develop African American economic power through the formation of collectives. In the 1940s, she joined the New York National Association for the Advancement of Colored People, serving first as a field secretary and then as the branch director. In her later years, she worked with Dr. King—despite their differences in leadership style—to establish the Southern Christian Leadership Conference. Baker was just one of many African American women involved in the modern civil rights movement in its early years, women who felt a strong connection to their communities and were skilled organizers.

Black Power and Black Power Politics

As we have seen in chapter 4, the civil rights movement had by the mid-1960s achieved some of its goals—most notably the passage of the 1964 Civil Rights Act and the 1965 Voting Rights Act—but there was a backlash from the White establishment. And it was within this tense political climate that a powerful, assertive, and radical African American voice emerged in the North, a voice critical of the nonviolent civil rights movement because it appeared to have few ties to the community it was purportedly serving. Some activists contended, in fact, that, while integrationists were well intended, the effect of their increasingly successful efforts was the destruction of Black communities and their institutions and the removal of Black politicians from positions of power. It also seemed to many people of color that they had to deny their racial identity if they were to gain access to the American dream. Another reaction was to respond to violence with violence.

The resurgent separatist movement first coalesced around Malcolm X, whose speeches and writings electrified African Americans, instilling in them a sense of pride in themselves and their race. And its growth was aided by the failure of Johnson's Great Society programs to deliver significant change and the increasingly violent White reaction to the efforts of civil rights activists. Especially galvanizing was the 1966 attempted assassination of

James Meredith (the young African American student who led the charge to integrate the University of Mississippi in 1962) on the second day of his March against Fear. In response, the civil rights leader Stokely Carmichael joined the march, giving in a speech made shortly thereafter the first call for "Black Power." The slogan quickly caught on, but, because it was adopted by activists of various ideological perspectives, it meant different things to different people: for example, ethnic solidarity, Black nationalism, and Black pan-nationalism. But, at its most general, *Black Power* meant the direct participation of African Americans in the political institutions that affected their daily lives: for example, many activists began to demand the establishment of civilian review boards to oversee predominantly White urban police forces and educational systems.

One specifically political response was the creation of Black political parties. For example, even in the 1960s, the Mississippi Democratic Party was a Whites-only organization. So, in 1964, the integrated Mississippi Freedom Democratic Party (MFDP) was created to challenge the exclusion of African Americans from state politics. During the 1964 Democratic National Convention in Atlantic City, New Jersey, the MFDP challenged the seating of the five White Mississippi delegates on the grounds that African Americans had been excluded from both the primary and the general elections. The challenge failed, but the MFDP persevered, eventually merging with the regular Democratic Party.

In 1966, the Student Nonviolent Coordinating Committee organized the Lowndes County Freedom Organization, an independent African American political party, for the sole purpose of registering Black voters and nominating people of color to run in the Lowndes County, Alabama, sheriff, tax assessor, and school board elections. Despite the fact that the county was 80 percent Black, few of the party's candidates won, owing largely to the violence with which African Americans attempting to vote were threatened. In 1970, it too merged with the regular Democratic Party.

Also in 1966, the Black Panther Party of Self-Defense was established by Huey Newton and Bobby Seals in Oakland, California. Taking a grassroots approach, Newton and Seals canvassed door-to-door throughout the city, spreading word of the organization's goals and demands, which included full employment and economic reparations for all African Americans and an end to police brutality. At its most militant, the party organized openly armed patrols meant to police the police. But it also offered such free services

Civil rights leader and community activist Malcolm X at a press conference given by Martin Luther King Jr. The event was held at the US Capitol as the Senate debated the passage of the Civil Rights Act of 1964. (Courtesy of the Prints and Photographs Division, Library of Congress: LC-DIG-ppmsc-01274.)

as school breakfast programs, clothing distribution, adult education classes, free medical clinics, drug and alcohol rehabilitation, and sickle-cell testing, a practice soon adopted by other Black Power organizations.

In 1972, in another attempt to transition to an independent Black politics, more than ten thousand African Americans attended the National Black Political Convention in Gary, Indiana. The convention was able to commit to a platform, but little else in the way of consensus was achieved, not even endorsing Shirley Chisholm's presidential run, and a third party was not established. Still, attendees left the convention with a newfound sense of racial pride and solidarity and a determination to maintain an independent bloc of Black voters.

Somewhat surprisingly, the various manifestations of the Black Power movement were largely dominated by men, likely a response to the historical dehumanization and subjection of African American men. African American women were expected to play only supporting roles. Still, some, such as Kathleen Neal Cleaver, Elaine Brown, and Ericka Huggins, managed to carve out spheres of influence for themselves, making greater progress in some ways than women in more traditional activist groups did.

African American Political Power during the 1970s

By the late 1960s, as the American political landscape began shifting to the right, support for civil rights reform began to wane. Still, during the 1970s, African American activists not only held their ground but also racked up some surprising successes, most of them owing to a reliance on lobbying and litigation rather than mass protest.

One of the priorities that remained high on the list for civil rights leaders during the 1970s was school desegregation. Even though substantial progress toward integration had been made in small towns and rural areas, where little residential segregation existed and the redistribution of students among schools caused little outcry, larger towns and cities remained highly segregated residentially, leaving planners few options. Hence the resort to litigation in the federal courts pressing for the use of busing in urban areas. A defense against busing was mounted by claiming that, although the Fourteenth Amendment banned racial discrimination, it did not mandate racial integration. Two lawsuits—*Swann v. Charlotte-Mecklenburg Board of Education* (1971) and *Keys v. School District No. 1, Denver, Colorado* (1973)—finally resolved the issue, the Supreme Court green-lighting, respectively, busing in the furtherance of integration and the imposition by federal judges of desegregation plans in recalcitrant school districts. Also, despite opposition, in 1976 Congress enacted legislation enabling the Department of Health, Education, and Welfare to cut off federal funding for school districts that refused to adopt busing plans.

Still, desegregating schools was not all smooth sailing. The White flight from the cities to the suburbs that had begun in the 1950s and 1960s intensified in the 1970s, leaving most urban schools even more heavily segregated than they had been. The only meaningful desegregation policy left to planners was the movement of students between city school districts and urban school districts. And *Milliken v. Bradley* (1974)—in which the Supreme Court ruled that, unless it could be demonstrated that suburban school districts had intentionally adopted policies designed to promote segregation, busing to further the desegregation of inner-city schools could not be forced on them—eliminated that option. As a result, during the 1980s and 1990s, the schools in most of the nation's large urban cities, where mostly African Americans lived, became even more segregated than they had been in the 1960s.

African American Elected Officials during the Late 1970s and Early 1980s

Before 1965, there were, it has been estimated, fewer than three hundred African American elected officials in the United States. However, the year 1967 marked a major turning point for Black Americans who wanted to hold a political office when Carl Stokes and Richard Hatcher were elected as the mayors of Cleveland, Ohio, and Gary, Indiana, respectively. Shortly thereafter, five African Americans were elected to Congress, including Edward W. Brooke, who became the first person of color to be seated in the US Senate since 1881.

Progress continued. In 1973, Coleman Young in Detroit and Thomas Bradley in Los Angeles became the first African American mayors of cities of more than a million residents. In 1983, Chicago elected its first African American mayor, Harold Washington. And, in 1985, state senator L. Douglas Wilder was elected lieutenant governor of Virginia, making him the first African American to be elected to that position in a southern state since

President Barack Obama, official portrait, 2012. (Official White House photo by Pete Souza.)

Reconstruction. The jury is still out on whether these are Pyrrhic victories. That is to say, Blacks in public office cannot push only Black concerns—at least if they wish to remain in office. Often they must forge the proverbial deal with the devil, looking to corporate America to fund pet projects.

Unfortunately, the growth in African American political power was gradually checked by a resurgence in the 1980s of the Republican Party—evidenced by the presidencies of Ronald Reagan (1980–1988) and George H. W. Bush (1988–1992)—which sought smaller, not bigger, government and took aim at programs that conservatives considered to be examples of government overreach, aided by a small but influential cadre of African American conservatives such as William Bell, Clarence Thomas, and Clarence Pendleton. (Prime targets were the Equal Employment Opportunity Commission and the US Commission on Civil Rights.) Still, most African American voters remained firmly committed to the Democratic Party, helping elect William Jefferson Clinton to two terms in the White House (1992–2000) and staying faithful through the presidency of George W. Bush (2000–2008) despite his attempts to curry their favor by appointing (admittedly conservative) African Americans to judgeships and his cabinet. And they were pivotal in bringing about the historic presidency of Barack Obama (2008–2016).

Conclusion

Both the political system and the judicial system were affected by the shift to the right in politics. Over the years, the courts had edged ever more in the direction of upholding the rights of and obtaining justice for African Americans, a movement culminating in the appointment of Earl Warren as chief justice of the Supreme Court in 1954. However, with the victory of Richard Nixon over Hubert Humphrey in 1968 and the retirement of Chief Justice Warren in 1969, the liberal construction of the federal judicial system came under attack. A series of conservative presidents began to fill judicial vacancies with conservative jurists. And, not surprisingly, the number of incarcerated African Americans began to rise. From 1954 to 2005, the African American prison population increased by almost 900 percent, from 98,000 to 910,000. Furthermore, by 2011, African Americans made up about 46 percent of the prison population although they constituted only about 12 percent of the overall US population.

What does all this say about the future of African American politics? The major takeaway is that integration—if that is the desired goal—should not come at the expense of African American social, political, and economic institutions. And political institutions—independent political institutions— are particularly important because they can revitalize and strengthen social and economic institutions.

16

The Creative Expressions of African Americans

The Origins, Development, and Impact of African American Music

Born in New Orleans on August 4, 1901, Louis Daniel "Satchmo" Armstrong was the eldest of two children born to Willie Armstrong, a turnpike worker, and Mary A. Armstrong, a direct descendant of enslaved persons. From a young age, Louis regularly sang and performed on the streets of New Orleans with his friends. As he turned five years old, his parents divorced, and thereafter he was raised by his mother and grandmother in "the Battlefield," a run-down and dangerous section of New Orleans. In 1913, he was arrested for firing a handgun into the air on New Year's Eve and sent to the Colored Waifs Home, a local African American reform school, where he learned to play the cornet. After his release in 1919, he worked odd jobs and began to play music in local bands, leaving New Orleans in 1922 to join first Joe "King" Oliver's Creole jazz band in Chicago and then Fletcher Henderson's jazz big band in New York. In 1925, Armstrong returned to Chicago, organized his own band, and began to record with the drummer Zutty Singleton and the pianist Earl Hines, two musicians who could match his adventurous rhythms and complex techniques with precision. His performances featured his intense trumpet and vocal solos, the latter pioneering the technique known as *scat singing*, a form of vocal improvisation utilizing nonsense syllables.

In 1929, Armstrong moved his band to New York, becoming an instant sensation. But the Depression and some bad management decisions took their toll economically. So, in 1932, under new management, he embarked on the first of what would be a series of highly successful European tours. When he did return to the States, he embraced the swing ethos and, fronting a big band, became more popular than ever. In 1947,

Jazz musician Louis Armstrong in Amsterdam, 1955. (Photo by Herbert Behrens, 1955. Courtesy of the Nationaal Archief.)

with the waning of the swing era, he formed the All-Stars, a Dixieland-style sextet that toured worldwide.

Armstrong's crossover appeal gained him roles in such films as *New Orleans* (1947), *Satchmo the Great* (1957), *Paris Blues* (1961), and *Hello, Dolly!* (1969). It also led to his being viewed as little more than a vaudevillian. But beneath the lighthearted humor and comic stage presence for which he became known was a mission: defying Jim Crow by bringing African American rhythmic elements and performance styles to audiences everywhere.

Learning Objectives

▼ ▼ ▼

1. What are the foundational roots of African American music?
2. How did African American music develop during the enslavement period?

3. How did gospel music emerge?
4. What were some of the fundamental principles of jazz music?
5. What factors led to the development of blues music?
6. How are the musical genres of rock and roll and rhythm and blues linked?
7. What has been the lasting impact of rap music?

▲ ▲ ▲

Music has always been a major influence on African American culture. Initially, it allowed the first enslaved Africans to keep their heritage alive. It also buoyed their spirits and helped create a sense of community among them.

Whereas European music was centered on melody, African American music was centered on rhythm, particularly the sound of the drum. Also important was the call-and-response or ring-shout format (see chapter 7), which fostered dialogue, especially in work songs, and thus improvisation. These traditions were passed down orally. Besides the drum, African American music also employed most prominently the banjo (and its predecessors) but also bells, horns, small flutes, pipes, and rattles.

Most distinctive about African American music was, however, the singing style, which was less rooted in lyrics and more expressive and percussive, including as it did such vocal gestures as shouts, shrieks, and slurs and such physical realizations as foot stomping and hand clapping. The latter should not be surprising as dancing was a vital part of African culture, one that contributed to a sense of community. Witness the link between music and dance in such celebratory practices as funeral percussions in the South and Election Day parades in the North.

Before moving on to specific forms that African American music took, especially after the end of the Civil War, we need to take note of the form of entertainment known as *minstrel shows*. The minstrel show was a form of racist entertainment developed during the early nineteenth century, essentially a variety show lampooning Blacks, characterizing them as lazy, dim-witted, and superstitious buffoons. Most of the roles were taken by White people in blackface. But the minstrel show did have a place for Black entertainers, for many years the only place for African Americans seeking a show business career. It was a compromise for them, but a necessary one.

Early lithograph depicting a performance of "Oh Carry Me Back to Ole Virginny," a standard minstrel tune during the nineteenth and early twentieth centuries. (Robertson, Seibert and Shearman Publishing Company, 1859. Courtesy of the Prints and Photographs Division, Library of Congress: LC-DIG-ppmsca-08346.)

From Spirituals to Gospel

The various musical expressions outlined above coalesced in what came to be known as the *spiritual,* a significant form of folk song created by enslaved people and their descendants and at first passed along orally. (The first compilation of spirituals was not published until 1867.) Spirituals took as their texts biblical songs and stories, and, while they emphasized optimism and affirmation, they also recognized sorrow. Especially important in their development were Old Testament texts, Blacks seeing their life circumstances mirrored in the sufferings of the Jews, the Chosen People. In other words, spirituals embodied the fundamental search of all people of color for an abiding religious faith that would sustain them in the face of the horrors of the world in which they are forced to live.

Gospel music, a new style of church music that developed in the late nineteenth century, was influenced by and built on older forms of African American music, especially spirituals, carrying on, as it did, the tradition of providing spiritual and communal uplift. But its growth was fueled by the revivals of the Holiness-Pentecostal movement. What distinguished the

Holiness movement was, as we saw in chapter 8, its emphasis on the healing power of God and its acceptance of prophesying and speaking in tongues. The freedom of expression that this type of religious experience afforded worshippers facilitated the creation of a corresponding form of music that relied on experimentation. Eventually, gospel music infused virtually all forms of African American religion. And, as it developed, it grew beyond the drums and the banjo to incorporate such instruments as tambourines, triangles, guitars, horns, pianos, and organs.

Gospel music was first introduced to a wider—and interracial—audience in 1871 by the first of the Fisk University Jubilee Singers' concert tours of the United States and Europe. Gospel songs began appearing in print in the 1870s, but it is the Methodist minister C. Albert Tindley, whose songs were first published in 1901, who is credited with the creation of gospel music for a larger audience. Most of the songs that Tindley composed were traditional in nature and relied heavily on African American spirituals. His "I'll Overcome Someday" is credited by many scholars with being the basis for the civil rights anthem "We Shall Overcome."

The individual who most influenced gospel music was Thomas Andrew "Georgia Tom" Dorsey. As a worship leader for Chicago's Pilgrim Baptist Church, he brought with him a musical style that merged elements of hymns and the blues to create a gospel blues. His gospel pieces—ranging from ragtime to boogie-woogie and based mostly on piano tunes—generated a new and captivating urban gospel style. His place in gospel music was cemented in the 1930s and 1940s when Mahalia Jackson—one of the greatest gospel singers of all time and for a number of years one of the highest-paid recording artists in the United States—began to promote his songs on her national tours.

Between the late 1950s and the early 1970s, gospel music grew in popularity. Large gospel choirs toured not just the United States but the world, performing not only in churches but also in large, secular halls. It took hold in recording studios, in major concert venues (Clara Ward and the Ward Singers appeared at the 1957 Newport Jazz Festival), and on network television shows (Mahalia Jackson appeared on *The Ed Sullivan Show* in 1960), reaching hundreds of thousands of people. Other noteworthy gospel artists, like James Cleveland, the Clark Sisters, and Dinah Washington, who at one time refused to perform outside their local churches, began to take advantage of this newfound audience. African American gospel music continues

Jazz musician Nat "King" Cole (seated, left); the first African American mayor of Cincinnati, Theodore "Ted" Berry (with microphone); and Cincinnati's light heavyweight world champion Ezzard Charles (right) at a local event during the 1950s. (Robert O'Neal Multicultural Arts Center [ROMAC] West End Collection. Courtesy of Toilynn O'Neal Turner.)

to grow and remain relevant even today. Indeed, many African American rhythm and blues singers began their careers singing gospel music. Witness Della Reese, Sam Cooke, Billy Preston, and Gladys Knight.

Jazz Music as the Birth of Improvisation

Initially, jazz was primarily a response by African Americans to their newfound freedom, especially in New Orleans, where it originated. But it was distinctive in that its appetite was voracious when it came to influences, drawing as it did on the improvisational elements of spirituals and gospel music, as well as on brass band music, dance music, orchestra music, folk music, work songs, minstrel tunes, and ragtime. And at the core of jazz music is the notion of improvisation.

Print advertisement for the Regal Theatre in Cincinnati's West End, a predominantly Black community. Built in 1908 and opened as the Casino Theatre in 1914, the venue was ultimately renamed the Regal Theatre in 1941. (Robert O'Neal Multicultural Arts Center [ROMAC] West End Collection. Courtesy of Toilynn O'Neal Turner.)

The major jazz bands that emerged in New Orleans played at parades, funeral processions, and other outdoor events. Eschewing stringed instruments, jazz bands relied on brass, reeds, and drums. Ferdinand J. La Menthe—later known as Jelly Roll Morton—is regarded by many scholars as the first jazz musician. Still, the most innovative jazz musician of the early twentieth century was Louis Daniel "Satchmo" Armstrong, who introduced, among other things, a singing style that echoed the pathbreaking vocals of the African American female blues singers Ma Rainey and Bessie Smith. But it was Edward Kennedy "Duke" Ellington who took jazz to new heights. Building on the innovations of previous composers and bandleaders such as Jelly Roll Morton, Fletcher Henderson, Joe "King" Oliver, and Louis Armstrong, Ellington put together one of the most outstanding and powerful jazz bands in history—essentially an orchestra-based band—and wrote not just popular music but also film scores and operas.

Interestingly, jazz led in the 1920s and 1930s to the development of swing, both Black and White band leaders pushing the music in a different direction and reaching increasingly wider audiences. By the 1940s, however, it began to be influenced by the growing political assertiveness of the African American–led civil rights movement. This new commitment to an African American consciousness led jazz musicians to experiment with a new form of music that became known as bebop or free music. When the swing era ended after World War II, a new generation of bebop artists, such as Dizzy Gillespie, Bud Powell, Kenny Clark, Max Roach, Charlie Parker, John Coltrane, Ornette Coleman, and Miles Davis, came to the fore.

The Blues Began in the Mississippi Delta

Another direction that African American music took after spirituals was the blues. Blues music, which emerged in the 1880s and 1890s, emphasized increasingly personal expression and musicians' skill. The appeal of the blues lay in its ability to make sense of the human condition.

The blues had secular as well as sacred origins. Besides spirituals and early gospel songs, it also drew on ragtime tunes and the music of minstrel shows. It also mixed secular and religious subject matter. In fact, it was known in some circles as *devil music* because of its explicit language and intense concentration on sexual desire.

A dancer at the Cotton Club in Cincinnati. (Robert O'Neal Multicultural Arts Center [ROMAC], West End Collection. Courtesy of Toilynn O'Neal Turner.)

The blues takes a cyclic form in which repetition mirrors the traditional call-and-response pattern. In early blues songs we find one line repeated four times. By the early years of the twentieth century, however, the blues had taken on an AAB form: that is, one line sung twice followed by a longer concluding line. A wide range of instruments can be used to back up the vocals, though guitars, banjos, pianos, and harmonicas are most commonly found, and audience participation is expected, whether that be hand clapping, foot stomping, finger snapping, or singing alone with the lyrics.

There are three main styles of blues music: down-home (or country) blues, classic women's blues, and urban blues. It should be noted that these are loose chronological classifications and not solid divisions.

Down-home blues was played mostly during the early twentieth century in the South and is mostly associated with the Mississippi Delta. The most important Delta blues player was Robert Johnson. A guitar prodigy, Johnson absorbed the styles of both little-known musicians such as Harvey "Hard Rock" Glenn, Myles Robson, and Ernest "Whiskey Red" Brown and legendary bluesmen such as Charley Patton and Willie Brown. He led an itinerant lifestyle, but a year or so before his death he sat for a series of recording sessions. Hence we have an aural record of some of his most famous songs, such as "Sweet Home Chicago," "Cross Road Blues," and "Hellhound on My Trail." Tragically, Johnson died in 1938 at the age of twenty-seven, but his legacy lives on among such musicians as Eric Clapton, Jimmy Paige, Jimi Hazel, Buddy Guy, Keith Richards, and the late Stevie Ray Vaughan, who consider him the best bluesman of all time.

Ma Rainey, the so-called mother of the blues, and Bessie Smith, known as the empress of the blues, spearheaded the style that dominated the 1920s and 1930s, women's blues. Ma Rainey (born Gertrude Pridgett) made her debut around 1900 at the age of fourteen as a performer in the musical revue *Bunch of Blackberries* at the Columbus, Georgia, Springer Opera House. In 1904, she married William Rainey, a comedian, dancer, and minstrel show actor, and they began touring as "Ma and Pa Rainey." Ma Rainey quickly became popular with both African American and White audiences, developing a hybrid style based on minstrel shows and vaudeville. After divorcing her husband, she embarked on a successful solo career. Bessie Smith, on the other hand, is remembered more as a straightforward blues singer who in her later years gravitated more toward jazz. She too was popular with mainstream audiences and, during her heyday in the 1920s, became the highest-paid Black entertainer in America.

With the Second Great Migration, which began in the early 1940s, more and more African Americans congregated in such northern cities as Chicago, New York, and Detroit, and, consequently, the blues musicians among them began to adopt a style and content that better reflected their urban surroundings. Typical of the change was the use of the electric guitar, which was introduced to the blues by the legendary T-Bone Walker and subsequently adopted by the likes of B. B. King, Buddy Guy, and Albert Collins. This sound continues to dominate blues music today, Black or White, having been carried on by musicians including Robert Cray, Keb' Mo', Albert King, Jonny Lang, Bonnie Raitt, and Vernon Reid.

Rock and Roll and Rhythm and Blues Capture a Generation

When Elvis Presley made his initial television appearances on *The Tommy Dorsey Show* and *The Ed Sullivan Show* in the fall of 1955, it was the first time that a majority of Americans had heard rock and roll music, even though the era of rock and roll had been ushered in a year earlier with Bill Haley & His Comets' recording of "Rock around the Clock." These musicians did, however, have African American predecessors. One of these was the doo-wop group the Chords, known today mostly for their 1954 hit "Sh-Boom," which rocketed up the charts to *Billboard's* top ten. Other, more successful African American performers—most of whom started out on the chitlin circuit, a group of theaters and nightclubs catering to Blacks and spotlighting Black entertainers—included Joe Turner, Chubby Checker, Fats Domino, Ray Charles, and Etta James. Arguably, however, the most important African American to play rock and roll was Charles Edward Anderson "Chuck" Berry.

As a teenager, the St. Louis native Berry was fascinated with jazz, blues, and country music, but in 1944 his plan to pursue a career in music hit a snag when he was arrested for armed robbery and wound up in prison. On his release in 1947, he took guitar lessons from a local teacher and studied the playing styles of Charlie Christian, T-Bone Walker, and Carl Hogan as well as the sounds of Nat "King" Cole, Muddy Waters, and Big Joe Turner. By 1952, he was playing regular gigs in various clubs around town. It was at this time that he met the pianist Johnnie Johnson and formed a trio that recorded such important early rock and roll songs as "Roll over Beethoven" (1956), "School Day" (1957), and "Rock and Roll Music" (1957). His influence on rock and roll was so great that he could count among his many admirers the Beatles, the Rolling Stones, and the Animals.

Then there was Little Richard (born Richard Wayne Penniman). Always musical, Richard began his performing career at the age of fourteen on the minstrel show circuit. Eventually moving from his hometown of Macon, Georgia, to Atlanta, he became a popular enough act that he began recording in the early 1950s, and in 1955 released the enormously popular "Tutti Frutti," which he followed up with such hits as "Long Tall Sally," "Slippin' and Slidin'," "She Got It," "Lucille," and "Good Golly, Miss Molly." As they were by Chuck Berry, many White rock musicians were influenced by Little Richard, including the Beatles, the Rolling Stones, and Mitch Ryder.

Rhythm and blues emerged simultaneously with rock and roll. Unlike rock and roll, however, it originated in the South in the African American church, like the blues moving north with the Great Migration and incorporating a more urban style. Before 1949, it was categorized by record companies and radio stations as *race music* (to signify that it had, in fact, been created by African American musicians). However, during the 1950s, *Billboard* magazine started to use *rhythm and blues,* partly because the term was less racially insensitive, and partly because the music was becoming popular among young White audiences who might be put off by the term *race music.* From the late 1950s through the early 1960s, rhythm and blues ruled the airways. It became so popular, in fact, that White artists began covering Black artists' songs. For example, one of the hit songs that skyrocketed Elvis Presley to stardom was "Hound Dog," which had been written and recorded three years earlier by the female African American blues singer Big Mama Thornton.

As the modern civil rights movement shifted into its second phase, rhythm and blues metamorphosed into soul. Two major styles of soul music emerged. The first style involved a lead singer being backed up by other singers in something like a call-and-response pattern. The second involved a group performance of a popular song or older ballad. Both incorporated an upbeat slow dance or stepping performance. Some of the earliest groups that pioneered soul music were the Flamingos, the Ravens, the Midnighters, and the Drifters. Also influenced by it were such diverse performers as James Brown, Aretha Franklin, Chuck Berry, Bo Diddley, Bobby "Blue" Bland, and Muddy Waters and, into the 1970s, Ike and Tina Turner, the Isley Brothers, the Fifth Dimension, Otis Redding, and Wilson Pickett.

Pivotal to this new era in African American music was the founding by Berry Gordy of the record label Motown in Detroit in 1959. The company was known for the so-called Motown sound, a sophisticated mix of rhythm and blues/soul and pop that had crossover appeal, and its releases, seventy-nine of which hit the *Billboard* top ten between 1960 and 1969, were hugely popular among both White and Black audiences. Motown transformed the music industry, in the process launching the careers of, among others, Marvin Gaye, Diana Ross and the Supremes, the Four Tops, Smokey Robinson and the Miracles, the Marvelettes, the Jackson Five,

Stevie Wonder, Gladys Knight and the Pips, the Temptations, and Martha Reeves and the Vandellas.

Beginning in the 1980s, rhythm and blues/soul became more and more influenced by electro music, a fusion of funk and early hip-hop that focused on synthesized drums and electronically produced music and that forced vocals, where present, into the background. Still, in the mid-1990s, soul made a comeback as neosoul, with such artists as Mary J. Blige and John Legend and the rhythm and blues group Mint Condition determined to recapture the music's historical roots.

Rap Music and Hip-Hop Culture

Rap music is the most commercially successful genre of African American music today. At its heart is a form of rhythmic spoken-word poetry that speaks to the reality of urban life. Also important is the concept of hip-hop, which refers to the background music, usually a sampling of elements (e.g., tracks or beats) from older records.

Some scholars date the origins of rap to the late 1960s and the Last Poets, a group of Black nationalist poets and musicians whose performances focused on the spoken word, and Gil Scott-Heron, who was known primarily as a spoken-word performer. Most scholars agree, however, that true rap music first emerged in the 1970s in the Bronx. The original purpose was to promote dancing and singing among young inner-city African Americans who had limited access to constructive, creative outlets for their energy and talent.

One of rap music's pioneers was DJ Kool Herc (born Clive Campbell), who began using sample raps on top of a mixture of beats and rhythms from two turntables that were playing various up-tempo songs. In his youth in Jamaica, Clive fell in love with dancehall or party reggae music, and after his mother moved him to the South Bronx, he was introduced to house party music and began his career as a DJ. At the same time, Afrika Bambaataa, also a South Bronx DJ, began to develop a version of rap that merged the politics, philosophy, and rhetoric of the Nation of Islam with the cultural nationalism of the Black Panthers. Bambaataa eventually created an organization known as the Zulu Nation that promoted rap music, break dancing, and graffiti art, spreading this emerging cultural movement throughout New York and then the East Coast generally.

The first commercially successful dance rap hit was the Sugarhill Gang's 1979 "Rapper's Delight," which popularized the term *hip-hop*. Soon after, Grandmaster Flash and the Furious Five emerged, adding the technique of "scratching" (the moving of records back and forth on a turntable) to the rap repertoire. During its early years, rap music was made mostly for entertainment purposes, but it gradually took on more and more of a political edge, acknowledging the reality of urban life for African Americans.

Initially, White America was indifferent to rap, as were the major record labels. It was Russell Simmons who, in the mid-1970s, saw its commercial potential and, inspired by Rudy Toppin, left college in 1979 to become a full-time promoter, encouraging his artists to retain their street credibility and not give in to mainstream norms in order to obtain success. In 1984, he and Rick Rubin formed Def Jam Recordings, whose artists, including Run-DMC and Public Enemy, became incredibly popular and sold millions of albums. Simmons also started a hip-hop clothing line, Phat Pharm; branched out to television, producing the HBO series *Def Comedy Jam*, which originally aired from 1992 to 1997; and, with Stan Lathan, created the Simmons Lathan Media Group, which produced such films as *The Addiction* (1995), *The Nutty Professor* (1996), and *Gridlocked* (1997). In 2000, Simmons sold his shares in Def Jam for over $100 million.

Like Simmons, Sean "P. Diddy" (Puff Daddy) Combs found enormous success by bringing rap music and hip-hop culture into the mainstream of the recording industry. Raised in the New Jersey suburb of Mount Vernon, Combs dropped out of Howard University in 1990 and took a full-time job with Uptown Records. In 1993, he founded his own record company, Bad Boy Records. Having signed such acts as Mary J. Blige, Craig Mack, and the Notorious B.I.G., he took rap in a more mainstream and commercial direction that was remarkably successful.

The rise of music video television channels also fueled the growth in popularity of rap, and the music's national and international availability led to the emergence of various subgenres, such as southern California's gangsta rap, led by the group NWA (Niggas with Attitude), one of the most popular rap groups of the late 1990s. Particularly troubling about gangsta rap was its violent imagery and objectification of African American women. But not all rap music was so hard-core during these years. Artists such as Queen Latifah, MC Lyte, and Salt-N-Pepa, for example, promoted positive images of African American women meant to empower all African Americans.

Conclusion

African American music has survived by adapting. And it continues to remain relevant. Witness the movement of rap music and hip-hop culture beyond the borders of the United States to become an international force in the music industry, particularly in Europe and throughout the African diaspora. The world truly has become a hip-hop planet.

17

The Creative Expressions of African Americans

Performance and Visual Art

Carol Diann Johnson was born on July 17, 1935, and raised in Harlem and the Bronx. Her talent was evident at an early age. In 1945, she received a Metropolitan Opera scholarship that enabled her to study at New York's High School of Music and Art, and four years later, as Diahann Carroll, she won first prize on the *Arthur Godfrey's Talent Scout* television show and began performing regularly on radio and in nightclubs.

Carroll debuted on Broadway in 1954 in the Truman Capote and Harold Arlen musical *House of Flowers*. The show closed after 165 performances, but Carroll's performance was so powerful that she was able to obtain a small role in the movie *Carmen Jones*. She began to study acting with Lee Strasberg, obtaining small roles in films and the lead in the Broadway musical *No Strings* in 1962, for which she won a Tony. She also kept up her singing career, recording several albums and continuing to sing in nightclubs.

During the mid-1960s, Carroll was a frequent guest on television talk shows, and in 1968, she became the first African American to star in a television situation comedy. *Julia*—about a widowed nurse with a young son—ran for three years and earned Carroll a Golden Globe. But what many critics consider her best performance was as the female lead in the 1974 film *Claudine,* in which she played opposite James Earl Jones. Her powerful portrayal of an uncompromising single welfare mother of six gained her a best actress Academy Award nomination. What was particularly significant about *Claudine* was that, in the era of blaxploitation, it was a film portraying Black life realistically.

It is arguably unfortunate that Carroll will probably be most remembered for playing the uncompromising and witty Dominique Deveraux on the television show *Dynasty* from 1984 to 1987. But Carroll herself considered the role a high point of her career because it allowed her to portray an African American character with as much depth and potent viciousness as her White counterparts on the show. As she said later in an interview: "I wanted to be the first Black bitch on television" (quoted in Carroll and Firestone, p. 5).

Carroll continued to be professionally active into the twenty-first century. But she is just one of many artists who sought to bring realistic portrayals of African American lives to the stage and the screen, large or small. Her influence has been profound. Most importantly, the majority of her roles highlighted a distinct aspect of African American history, culture, and creativity that crystallized during and after the Black Arts movement of the 1960s.

Learning Objectives

▼ ▼ ▼

1. What are some of the major themes that formed the aesthetics of African American visual and performance art?
2. How did African American art develop from the sixteenth century to the antebellum years?
3. What were some of the major trends of African American visual and performance art from the nineteenth century to the Reconstruction Era?
4. How did African American visual and performance art change between the post-Reconstruction period and the Harlem Renaissance Era?
5. How should we characterize African American visual and performance art during the 1930s and 1940s?
6. How was African American visual and performance art shaped by the civil rights movement?
7. What trends have characterized African American art since the 1970s?

▲ ▲ ▲

Traditionally, what is art and what is not has often been determined by the ruling classes. And, in the United States, racism, sexism, and classism have played a major role in this determination. Consequently, art created by Africans and African Americans has historically been relegated to an inferior status—when it has been regarded as art at all. It was only in the 1940s that the unique nature of African American art began to be recognized. Unfortunately, many White scholars approach African or African American aesthetics from a Eurocentric perspective, which does not take into account the cultural context from which these works emerge.

African American Art through the Civil War and Reconstruction

African American art during the colonial period took many forms, some of which were based in African traditions: musical instruments (especially drums), iron and ceramic figures, and domestic architecture. But some took a more mainstream form.

Among visual artists, consider, for example, Scipio Moorhead, an enslaved African American artist who lived in Boston for several years. His only surviving work is a portrait of Phillis Wheatley (see chapter 2). Moorhead also gained notoriety when Wheatley dedicated one of her earliest books, *Poems on Various Subjects, Religious and Moral, 1773,* to "S. M. a young African Painter, on seeing his Works." Another prominent artist was Joshua Johnson, a biracial painter in the naive style who lived in Baltimore and is often viewed as the first person of color to make a living as a portrait painter in the United States. Among later generations, there was a small but growing cadre of academically trained African American artists. One such was Patrick Reason, an engraver who produced portraits of such luminaries as Granville Sharp, a British abolitionist; Governor DeWitt Clinton of New York; and Henry Bibb, a formerly enslaved African American and abolitionist from Kentucky. Also noteworthy was William Simpson, who became well known for powerful portraits of African Americans during the antebellum period.

The biracial Mary Edmonia Lewis (born ca. 1843–1854) was the first African American sculptor to achieve national prominence. Although she was orphaned before she reached the age of ten, by her early teens she lived an economically privileged life, her older brother, Samuel, having made a fortune in the Gold Rush. She attended Central College in McGrawville, New York, and then Oberlin College before moving to Boston to pursue a career as a sculptor. She spent most of her career in Rome. She is best known for *The Death of Cleopatra,* which was exhibited at the 1876 Philadelphia World's Fair, and the portrait bust commissioned by Ulysses S. Grant in 1877.

Robert S. Duncanson (born in 1821) started life as a tradesman in his family's house painting and household repair business, but he aspired to be a landscape painter. He began his career by reproducing popular art prints but soon began producing work of his own. He slowly gained a regional reputation and, in 1851, was commissioned by the Cincinnatian Nicholas Longworth to paint eight large landscape murals and two floral vignettes to be displayed at the Longworth family estate. From that point forward, his career flourished.

Among African Americans, the road to success was hard enough for visual artists, but the obstacles for those seeking a career in the theater were almost overwhelming. Essentially the only option open to them was the minstrel show, which perpetuated every racial stereotype imaginable (see chapter 16). Initially, these shows were dominated by Whites. But, during the 1840s and 1850s, African American minstrel troupes began to emerge, and they remained popular well into the 1940s. Ironically, as White troupes gradually moved away from subject matter based on plantation life, African American troupes embraced it, and the addition of gospel songs gave performances an authenticity that Black audiences especially appreciated.

African American Arts and Culture through World War II

Little changed for African American artists until the emergence in the 1920s of what became known as the Harlem Renaissance. A high point of the movement was the publication in 1925 of the anthology *The New Negro,* which featured fiction, poetry, and essays on African and African American art and literature by such Black authors as Langston Hughes and Zora Neale Hurston. But the Harlem Renaissance was more than just a literary and scholarly endeavor. It represented a revival of African American culture generally, including music, dance, art, fashion, theater, and even politics.

One actor/singer who got his start during this period was Paul Robeson, a graduate of Rutgers University and Columbia Law School. He first made his name in a 1920 Broadway revival of Eugene O'Neill's *The Emperor Jones* (and a filmed version from the same year) and went on to gain fame in London as Joe in the 1928 London premiere, the 1932 Broadway revival, and the 1936 film version of *Show Boat* and as Othello in a 1959 production of *Othello* at Stratford-upon-Avon. He was also committed to the cause of social justice, receiving from the National Association for the Advancement of Colored People its prestigious Spingarn Medal in 1945, and he was prominent in Henry Wallace's 1948 Progressive Party bid for the presidency. But he was also at the time a committed Communist and an apologist for the Soviet Union, and he ran afoul of the House Un-American Activities Committee in the 1950s and was blacklisted. Nevertheless, after the end of McCarthyism, he embarked on comeback tours that ended only with the failure of his health in the early 1960s.

Other African American artists joined with Robeson in feeling that art should serve a political purpose. The visual artist Aaron Douglas, considered by some to be a pioneering "Africanist," designed and illustrated *The New Negro* (an anthology edited by Alain L. Locke) and contributed regularly to such prominent publications as the *Crisis* and *Opportunity*. In 1928, he became the first president of the Harlem Artists Guild, which helped African Americans obtain work with the Works Progress Administration. He is most known today for the murals he created in the 1930s for Fisk University and the 135th Street Branch of the New York Public Library (known today as the Schomburg Center for Research in Black Culture).

Also significant was Archibald J. Motley Jr., the first African American to have a solo exhibition in New York City. Motley is known mostly for his chronicling of Black life in Chicago. But, after winning a Guggenheim Fellowship in 1929, he spent a year in Paris producing genre scenes. Although he never lived in Harlem, his depiction of contemporary African American social life caused him to be associated with the Harlem Renaissance.

Another African American artist who gained fame during the 1930s and 1940s while working outside New York was Allan Rohan Crite. Born in Plainfield, New Jersey, of African, Native American, and European descent, Crite enjoyed an illustrious career as a painter, draftsman, and printmaker. After studying at the Massachusetts School of Art, Boston University, and Harvard University, he worked under the direction of the Works Progress Administration in the 1930s and, in the early 1940s, began a thirty-year career as a technical illustrator for the Department of the Navy. What is interesting about his work is that, like Douglas and Motley, he had to walk a fine line between the conservative tone expected of public art projects and his own radical political perspective.

Probably one of the most important artists to emerge from the Harlem Renaissance was Jacob Armstead Lawrence, a self-styled "dynamic cubist" best known for his narrative paintings depicting important moments in African American history. In the 1930s, Lawrence began working in a series format, first completing forty-one paintings depicting the life of Toussaint L'Ouverture, the revolutionary who established the Haitian Republic. He also produced series that followed the lives of the abolitionists Frederick Douglass, Harriet Tubman, and John Brown.

When it came to film, African American actors had few opportunities in mainstream motion pictures, and those opportunities were restricted to the expected stereotypical roles. Witness Hattie McDaniel and Butterfly McQueen in *Gone with the Wind* (1939). Winning an Oscar, but criticized for taking on the role of Mammy, McDaniel quipped that it was better to play a maid and make $700 a week than to be a maid and make $7.00 a week. But, in the 1930s and 1940s, both African American and White producers turned to making what were known as *race films,* such as *Stormy Weather* (1942) and *Cabin in the Sky* (1943), which specifically targeted Black audiences. During and after World War II, Hollywood developed more sophisticated race-focused movies and more progressive roles for African American actors. Of particular significance was the War Department's *The Negro Soldier* (1944).

African American Visual and Performance Art after World War II

African American abstract artists differentiated their work from that of White artists by integrating African design techniques, even before the advent of the modern civil rights movement. At the forefront of this movement was Hale Woodruff (born in 1900), who was known mostly for his murals but also had a long teaching career at Atlanta University. Also significant was Beauford Delaney (born in 1901), who began as a modernist but gravitated toward abstract expressionism in his later years.

The Black Arts movement of the 1960s and 1970s built on the foundations provided by Woodruff and Delaney to spread the message of Black pride. The beginnings of the movement can be traced to 1965, when the poet and activist Amiri Baraka (born Leroi Jones) established the Black Arts Repertory Theatre/School in Harlem. Another important troupe was the Negro Art Players, the mission of which was to produce plays written by African Americans, probably the most significant being Lorraine Hansberry's *A Raisin in the Sun*. Also notable is Ntozake Shange's *For Colored Girls Who Have Considered Suicide/When the Rainbow Is Enuf*, only the second play by an African American woman to reach Broadway. Other significant African American playwrights were August Wilson, best known for *Ma Rainey's Black Bottom*, and Charles Fuller, whose *A Soldier's Tale* won a Pulitzer Prize.

African Americans worked behind the scenes as well. Besides being a playwright, George C. Wolfe produced such critically acclaimed plays as *The Colored Museum* (1986), *Jelly's Last Jam* (1992), and the Tony Award–winning *Angels in America* (1994). During the late 1980s and early 1990s, Anna Deavere Smith pioneered a new form of theater with her one-woman plays: for example, *Twilight: Los Angeles* (1992) and *Fires in the Mirror* (1994). (She also received a MacArthur Foundation fellowship in 1996.)

The Black renaissance of the 1980s and 1990s was, in many ways, different from the Black Arts movement of the 1960s and 1970s. For instance, it was more open to the works of women as well as to those of gay and lesbian artists. Also, whereas poets and dramatists dominated the Black Arts movement, novelists such as Toni Morrison, Toni Cade Bambara, and Alice Walker took center stage at the end of the century.

In 1980, the African American businessman Robert L. Johnson founded the cable network Black Entertainment Television. And, during the 1980s, more and more African Americans began appearing on television. But, at least in mainstream television, most often they took supporting roles, only occasionally—on shows such as *Diff'rent Strokes* and *Benson*—being featured as main characters. The one exception was *The Cosby Show*, which centered on an upper-middle-class Black family and tackled issues few other shows were willing to touch. The advertising industry also finally recognized the purchasing power of Blacks and began to feature them in commercials.

Ultimately, however, nothing was more important in expanding the presence of African Americans on television during the last twenty years of the twentieth century than the growth of talk shows. The most important of these shows, *The Oprah Winfrey Show*, was launched in 1985. It won numerous Emmy Awards and was aired in hundreds of countries around the globe. Oprah Winfrey also created her own production company, which produced television shows and films aimed at an African American audience. By the end of the 1990s, Winfrey had become, according to *Time* magazine, one of the most influential people in the world, not to mention one of the richest.

Most successful, however, were films featuring African American comedians, generally male. The success of, for example, *She's Gotta Have It* (1986) helped usher in a period of popular but still relevant movies examining African American lives from a variety of perspectives. In a series of popular movies such as *48 Hrs.* (1982) and the *Beverly Hills Cop* (1984, 1987) films, Eddie Murphy used humor to bridge the cultural gap between him and his White crime-solving partners. On a more serious note, the independent film producer Spike Lee released such acclaimed movies as *Do the Right Thing* (1989) and *Malcolm X* (1992), which were unflinching in their portrayals of continued racism. Similarly inspired films followed; for example, *Boyz n the Hood* (1991), *Straight Out of Brooklyn* (1991), *Menace II Society* (1993), and *New Jack City* (1998).

Conclusion

By the end of the twentieth century, the playing field had by no means been leveled, but the opportunities for African American artists had increased exponentially. The 1990s saw, for example, the emergence of such now-respected actors as Denzel Washington, Morgan Freeman, Cuba Gooding Jr., Forest Whitaker, Samuel L. Jackson, Wesley Snipes, Laurence Fishburne, Will Smith, Whoopi Goldberg, Angela Bassett, and Halle Berry. And great strides are continuing to be made in the early years of the twenty-first century.

Bibliography

Acham, Christine. *Revolution Televised: Prime Time and the Struggle for Black Power.* Minneapolis: University of Minnesota Press, 2004. A chronicle of a complex period in television history that challenged the dominant White constructions of African American identity.

Ahlstrom, Sydney. *A Religious History of the American People.* New Haven, CT: Yale University Press, 1972. The most comprehensive study of American religious history.

Akbar, Na'im. *Breaking the Chains of Psychological Slavery.* Tallahassee, FL: Mind Productions, 1996. A controversial book claiming that the psyches of many African Americans still rest in an enslavement framework.

———. *Light from Ancient Africa.* Tallahassee: Mind Productions, 1994. An account proposing the African origins of psychology.

———. "Power Themes among Negro and White Paranoid and Non-Paranoid Schizophrenics." Ph.D. diss., University of Michigan, 1970. A classic study of Afrocentric and Black psychology.

Akyeampong, Emmanuel Kwaku, ed. *Themes in West Africa's History.* Athens: Ohio University Press, 2006. An interdisciplinary approach to West African history.

Aldridge, Delores P., and Carlene Young, eds. *Out of the Revolution: The Development of Africana Studies.* New York: Lexington, 2000. A collection that provides a comprehensive understanding of the impetus, development, impact, and legacy of the field of Black studies.

Alexander, Estrelda Y. *One Hundred Years of African American Pentecostalism.* Downers Grove, IL: IVP Academic, 2011. A chronicle of the origins and development of African American Pentecostalism.

Alkalimat, Abdul. *The African American Experience in Cyberspace: A Resource Guide to the Best Web Sites on Black Culture and History.* London: Pluto, 2003. An important resource in its day.

Allen, James, Hilton Als, John Lewis, and Leon F. Litwack. *Without Sanctuary: Lynching Photography in America.* Santa Fe, NM: Twin Palms, 2000. Vivid depictions of the various forms of lynching.

Allen, Robert L. *Black Awakening in Capitalist America.* London: Gollancz, 1969. An examination of the African American response to capitalism during the Black Power phase of the civil rights movement.

Allen, William Francis, Charles Pickard Ware, and Lucy McKim Garrison, comps. *Slave Songs of the United States.* 1867. Bedford, MA: Applewood, 1995. An examination of the history and impact of the songs sung by thousands of enslaved African Americans.

Anderson, Carol. *Eyes Off the Prize: The United Nations and the African American Struggle for Human Rights, 1944–1955.* Cambridge: Cambridge University Press, 2003. An examination of the civil rights movement in the context of the emerging Cold War.

Anderson, Elijah. *Streetwise: Race, Class, and Change in an Urban Community.* Chicago: University of Chicago Press, 1990. An exploration of the dilemma of both Blacks and Whites, the underclass and the middle class, caught up in the new struggle for common ground in urban America.

Anderson, John D. *The Education of Blacks in the South, 1860–1931.* Chapel Hill: University of North Carolina Press, 1998. A critical account of the education and philosophy promoted by the Hampton and Tuskegee Institutes.

Anderson, Talmadge. *Introduction to African American Studies.* Dubuque, IA: Kendall/Hunt, 1993. A short but potent exploration of the various fields of Black studies.

Ani, Marimba. *Yurugu: An African-Centered Critique of European Cultural Thought and Behavior.* Trenton, NJ: Africa World, 1994. A survey of the impact of African culture on Europe.

Aronson, Elliot, Timothy D. Wilson, and Robin M. Akert. *Social Psychology.* New York: Pearson/Prentice Hall, 2002. An introduction to the field of psychology for all readers.

Asante, Molefi K. *The Afrocentric Idea.* Philadelphia: Temple University Press, 1998. A continuation of Asante's explorations of the idea of Afrocentricity.

———. *Afrocentricity: The Theory of Social Change.* Buffalo, NY: Amulefi, 1980. A classic volume that introduced the concept of Afrocentric learning.

———. *Kemet, Afrocentricity, and Knowledge.* Trenton, NJ: African World, 1990. A classic work that expands the concept and notions of Afrocentricity.

Asante, Molefi K., and K. W. Asante, eds. *African Culture.* Westport, CT: Greenwood, 1985. A collection that treats African culture symbolically as one cultural river with numerous tributaries determined by their specific responses to history and the environment.

Asante, Molefi K., and Ama Mazama, eds. *Encyclopedia of Black Studies.* Thousand Oaks, CA: Sage, 2005. One of the most comprehensive accounts of the field of Black studies.

Asante, Molefi K., and Arthur L. Smith. *Rhetoric of Black Revolution.* Boston: Allyn & Bacon, 1969. A classic volume that captures the views and ideas of numerous African American revolutionary leaders.

Auletta, Ken. *The Underclass.* New York: Overlooked, 1982.

Babbie, Earl. *The Practice of Social Research*. Belmont, CA: Wadsworth, 2007. An explanation of how to design and construct projects.

Baldwin, Joseph. *The African Personality in America: An African-Centered Framework*. Tallahassee: Nubian Nation, 1992. A study providing an African-centered philosophical and psychological framework for the African American experience in the West.

Baldwin, Lewis V. *The Mark of a Man: Peter Spencer and the African Union Methodist Tradition*. Lanham, MA: University Press of America, 1987. The most comprehensive study of the religious figure Peter Spencer.

Bambara, Toni Cade. *The Black Woman: An Anthology*. New York: Washington Square, 2005. A collection of early, emerging works from some of the most celebrated female African American writers.

Bandele, Ramla M. *Black Star: African American Activism in the International Political Economy*. Urbana: University of Illinois Press, 2008. An account of how the first African American mass political organization was able to gain support from throughout the African diaspora to finance the Black Star Line.

Banks, William M. *Black Intellectuals: Race and Responsibility in American Life*. New York: W. W. Norton, 1998. An analysis of Black life beginning with the arrival of enslaved Africans, when medicine men and conjurers were still held to command ancient, powerful wisdom.

Barlow, William. *Looking Up at Down: The Emergence of Blues Culture*. Philadelphia: Temple University Press, 1989. An exploration of the lyrics, musical styles, and musicians and performers who created blues music.

———. *Voice Over: The Making of Black Radio*. Philadelphia: Temple University Press, 1999. An exploration of the entire landscape of Black radio through the end of the twentieth century.

Barnes, Sandra L. *Black Megachurch Culture: Models for Education and Empowerment*. New York: Peter Lang, 2010. An examination of the cultural components of the growing numbers of large African American churches.

Bay, Mia. *To Tell the Truth Freely: The Life of Ida B. Wells*. New York: Hill & Wang, 2009. A discussion of the life and legacy of Ida B. Wells.

Belgrave, Faye Z., and Kevin W. Allison. *African American Psychology: From Africa to America*. Thousand Oaks, CA: Sage, 2006. A comprehensive coverage of African American psychology as a field that integrates African and American influences on the psychology of African Americans.

Belz, Carl. *The Story of Rock*. New York: Oxford University Press, 1969. A history of rock and roll music.

Benedict, Ruth. *Race: Science and Politics*. New York: Viking, 1945. An anthropological approach to the link between race, science, and politics.

Benjamin, Lois. *The Black Elite: Still Facing the Color Line in the Twenty-First Century*. Lanham, MA: Rowman & Littlefield, 2005. A detailed account of the lived experiences of African Americans and how they grapple daily with what W. E. B. Du Bois called the *double consciousness*, living within and between two worlds.

————. *Three Black Generations at the Crossroads: Community, Culture, and Consciousness.* 2000. 2nd ed. Lanham, MA: Rowman & Littlefield, 2008. An exploration of how values within the Black American community have shifted and how to deal with what remains of the color line.

Bennett, Lerone. *Forced into Glory: Abraham Lincoln's White Dream.* Chicago: Johnson, 2000. A detailed critique of the motives of Abraham Lincoln.

Berger, Peter L., and Brigitte Berger. *Sociology.* New York: Basic, 1972. One of the first comprehensive surveys of the field of sociology.

Berger, Peter L., and Thomas Luckmann. *The Social Construction of Reality.* Garden City, NY: Doubleday, 1967. An intriguing look at everything that passes for knowledge from a sociological perspective.

Berlin, Ira. *Many Thousands Gone: The First Centuries of Slavery in North America.* Cambridge, MA: Belknap Press of Harvard University Press, 1998. An impressive synthesis of the experience of life under slavery during the seventeenth and eighteenth centuries.

Berlin, Ira, and Ronald Hoffman, eds. *Slavery and Freedom in the Age of the American Revolution.* Charlottesville: University Press of Virginia, 1983. A collection focused on African American life during the American Revolution.

Berlin, Ira, and Leslie S. Rowland, eds. *Families and Freedom: A Documentary History of African-American Kinship in the Civil War Era.* New York: Cambridge University Press, 1997. A collection of documents highlighting the frustrations and struggles of the 4 million formerly enslaved people of color.

Bernal, Martin. *Black Athena.* Vol. 1, *The Afroasiatic Roots of Classical Civilization.* Vol. 2, *The Archaeological and Documentary Evidence.* Vol. 3, *The Linguistic Evidence.* New Brunswick, NJ: Rutgers University Press, 1987–2006. A unique and controversial perspective on the history of early African civilization.

Bibb, Henry. *Narrative of the Life and Adventures of Henry Bibb, an American Slave, Written by Himself.* New York: Henry Bibb, 1849. An examination of the complex life of Henry Bibb.

Billingsley, Andrew. *Black Families in White America.* Englewood Cliffs, NJ: Pearson/ Prentice Hall, 1968. A demonstration of how closely the fate of Black American families is related to the ultimate fate of America itself.

————. *Climbing Jacob's Ladder: The Enduring Legacy of African American Families.* New York: Touchstone, 1994. A groundbreaking volume that traces the history of the Black American family from its roots in Africa to the 1990s, arguing that Black families cannot be measured against White norms.

————. *Mighty Like a River: The Black Church and Social Reform.* New York: Oxford University Press, 1999. A study of how the African American church has shaped American society.

Black, Marilyn Richardson. *Women and Religion: A Bibliography.* Boston: G. K. Hall, 1980. A resource for those interested in the rich history of Black American women and religion.

Blackmon, Douglass A. *Slavery by Another Name: The Re-enslavement of Black Americans from the Civil War to World War II.* New York: Doubleday, 2008. A groundbreaking consideration of the labor system based on slavery that thrived from the end of the Civil War until the outbreak of World War II.

Blackwell, James E., and Morris Janowitz. *Black Sociologists.* Chicago: University of Chicago Press, 1974. A classic volume that examines the field of Black sociology generally as well as several of its founding members.

Blassingame, John W. *New Perspectives on Black Studies.* Chicago: University of Illinois Press, 1971. An account of the origins and development of the field of Black studies.

———. *The Slave Community: Plantation Life in the Antebellum South.* New York: Oxford University Press, 1979. An examination of African American culture and the Black family through the Civil War.

Blauner, Robert. *Racial Oppression in America.* New York: Harper & Row, 1972. An account of how new theories of race relations developed historically by revealing the strategic role of racism and racial oppression in American society.

Blight, David W. *Race and Reunion: The Civil War in American Memory.* Cambridge, MA: Harvard University Press, 2001. A consideration of how White Americans remembered the Civil War, the sectional division between the states, and the contributions of African Americans to the history of the United States.

Bobo, Jacqueline, ed. *The Black Studies Reader.* New York: Routledge, 2004. A collection examining the discipline of Black studies from a variety of perspectives.

Bogin, Ruth. "'Liberty Further Extended': A 1776 Antislavery Manuscript by Lemuel Haynes." *William and Mary Quarterly* 40, no. 1 (January 1983): 85–105.

Bogle, Donald. *Brown Sugar: Eighty Years of America's Female Superstars.* New York: Crown, 1980. An account of the struggles of the African American women who made it in the entertainment industry against overwhelming odds.

Bolster, W. Jeffrey. *Black Jacks: African American Seamen in the Age of Sail.* Cambridge, MA: Harvard University Press, 1997. An exploration of the lives of African American seamen from 1740 to 1865.

Bond, Horace Mann. *Negro Education in Alabama: A Study in Cotton and Steel.* Tuscaloosa: University of Alabama Press, 1994. A history of Black American education from preschool through college.

Boney, William Jerry, and Glenn A. Igleheat, eds. *Baptists and Ecumenism.* Valley Forge, PA: Judson, 1980. One of the first studies to examine the topic of Baptist ecumenism.

Bowser, Paul, and Charles Musser. *Oscar Micheaux and His Circle: African American Filmmaking and Race Cinema of the Silent Era.* Bloomington: Indiana University Press, 2005. A comprehensive account of the life and times of Oscar Micheaux.

Bragg, George F. *History of the Afro-American Group of the Episcopal Church.* Baltimore: Church Advocate Press, 1922. An account of the origins and development of the African American Episcopal Church.

Branch, Taylor. *Parting the Waters: America in the King Years, 1954–63.* New York: Simon & Schuster, 1988. A well-researched study that places King at the center of American politics during the 1950s and 1960s.

Brazile, Donna. *Cooking with Grease: Stirring the Pot in American Politics.* New York: Simon & Schuster, 2004. A behind-the-scenes memoir of the life and times of a political organizer and the first African American woman to head a major presidential campaign.

Bringhurst, Newell G. *Saints, Slaves, and Blacks: The Changing Place of Black People within Mormonism.* Westport, CT: Greenwood, 1981. An exploration of the experience of African Americans within the Mormon faith.

Brooks, Tilford. *America's Black Music Heritage.* New York: Pearson/Prentice Hall, 1984. An examination of a constantly changing art form.

Brothers, Thomas, ed. *Louis Armstrong: In His Own Words.* New York: Oxford University Press, 1999. An introduction to the master trumpeter, bandleader, and entertainer.

Brown, Cecil. *Dude: Where Is My Black Studies Department? The Disappearance of Black Americans from U.S. Universities.* Berkeley, CA: North Atlantic Books, 2007. An examination of the disappearance of Black studies programs, especially in the California higher-education system.

Brown, Michael K. *Race, Money, and the American Welfare State.* Ithaca, NY: Cornell University Press, 1999. An account proposing that our welfare system has in fact denied African Americans the social provision it gives White citizens while stigmatizing them as recipients of government benefits.

Bullard, Robert. *Dumping in Dixie: Race, Class, and Environmental Quality.* Boulder, CO: Westview, 1990. A detailed examination of the environmental justice movement focusing on the topics of environmental racism, different organizing strategies, and success stories.

Bullock, Henry Allen. *A History of Negro Education in the South from 1619 to the Present.* Cambridge, MA: Harvard University Press, 1967. An educational history of southern African Americans from 1619 to the 1950s.

Bundles, A'Lelia. *On Her Own Ground: The Life and Times of Madam C. J. Walker.* New York: Scribner, 2001.

Burkett, Randall K. *Garveyism as a Religious Movement: The Institutionalization of a Black Civil Religion.* Metuchen, NJ: Scarecrow, 1978. A consideration of the Garvey movement as a religious crusade.

Burkett, Randall K., and Richard Newman, eds. *Black Apostles: Afro-American Clergy Confront the Twentieth Century.* Boston: G. K. Hall, 1978. A collection of essays on both famous and obscure African American religious leaders.

Burnham, Kenneth E. *God Comes to America: Father Divine and the Peace Mission Movement.* Boston: Lambeth, 1979. This is the most comprehensive study of Father Divine, the twentieth-century African American spiritual leader.

Burroughs, Nannie Helen. "How Sisters Are Hindered from Helping." 1900. https://awpc.cattcenter.iastate.edu/2019/09/26/how-the-sisters-are-hindered-from-helping.

"Burroughs, Nannie Helen." In *Black Women in America: An Historical Encyclopedia* (2nd ed.), ed. Darlene Clark Hine, Elsa Barkley Brown, and Rosalyn Terborg-Penn, 3 vols., 1:201–5. Bloomington, IN: Indiana University Press, 1993.

Butler, John Sibley. *Entrepreneurship and Self-Help among Black Americans: A Reconsideration of Race and Economics.* Albany: State University of New York Press, 1991. An account of the development of Black enterprises and community organizations starting before the Civil War.

Cain, Herman. *This Is Herman Cain! My Journey to the White House.* New York: Threshold, 2011. An account of the life and times of the former Republican Party presidential candidate Herman Cain.

Carlisle, Rodney. *The Roots of Black Nationalism.* Port Washington, NY: Kenniket, 1975. An examination of the origins and development of the Black American nationalist movement.

Carmichael, Stokely, and Charles V. Hamilton. *Black Power: The Politics of Liberation in America.* New York: Vintage, 1992. An outline of how to change the political system for the benefit of the lower classes of various races and ethnicities.

Carr, Ian. *Miles Davis: The Definitive Biography.* New York: Thunder's Mouth, 1998. A comprehensive account of the life and times of Miles Davis.

Carr, Robert. *Black Nationalism in the New World: Reading the African American and West Indian Experience.* Durham, NC: Duke University Press, 2002. An account of Black nationalism in the New World that employs geography, political economy, and subaltern studies to explore heated debates over African American and West Indian culture, identity, and politics.

Carroll, Diahann, and Ross Firestone. *Diahann: An Autobiography.* New York: Little, Brown, 1986.

Carson, Clayborne. *The Autobiography of Martin Luther King, Jr.* New York: Warner, 2001. The most up-to-date biography of Martin Luther King Jr.

Carson, Clayborne, Emma Lapsansky-Werner, and Gary B. Nash. *African American Lives: The Struggle for Freedom.* 2 vols. New York: Pearson, 2005. An examination of the lives of African Americans that employs a first-person perspective.

Carter, Dan T. *Scottsboro: A Tragedy of the American South.* Baton Rouge: Louisiana State University Press, 1969. An account of the origins, development, and impact of the Scottsboro case, in which nine African American teenagers were falsely accused of raping two White women aboard a train near Scottsboro, Alabama, in 1931.

Cecelski, David S. *Along Freedom Road: Hyde County, North Carolina, and the Fate of Black Schools in the South.* Chapel Hill: University of North Carolina Press, 1994. An account of the successful protest movement against segregated public schools in a North Carolina county during the late 1960s.

Cecelski, David S., and Timothy B. Tyson, eds. *Democracy Betrayed: The Wilmington Race Riot of 1898 and Its Legacy.* Chapel Hill: University of North Carolina Press, 1998. A detailed description of the Wilmington Race Riot.

Charters, Ann. *Nobody: The Story of Bert Williams.* New York: Macmillan, 1970. An account of the life and legacy of Bert Williams.

Chernoff, John Miller. *African Rhythm and African Sensibilities: Aesthetics and Social Activism in African Musical Idioms.* Chicago: University of Chicago Press, 1979. An examination of the social, political, and spiritual meanings of African/African American music.

Chisholm, Shirley. *Unbought and Unbossed.* Boston: Houghton Mifflin Harcourt, 1970. A chronicle of the author's long political struggle.

Chude-Sokei, Louis. *The Last Darky: Bert Williams, Black-on-Black Minstrelsy, and the African Diaspora.* Durham, NC: Duke University Press, 2006. The definitive book on Bert Williams.

Clark, E. Culpepper. *The Schoolhouse Door: Segregation's Last Stand at the University of Alabama.* New York: Oxford University Press, 1995. A riveting account of George Wallace's refusal to integrate the University of Alabama and the response of the federal government.

Clark, John Henrik. *Africans at a Crossroads: African World Revolution.* Trenton, NJ: African World Press, 1991. A collection of essays on the African and African American freedom struggle.

Clark, Kenneth. *The Dark Ghetto.* New York: Harper & Row, 1965. An examination of how the ghetto separates Black Americans not only from White Americans but also from opportunities and resources.

Clark, Kenneth, and Mamie Phipps Clark. "Racial Identification and Preference in Negro Children." *Journal of Negro Education* 19, no. 3 (Summer 1950): 341–50.

Clark, Septima. *Ready from Within: A First Person Narrative.* Lawrenceville, NJ: Africa World, 1990. A chronicle of the role that Septima Clark played in the civil rights movement.

Cohen, Ronald D. *Children of the Mill: Schooling and Society in Gary, Indiana, 1906–1960.* Bloomington: Indiana University Press, 1990. A study of the unique educational history of Gary, Indiana, in the early and mid-twentieth century.

Cole, Johnetta B. *Conversations: Straight Talk with America's Sister President.* New York: Anchor, 1994. A call to women of color to take action.

Collins, Patricia Hill. *Black Feminist Thought: Knowledge, Consciousness, and the Politics of Empowerment.* New York: Routledge, 1990. A detailed sociological examination of the tradition of Black feminism.

"A Colored Woman, However Respectable, Is Lower Than the White Prostitute" (1902). In *Black Women in White America,* ed. Gerda Lerner, 166–69. New York: Vintage Books, 1972. Drawn from a collection of famous and little-known documents on the diverse experiences of women of color, this piece describes the negative view of African American women in the early 1900s.

Cone, James H. *Black Theology and Black Power.* Maryknoll, NY: Orbis, 1997. A detailed study of the links between Black theology and the Black Power phase of the civil rights movement.

———, ed. *A Black Theology of Liberation*. Maryknoll, NY: Orbis, 1993. A collection of essays on the origins and impact of African American theology in the United States.

———. *Martin and Malcolm and America: A Dream or a Nightmare?* Maryknoll, NY: Orbis, 1992. A study that compares and contrasts the life, impact, and civil rights activities of Martin Luther King Jr. and Malcolm X in great detail.

———. *The Spirituals and the Blues: An Interpretation*. Maryknoll, NY: Orbis, 1992. An exploration of two classic aspects of African American culture—spirituals and the blues.

Cone, James H., and Gayraud S. Wilmore, eds. *Black Theology: A Documentary History.* Vol. 2, *1980–1992*. Maryknoll, NY: Orbis, 1993. The first single volume of primary sources on the emergence of Black theology.

Conyers, James L., ed. *Africana Studies: A Disciplinary Quest for Both Theory and Method.* Jefferson, NC: McFarland, 2005. A collection of fifteen essays about how to develop and structure a potent Africana studies program.

Cooper, Anna Julia. *A Voice from the South: By a Black Woman of the South*. 1892. New York: Oxford University Press, 1990.

Cooper, Arnold. *Between Struggle and Hope: Four Black Educators in the South, 1894–1915.* Ames: Iowa University Press, 1989. An account that highlights the background of four leading but little-known African American educators.

Cornish, Dudley T. *The Sable Arm: Negro Troops in the Union Army, 1861–1865*. New York: W. W. Norton, 1856. A study of the participation of African American men in the Union Army.

Cose, Ellis. *The Rage of a Privileged Class*. New York: HarperCollins, 1993. An examination of the outrage and pain of the African American middle class.

Cox, Harvey. *Fire from Heaven: The Rise of Pentecostal Spirituality and the Reshaping of Religion in the Twenty-First Century.* Cambridge, MA: Da Capo, 1995. An exploration of the history of the Pentecostal movement in the United States.

Cripps, Thomas. *Making Movies Black: The Hollywood Message Movie from World War II to the Civil Rights Era.* New York: Oxford University Press, 1993. An examination of how certain Hollywood movies anticipated and helped form America's changing ideas about race.

Cronon, E. David. *Black Moses: The Story of Marcus Garvey and the Universal Negro Improvement Association.* Madison: University of Wisconsin Press, 1955. A detailed exploration of the life of Marcus Garvey.

Cross, William E., Jr. *Shades of Black: Diversity in African American Identity.* Philadelphia: Temple University Press, 1991. An examination of the diversity and texture that has always been the hallmark of Black psychology that explodes the myth that self-hatred is the dominant theme in Black identity.

Cruse, Harold. *The Crisis of the Negro Intellectual.* 1967. New York: William Morrow, 1984. A critique of both integrationists and Black nationalists claiming that Black Americans will assume their proper place within American life only when they develop their own distinctive centers of cultural and economic influence.

Curry, Leonard. *The Free Black in Urban America, 1800–1850: The Shadow of the Dream.* Chicago: University of Chicago Press, 1981. A comprehensive analysis of urban African American life in the antebellum period.

Dallek, Robert. *Ronald Reagan: The Politics of Symbolism.* Cambridge, MA: Harvard University Press, 1984. A detailed examination of the former president.

Daniel, William A. *The Education of Negro Ministers.* New York: George H. Doran, 1925. An exploration of the educational history of a number of early African American ministers.

Daugherity, Brian J., and Charles C. Bolton, eds. *With All Deliberate Speed: Implementing Brown v. Board of Education.* Fayetteville: University of Arkansas Press, 2008. A collection exploring the integration of public school systems nationwide.

Davidson, James West. *"They Say": Ida B. Wells and the Reconstruction of Race.* New York: Oxford University Press, 2009. A brief but comprehensive examination of the life of Ida B. Wells.

Davis, Angela Y. *Blues Legacies and Black Feminism: Gertrude "Ma" Rainey, Bessie Smith, and Billie Holiday.* New York, Vintage, 1998. An examination of three African American women's lives through a Black feminist lens.

———. *Women, Culture, and Politics.* New York: Random House, 1984. A powerful collection of speeches and writings on the intersection of race, gender, class, culture, and politics.

———. *Women, Race, and Class.* New York: Penguin/Random House, 1981. An examination of the interconnections of gender, race, and class oppression.

Davis, David Brion. *The Problem of Slavery in the Age of Revolution, 1770–1823.* Ithaca, NY: Cornell University Press, 1975. A discussion of the influence of the Enlightenment and the Industrial Revolution on the institution of slavery and the antislavery movement.

Davis, F. James. *Who Is Black? One Nation's Definition.* University Park: Pennsylvania State University Press, 1991. An examination of the complex notions of defining African American identity.

Davis, Miles, and Quincy Troupe. *Miles: The Autobiography.* New York: Simon & Schuster, 1989. The most comprehensive account of the life of Miles Davis.

DeConde, Alexander. *Ethnicity, Race, and American Foreign Policy.* Boston: Northeastern University Press, 1995. A study of the intertwining of ethnicity, race, and American foreign policy.

Delany, Martin. *The Condition, Elevation, Emigration, and Destiny of the Colored People of the United States, Politically Considered.* Philadelphia, 1852. Delany's examination of his mind-set during the antebellum years.

D'Emilio, John. *Lost Prophet: The Life and Times of Bayard Rustin.* New York: Simon & Schuster, 2003. A study of the life and times of Bayard Rustin.

DeVeaux, Scott. *The Birth of Bebop: A Social and Musical History.* Berkeley: University of California Press, 1997. An examination of the era of swing and bebop jazz, focusing on the position of African American musicians, in particular.

Dew, Charles B. *Bonds of Iron: Masters and Slaves at Buffalo Forge.* New York: W. W. Norton, 1994. An outstanding account of one type of industrial enslavement system in the South.

Diop, Cheikh Anta. *The Cultural Unity of Black Africa.* Chicago: Third World, 1978. An overview of the cultural norms of African societies.

Dixon, Kwame, and John Burdick, eds. *Comparative Perspectives on Afro-Latin America.* Gainesville: University Press of Florida, 2012. A collection discussing the cultural and political issues faced by the various African populations throughout different regions of Latin America.

Douglass, Davison M. *Reading, Writing, and Race: The Desegregation of the Charlotte Schools.* Chapel Hill: University of North Carolina Press, 1995. A discussion of the desegregation of the public school system in Charlotte, North Carolina, from the *Brown* decision to the early 1970s.

Douglass, Frederick. *My Bondage and My Freedom.* 1855. Reprint, New Haven, CT: Yale University Press, 2014.

———. *Narrative of the Life of Frederick Douglass, an American Slave.* 1845. Reprint, Boston: Bedford, 1993. A classic autobiography that examines the author's struggles against political oppression and heightened racism in the North during the antebellum and Civil War years.

Drake, St. Clair. *Black Folk Here and There.* Los Angeles: University of California, Center for African Studies, 1990. A study of the Black experience that attempts to combine symbolic anthropology and comparative history.

Drake, St. Clair, and Horace R. Cayton. *Black Metropolis.* 1945. New York: Harper & Row, 1962. A landmark study of race and urban life.

Duberman, Martin. *Paul Robeson: A Biography.* New York: New Press, 1995. The most comprehensive account of the life and times of Paul Robeson.

Du Bois, W. E. B. *Black Folk: Then and Now.* New York: Henry Holt, 1939. A pathbreaking examination of the lives of people of African descent before their capture and enslavement.

———. *Black Reconstruction in America: An Essay toward a History of the Part Which Black Folk Played in the Attempt to Reconstruct Democracy in America, 1860–1880.* New York: Russell & Russell, 1935. A classic account of the Reconstruction Era challenging the traditional interpretation that it was a tragic period characterized by political corruption and uneducated southern African Americans.

———. *The Negro Church.* Walnut Creek, CA: Altimira, 1903. A groundbreaking study of African American religion.

———. *The Philadelphia Negro: A Social Study.* 1899. New York: Schocken, 1967. A classic early attempt at urban sociology.

———. *The Souls of Black Folk.* 1903. New York: New American Library, 1969. A classic examination of the double-consciousness of African Americans.

———. "The Talented Tenth: Memorial Address." In *W.E.B. DuBois: A Reader,* ed. David Levering Lewis, 347–57. New York: Henry Holt and Company,

1995. This document reflects Du Bois's reexamination of his concept of the "Talented Tenth."

———. *The World and Africa.* New York: International, 1946. One of the earliest examinations of parts of Africa before it was colonized.

Dyson, Eric Michael. *Between God and Gangsta Rap: Bearing Witness to Black Culture.* New York: Oxford University Press, 1996. An argument that the richness of African American culture can be found in the interstices between God and gangsta rap.

Egerton, Douglas R. *Death or Liberty: African Americans and Revolutionary America.* New York: Oxford University Press, 2009. An account of little-known African Americans who shaped the Black American experience during the American Revolution.

———. *Gabriel's Rebellion: The Virginia Slave Conspiracies of 1800 and 1802.* Chapel Hill: University of North Carolina Press, 1993. An examination of the foiled rebellion planned by Gabriel Prosser, an enslaved person, and its legacy.

Egerton, John. *Speak Now against the Day: The Generation before the Civil Rights Movement in the South.* New York: Alfred A. Knopf, 1994. An outstanding survey of the period before the modern civil rights movement began.

Ellington, Duke. *Music Is My Mistress.* New York: Da Capo, 1973. The story of Duke Ellington told in his own words.

Ely, Melvin Patrick. *The Adventures of Amos 'n' Andy: A Social History of an American Phenomenon.* New York: Free Press, 1991. A fascinating account of America's shifting color lines.

Erskine, Noel. *Black People and the Reformed Church in America.* Lansing, IL: Reformed Church Press, 1978. An examination of the experience of African Americans in the Reformed church movement.

Essig, James D. *The Bonds of Wickedness: American Evangelicals against Slavery, 1770–1808.* Philadelphia: Temple University Press, 1982. An account of the attack on the system of human bondage from a religious standpoint.

Evans, Mari. *Black Women Writers, 1950–1980: A Critical Evaluation.* New York: Anchor, 1984. A collection of the writings of African American women from the 1950s to the 1980s.

Exum, William H. *Paradoxes of Protest: Black Studies Activism in a White University.* Philadelphia: Temple University Press, 1985. A firsthand account of the development of the Black studies program at New York University during the 1960s and 1970s

Fairclough, Adam. *Teaching Equality: Black Schools in the Age of Jim Crow.* Athens: University of Georgia Press, 2001. An overview of the contributions that African American teachers made to the modern civil rights movement.

Fanon, Frantz. *Black Skin, White Masks.* New York: Grove, 1967. A study of the Black psyche in a White world that was a major influence on civil rights, anticolonial, and Black consciousness movements around the world.

———. *The Wretched of the Earth.* 1961. New York: Grove, 1963. An inspiration for anticolonial movements worldwide written at the height of the Algerian war for independence from French colonial rule.

Felder, Cain Hope. *Troubling Biblical Waters: Race, Class, and Family.* New York: Orbis, 1997. A comprehensive examination of the significance of the Bible for African Americans.

Ferris, William. *Blues from the Delta.* New York: Da Capo, 1998. A study detailing the richness and power of the blues.

Fitzgerald, Michael W. *Splendid Failure: Postwar Reconstruction in the American South.* Chicago: Ivan R. Dee, 2007. An exceptional summary of the post-Reconstruction years.

Foner, Eric. *Reconstruction: America's Unfinished Revolution, 1863–1877.* New York: Harper & Row, 1998. Perhaps the best comprehensive analysis of the Reconstruction Era.

Foner, Philip S. *History of Black Americans, from Africa to the Emergence of the Cotton Kingdom.* Westport, CT: Greenwood, 1975. An exploration of the history of African Africans from 1783 to 1820, the first of a three-volume study.

———. *The Life and Writings of Frederick Douglass.* Vol. 1, *The Early Years.* New York: International, 1955.

Forman, Murray, and Mark Anthony Neal, eds. *That's the Joint: The Hip Hop Studies Reader.* New York: Routledge, 2004. A collection of the most important hip-hop scholarship produced to date.

Franklin, Donna. *Ensuring Inequality: The Structural Transformation of the African American Family.* New York: Oxford University Press, 1997. An investigation of the various stresses on the African American family.

Franklin, John Hope. *Reconstruction after the Civil War.* Chicago: University of Chicago Press, 1961. An outstanding summary of the post–Civil War years.

Franklin, John Hope, and Evelyn Brooks Higginbotham. *From Slavery to Freedom: A History of African Americans.* 1947. 9th ed. 2 vols. New York: McGraw Hill, 2011. A general history of African Americans in the United States to the Civil War.

Franklin, John Hope, and Genna Rae McNeil. *African Americans and the Living Constitution.* Washington, DC: Smithsonian Institution Press, 1995. A collection of essays examining the impact of the 1954 *Brown* decision.

Franklin, Raymond S. *Shadows of Race and Class.* Minneapolis: University of Minnesota Press, 1991. A powerful analysis that makes new connections between race and class and also proposes a different way to examine urban change.

Fraser, James W., ed. *The School in the United States: A Documentary History.* New York: Routledge, 2014. An outstanding array of primary documents chronicling the history of education in the United States.

Frazier, E. Franklin. *Black Bourgeoisie.* New York: Free Press, 1957. The book that established Frazier as the leading sociologist concerned with the plight of African Americans.

————. *The Negro Church in America.* New York: Schocken, 1964. One of the first comprehensive studies of African American church history.

————. *The Negro Family in Chicago.* Chicago: University of Chicago Press, 1932. The first comprehensive study of the family life of African Americans.

————. *The Negro in the United States.* New York: Macmillan, 1949. One of the first comprehensive sociological studies of African Americans.

Frederickson, David F., David C. Miller, and Howard Wolpe. *The United States and Africa: A Post–Cold War Perspective.* New York: W. W. Norton, 1998. A penetrating examination of the moral and practical concerns driving American foreign policy that outlines the steps needed to establish positive, not merely reactive, relations between the United States and the nations of Africa.

Frederickson, George M. *Black Liberation: A Comparative History of Black Ideologies in the United States and South Africa.* New York: Oxford University Press, 1996. A powerful account of how Blacks in the United States and South Africa came to grips with the challenge of White supremacy.

Freire, Paulo. *Pedagogy of the Oppressed.* New York: Continuum, 1970. A groundbreaking study proposing a more inclusive way to teach and transform minority students.

Frey, Sylvia R. *Water from the Rock: Black Resistance in a Revolutionary Age.* Princeton, NJ: Princeton University Press, 1991. A characterization of the War of Independence in the South as a three-way struggle among patriots, loyalists, and African Americans.

Fulop, Timothy E., and Albert J. Raboteau, eds. *African-American Religion: Interpretative Essays in History and Culture.* New York: Routledge, 1996. A collection of essays on the impact of African American religion in the United States.

Gaines, Jane M. *Fire and Desire: Mixed-Race Movies in the Silent Era.* Chicago: University of Chicago Press, 2001. A powerful look at the Black independent film movement during the silent period.

Gaines, Kevin. *Uplifting the Race.* Chapel Hill: University of North Carolina Press, 1996. A study of the link between class distinctions and patriarchal authority and the development of racial uplift ideologies within the Black American community that prevented the achievement of concrete social change.

Gallup, George, and Jim Castelli. *The People's Religion: American Faith in the 90s.* New York: Macmillan, 1989. An examination of the influence of religion in American society.

Garvey, Amy Euphemia Jacques. "Woman as Leaders" (1925). In *Let Nobody Turn Us Around: An African American Anthology* (2nd ed.), ed. Manning Marable and Leith Mullings, 251–52. New York: Rowman & Littlefield, 2009.

Gates, Henry Louis, Jr. *Schomburg Library of Nineteenth-Century Black Women Writers.* 30 vols. New York: Oxford University Press, 1991–1998. A collection of rare works of fiction, poetry, autobiography, biography, essays, and journalism written by nineteenth-century Black women.

Genovese, Eugene D. *From Rebellion to Revolution: Afro-American Slave Revolts in the Making of the Modern World.* Baton Rouge: Louisiana State University Press, 1979. A study that places the major American slave revolts and conspiracies into an Atlantic context.

Giddings, Paula. *When and Where I Enter: The Impact of Black Women on Race and Sex in America.* New York: William Morrow, 1984. An exploration of the stories of African American women who transcended the dual discrimination of race and gender.

Giddins, Garry. *Visions of Jazz: The First Century.* New York: Oxford University Press, 1998. An examination of the lives of the major figures in jazz history.

Gilbert, Erik, and Jonathan T. Reynolds. *Africa in World History: From Prehistory to the Present.* New York: Pearson, 2004. A groundbreaking study that situates Africa in the wider context of world history.

Gillespie, John Birks, and Wilmot Alfred Fraser, eds. *To Be or Not . . . to Bop: Memoirs—Dizzy Gillespie with Alfred Frazer.* New York: Doubleday, 1979. A good guide to the influence of Dizzy Gillespie on jazz music.

Gilliam, Reginald E., Jr. *Black Political Development.* Port Washington, NY: Dunellen, 1975. A comprehensive overview of African American political thought.

Glaude, Eddie S. *Exodus! Religion, Race, and Nation in Early Nineteenth-Century Black America.* Chicago: University of Chicago Press, 2000. An examination of how the biblical book of Exodus inspired a pragmatic tradition of racial advocacy among African Americans.

Gooding-Williams, Robert, ed. *Reading Rodney King: Reading Urban Uprising.* New York: Routledge, 1993. An exploration of the connections between the Rodney King incident and the ordinary workings of cultural, political, and economic power in contemporary America.

Gordon, Vivian V. *The Self-Concept of Black Americans.* Washington, DC: University Press of America, 1977. An exploration of the psychological makeup of African Americans.

Grant, Jacqueline. *White Women's Christ and Black Women's Jesus: Feminist Christologist and Womanist Response.* Atlanta: Scholars Press, 1990. A feminist approach to the impact of Christology on Black and White women.

Greth, H. H., and C. Wright Mills, eds. *From Max Weber: Essays in Sociology.* New York: Galaxy, 1958. An overview of the works of Max Weber, one of the founders of the field of sociology.

Grier, William H., and Price M. Cobbs. *Black Rage.* New York: Basic, 1968. One of the first examinations of the full range of Black life from the vantage point of psychiatry.

Grusky, David B., ed. *Social Stratification: Class, Race, and Gender in Sociological Perspective.* Boulder, CO: Westview, 2001. A refreshing take on existing theories of social stratification that incorporates the latest data and pursues new perspectives.

Guinier, Lani. *Tyranny of the Majority: Fundamental Fairness and Representative Democracy.* New York: Free Press, 1995. A collection of essays on the topic of representative democracy.

Guthrie, Robert V. *Being Black.* San Francisco: Canfield, 1970. An interdisciplinary approach to the psychology of African Americans.

Gutman, Herbert G. *The Black Family in Slavery and Freedom, 1750–1925.* New York: Random House, 1977. A history of Black families in America.

Guy-Sheftall, Beverly, ed. *Words of Fire: An Anthology of African American Feminist Thought.* New York: New Press, 1995. A collection of essays and documents chronicling the history of Black feminism from the early 1830s to the 1990s.

Hacker, Andrew. *Two Nations: Black and White, Separate, Hostile, Unequal.* New York: Ballantine, 1995. An examination of how the United States has become more divided over the concepts of race and class over the past few decades.

Hale, Janice E. *Unbank the Fire: Visions for the Education of African American Children.* Baltimore: Johns Hopkins University Press, 1994. An exploration of the different learning styles of African American children that is rooted in their culture.

Hall, Perry A. *In the Vineyard: Working in African American Studies.* Knoxville: University of Tennessee Press, 1999. An insiders' viewpoint on the movement of those students and their supporters who pushed universities to understand and embrace the mission and goals of Black studies programs.

Hall, Prince. "Slave Petition for Freedom to Massachusetts Legislature, January 13, 1777." In *The First Principles Series: The American Founding—Primary Source,* 1–2. Washington, DC: Heritage Foundation, 2021.

Harding, Vincent. *There Is a River: The Black Struggle for Freedom in America.* New York: Harcourt Brace, 1981. A metaphor for this examination comparing the history of African Americans in the United States to the movements of a mighty river.

Hare, Nathan. *The Black Anglo Saxons.* New York: Marzani & Munsell, 1965. A powerful and unique perspective on the African American middle class.

———. "Questions and Answers about Black Studies." In *The African American Studies Reader* (2nd ed.), ed. Nathaniel Norment Jr. Durham, NC: Carolina Academic Press, 2007. A discussion of the steps needed to create a Black studies program.

Hare, Nathan, and Julia Hare. *The Endangered Black Family: Coping with the Unisexualization and Coming Extinction of the Black Race.* San Francisco: Black Think Tank, 1984. A careful examination of the transformation of the Black American family.

Hare, Nathan, and Julia Hare. *The Miseducation of the Black Child.* San Francisco: Black Think Tank, 1991. An intriguing study of how to raise African American children in a Eurocentric world.

Harley, Sharon. "Nannie Helen Burroughs: 'The Black Goddess of Liberty.'" *Journal of Negro History* 81, nos. 1–4 (1996): 62–71. An examination of the life and impact of Burroughs.

Harris, Joseph E. *African American Reaction to the War in Ethiopia, 1936–1941.* Baton Rouge: Louisiana State University Press, 1994. A study of African American sympathies with Ethiopia, particularly during the Italo-Ethiopian War of 1936–1941.

Harris, Michael D. *Colored Pictures: Race and Visual Representation.* Chapel Hill: University of North Carolina Press, 2003. An examination of the role of visual representation in the construction of Black American identities, both real and imagined, in the United States.

Harris, Michael D., and Moyo Okediji. *Colored Pictures: Race and Visual Representation.* Chapel Hill: University of North Carolina Press, 2003. An investigation of the visual representation and construction of African American identities in the United States.

Harris, William M., and Darrell Millner, eds. *Perspectives on Black Studies.* Washington, DC: University Press of America, 1977. A review of the origins and development of Black studies.

Harris-Lacewell, Melissa Victoria. *Barbershops, Bibles, and BET: Everyday Talk and Black Political Thought.* Princeton, NJ: Princeton University Press, 2004. An examination of four political ideologies that constitute the framework of contemporary Black political thought.

Harris-Perry, Melissa V. *Sister Citizen: Shame, Stereotypes, and Black Women in America.* New Haven, CT: Yale University Press, 2011. A multidisciplinary approach to Black women's political and emotional responses to pervasive negative race and gender images.

Hatch, Nathan O. *The Democratization of American Christianity.* New Haven, CT: Yale University Press, 1989. An examination of the link between religion and culture during the early American republic.

Hawthorne, Walter. *Planting Rice and Harvesting Slaves: Transformations along the Guinea-Bissau Coast, 1400–1900.* Portsmouth, NH: Heinemann, 2003. An account of the participation of the Portuguese in the early years of the Atlantic slave trade.

Hay, Samuel A. *African American Theater: An Historical and Critical Analysis.* Cambridge: Cambridge University Press, 1994. The first comprehensive history of Black theater.

Hayes, Floyd W., III. *A Turbulent Voyage: Readings in African American Studies.* San Diego: Collegiate, 2001. An introduction to Black studies.

Hennessey, Thomas. *From Jazz to Swing: African American Jazz Musicians and Their Music, 1899–1935.* Detroit: Wayne State University Press, 1994. An exploration of jazz from its beginnings.

Herskovits, Melville. *The Myth of the Negro Past.* 1941. Reprint, Boston: Beacon, 1990. A combined historical and anthropological study of the plight of African Americans.

Higashida, Cheryl. *Black Internationalist Feminism: Women Writers of the Black Left, 1945–1995.* Urbana: University of Illinois Press, 2011. A discussion of how

African American women writers affiliated themselves with the post–World War II Black Communist Left and developed a distinct strand of feminism.

Higginbotham, A. Leon. *In the Matter of Color: Race and the American Legal Process: The Colonial Period*. New York: Oxford University Press, 1978. A classic legal study on the passage of enslavement laws during the colonial period.

Higginbotham, Evelyn Brooks. *Righteous Discontent: The Women's Movement in the Black Baptist Church, 1880–1920*. Cambridge, MA: Harvard University Press, 1993. An examination of the role African American women played in the Black Baptist church movement.

Hill, Kenneth H. H. *Religious Education in the African American Tradition*. Atlanta: Chalice, 2007. A comprehensive study of African American religion.

———. *Research on the African American Family: A Holistic Perspective*. With Andrew Billingsley, Eleanor Engram, Michelene R. Malson, Roger H. Rubin, Carol B. Stack, James B. Stewart, and James E. Teele. Westport, CT: Auburn House, 1993. A collection concerned with the state of the African American family.

Hill, Robert. *The Strengths of Black Families*. New York: Emerson Hall, 1972. A challenge to the 1965 Moynihan Report about the nature of the African American family.

Himes, Joseph S. *Racial and Ethnic Relations*. Dubuque: W. C. Brown, 1974. One of the first comprehensive studies of racial and ethnic relations.

Hine, Darlene Clark, ed. *Black Women in America: An Historical Encyclopedia*. 2 vols. Bloomington: Indiana University Press, 1994. A collection containing over two thousand entries on the lives and legacies of hundreds of African American women.

———. *A Shining Thread of Hope: The History of Black Women in America*. New York: Broadway, 1999. A groundbreaking study of the lives of African American women.

Hine, Darlene Clark, William C. Hine, and Stanley Harrold. *The African American Odyssey*. 6th ed. 2 vols. New York: Pearson, 2014. A history of African Americans from their African origins to the American Civil War.

Hinks, Peter P. *To Awaken My Afflicted Brethren: David Walker and the Problem of Antebellum Slave Resistance*. University Park: Penn State University Press, 1996. A study of the impact and legacy of the nineteenth-century abolitionist David Walker.

Hirshey, Gerri. *Nowhere to Run: The Story of Soul Music*. New York: Penguin, 1985. An examination of rhythm and blues singers and groups.

Holt, Thomas. *Black over White: Negro Political Leadership in South Carolina*. Urbana: University of Illinois Press, 1979. A study that illustrates the complex situations most African American politicians faced during the Reconstruction years.

hooks, bell. *Ain't I a Woman: Black Women and Feminism*. Boston: South End, 1981. A groundbreaking analysis of the complex relations between various forms of oppression from the perspective of Black feminist history and theory.

———. *Feminist Theory from Margin to Center.* Boston: South End, 1984. A call for a new direction for Black feminism.

Hopkins, Dwight N., and George C. L. Cummings, eds. *Cut Loose Your Stammering Tongue: Black Theology in the Slave Narratives.* Westminster, KY: John Knox, 2003. A collection of essays capturing the African American religious experience from personal viewpoints.

Horton, James O., and Lois E. Horton. *In Hope of Liberty: Culture, Community, and Protest among Northern Free Blacks, 1700–1860.* New York: Oxford University Press, 1997. An examination of the experiences of northern free Black Americans during the late nineteenth century.

Hudson, Winthrop. *Religion in America.* New York: Scribner's, 1981. An examination of religion in America from 1607 to the present.

Huggins, Nathan. *Black Odyssey: The Afro-American Ordeal in Slavery.* New York: Pantheon, 1977. A classic book on the plight of Africans and African Americans during the period of enslavement in the Americas.

———. *Harlem Renaissance.* New York: Oxford University Press, 1971. An examination of the origins and development of the Harlem Renaissance.

Hull, Gloria T., Patricia Bell Scott, and Barbara Smith, eds. *All the Women Are White, All the Blacks Are Men, but Some of Us Are Brave: Black Women's Studies.* Old Westbury, NY: Feminist, 1982. A collection that sets out the curricular and research agenda for the establishment of a Black women's studies program.

Hunter, Tera W. *To 'Joy My Freedom: Southern Black Women's Lives and Labors after the Civil War.* Cambridge, MA: Harvard University Press, 1997. An examination of the leisure, social, and work lives of African American women.

Hurston, Zora Neale. *Their Eyes Were Watching God.* New York: Harper Perennial, 1937.

Iton, Richard. *In Search of the Black Fantastic: Politics and Popular Culture in the Post–Civil Rights Era.* New York: Oxford University Press, 2008. A discussion of how Black artists have continued to play a significant role in the making and maintenance of critical social spaces.

Jackson, Cynthia L. *African American Education: A Reference Handbook.* Santa Barbara: ABC-CLIO, 2001. An examination of the preschool-through-college experiences of hundreds of African Americans from 1954 to the present.

Jackson, James S. *Life in Black America.* Newbury Park, CA: Sage, 1991. An interdisciplinary approach that aims to correct misconceptions about Black lives.

Jackson, Jesse. "Keep Hope Alive." In *Let Nobody Turn Us Around: An African American Anthology* (2nd ed.), ed. Manning Marable and Leith Mullings, 535–45. New York: Rowman & Littlefield, 2009.

Jacobs, Harriet. *Incidents in the Life of a Slave Girl: Written by Herself,* ed. George Hendrick and Willene Hendrick. St. James, NY: Brandywine, 1999. An annotated version of Harriet Jacobs's classic book.

Jacobs, Sylvia M. *The African Nexus.* Westport, CT: Greenwood, 1981. A detailed examination of African Americans' views on the European colonization of Africa.

————, ed. *Black Americans and the Missionary Movement in Africa.* Westport, CT: Greenwood, 1982. A collection of essays on the involvement of Black Americans in missionary work in Africa during the nineteenth and twentieth centuries.

Jay-Z. *Decoded.* New York: Spiegel & Grau, 2011. A collection of lyrics that together tell the story of a culture, an art form, a moment in history, and one of the most provocative and successful artists of our time.

Jeffries, Judson, ed. *Black Power in the Belly of the Beast.* Champaign: University of Illinois Press, 2006. A collection examining the emergence of the Black Power movement and its link to the development of several Black studies programs.

Jenkins, Adelbert H. *The Psychology of the Afro-American.* New York: Pergamon, 1982. A comprehensive study of Black psychology.

Johnson, Charles S. *Growing Up in the Black Belt.* Washington, DC: American Council on Education, 1941. A classic exploration of the lives of African American children and young adults in the South before World War II.

————. *The Negro in Chicago: A Study of Race Relations and a Race Riot.* New York: Baker & Taylor, 1922. An examination of the racial violence in Chicago during the Red Summer of 1919.

————. *Shadow of the Plantation.* Chicago: University of Chicago Press, 1934. A class examination of the lives of southern African Americans from a sociological perspective.

Johnson, Karen A. *Uplifting the Women and the Race: The Educational Philosophies and Social Activism of Anna Julia Cooper and Nannie Helen Burroughs.* New York: Garland, 2000. A detailed examination of the life and political activities of two activists.

Johnson, Paul E., ed. *African American Christianity: Essays in History.* Berkeley: University of California Press, 1994. A collection of essays on African American religious history from the enslavement period to today.

Johnson, Vernon D., and Bill Lyne, eds. *Walkin' the Talk: An Anthology of African American Studies.* New York: Pearson/Prentice Hall, 2003. A detailed and interdisciplinary approach to the experience of Americans of African descent that is rooted in primary sources.

Jones, Jacqueline. *Labor of Love, Labor of Sorrow: Black Women, Work, and the Family from Slavery to the Present.* New York: Vintage, 1995. A powerful account of the changing role of Black women.

Jones, Norrece T., Jr. *Born a Child of Freedom, yet a Slave: Mechanisms of Control and Struggles of Resistance in Antebellum South Carolina.* Middleton, CT: Wesleyan University Press, 1990. An examination of how masters used violence to control their captives and the captives resisted their enslavement.

Jones, Reginald L., ed. *Black Adult Development and Aging.* Berkeley, CA: Cobb & Henry, 1989. A detailed study of the aging process among Black Americans.

————, ed. *Black Psychology.* New York: Harper & Row, 1972. A pathbreaking examination of Black psychology.

Jordan, Winthrop D. *White over Black: American Attitudes toward Negroes, 1550–1852.* Chapel Hill: University of North Carolina Press, 1968. An intriguing and detailed analysis of the cultural and psychological forces that led Whites to enslave Africans.

Kagan, Jerome, and Ernest Havemann. *Psychology.* New York: Harcourt Brace Jovanovich, 1976. A detailed history of the field of psychology.

Kaluger, Charles, and Charles M. Unkovic. *Psychology and Sociology.* St. Louis: C. V. Mosby, 1969. A single-volume edition of this classic examination of the fields of psychology and sociology.

Karenga, Maulana. *Introduction to Black Studies.* Los Angeles: University of Sankore Press, 1993. One of the first comprehensive studies of the field of Black studies.

———. *Kawaida Theory: An Introductory Outline.* Inglewood, CA: Kawaida, 1980. An introduction to an Afrocentric psychology.

Keiler, Allan. *Marian Anderson: A Singer's Journey.* New York: Scribner, 2000. A detailed documentation of the contralto's life.

Kelley, Robin D. G. *Hammer and Hoe: Alabama Communists during the Great Depression.* Chapel Hill: University of North Carolina Press, 1990. A study of the radicalization of steelworkers and farmers during the 1930s and the appeal of communism to African American workers.

———. *Thelonious Monk: The Life and Times of an American Original.* New York: Free Press, 2009. The first account of Thelonious Monk based on exclusive access to the Monk family papers and private recordings.

———. *Yo' Mama's DisFunktional! Fighting the Culture Wars in Urban America.* Boston: Beacon, 1998. A study that undermines widespread misunderstandings of Black culture and shows how they have contributed to the failure of urban social policy.

Kellogg, Charles F. *NAACP: A History of the National Association for the Advancement of Colored People.* Baltimore: Johns Hopkins University Press, 1967. A history of the National Association for the Advancement of Colored People.

Kennedy, Randall. *The Persistence of the Color Line: Racial Politics and the Obama Presidency.* New York: Pantheon, 2011. A study highlighting the complex relationship between the first Black president and his African American constituency.

Keyes, Cheryl L. *Rap Music and Street Consciousness.* Urbana: University of Illinois Press, 2002. The first musicological history of rap, tracing the genre from its roots in West African traditions, Jamaican dance hall, and African American vernacular expressions to its permeation of the cultural mainstream as a major hip-hop lifestyle.

King, Martin Luther, Jr. *Where Do We Go from Here? Chaos or Community.* New York: HarperCollins, 1967. A short but powerful book that lays out King's thoughts, plans, and dreams for America's future.

King, Wilma. *Stolen Childhood: Slave Youth in Nineteenth-Century America.* Bloomington: Indiana University Press, 1995. The most current book on the enslavement of African American children.

Kitwana, Bakari. *The Hip Hop Generation: Young Blacks and the Crisis in American Culture*. New York: Basic Civitas, 2003. An account of how a generation of young African American men is disproportionately incarcerated and unemployed that also offers a perspective on the collapse of gender relations.

Klein, Herbert S. *The Atlantic Slave Trade*. New York: Cambridge University Press, 1999. A classic and detailed study on the Atlantic Slave Trade.

Klein, Julie T. *Interdisciplinarity: History, Theory, Practice*. Detroit: Wayne State University Press, 1990. An introduction to an interdisciplinary approach to research and writing.

Klineberg, Otto. *Race Differences*. New York: Harper & Bros., 1935. A classic and groundbreaking book that was one of the first to offer a comprehensive perspective on the topic of racial difference.

Kornweibel, Theodore, Jr. *Seeing Red: Federal Campaigns against Black Militancy, 1919–1925*. Bloomington: Indiana University Press, 1998. An account of how the African American movement for civil rights and equality as well as early Black nationalist, socialist, and other radicals were the targets of spying, harassment, and persecution.

Ladner, Joyce A., ed. *The Death of White Sociology*. New York: Vintage, 1973. A critique of mainstream sociology.

Landry, Bart. *Black Working Wives: Pioneers of the American Family Relations*. Berkeley: University of California Press, 2000. An examination of how the lifestyle of middle-class Black women in two-parent families was different from that of their White counterparts.

———. *The New Black Middle Class*. Berkeley: University of California Press, 1968. A consideration of the social stratification of African American families.

Lefkowitz, Mary R., and Guy MacLean Rogers, eds. *Black Athena Revisited*. Chapel Hill: University of North Carolina Press, 1996.

Lerner, Gerder, ed. *Black Women in White America: A Documentary History*. New York: Vintage, 1972. A collection of writings revealing the rich and diverse lives of African American women.

Levine, Lawrence. *Black Culture and Black Consciousness: Afro-American Folk Thought from Slavery to Freedom*. New York: Oxford University Press, 1977. A discussion of the rich and complex African American oral tradition.

Lewis, David Levering. *W. E. B. Du Bois: A Reader*. New York: Holt, 1995.

———. *W. E. B. Du Bois: Biography of a Race, 1868–1919*. New York: Henry Holt and Company, 1993. An account of Du Bois's formative years, the evolution of his philosophy, and his roles as a founder of the National Association for the Advancement of Colored People and an architect of the American civil rights movement

———. *W. E. B. Du Bois: The Fight for Equality and the American Century, 1919–1963*. New York: Henry Holt, 2001. Perhaps the most comprehensive analysis of Du Bois's life and times.

Lincoln, C. Eric, ed. *The Black Experience in Religion.* Garden City, NY: Doubleday, 1974. A collection that showcases a variety of views of the African American religious experience.

———. *The Black Muslims in America.* Trenton, NJ: Africa World, 1961. A concise examination of the Black American Muslim movement in the United States.

———. *Race, Religion, and the Continuing American Dilemma.* New York: Hill & Wang, 1984. A study that places the African American church movement at the center of America's moral systems.

Litwack, Leon F. *Trouble in Mind: Black Southerners in the Age of Jim Crow.* New York: Alfred A. Knopf, 1998. A description of the lives of African Americans in a White supremacist society.

Litwack, Leon F., and August Meier. *Black Leaders in the Nineteenth Century.* Urbana: University of Illinois Press, 1988. Eighteen brief but powerful biographical essays.

Locke, Alain L., ed. *The New Negro.* 1925. New York: Simon & Schuster, 2007. The book that introduced the Harlem Renaissance to the nation.

Logan, Rayford W. *The Betrayal of the Negro: From Rutherford B. Hayes to Woodrow Wilson.* New York: Collier, 1965. A classic examination of the political history of African Americans from the end of Reconstruction to the presidency of Woodrow Wilson.

Lomax, Alan. *The Land Where the Blues Began.* New York: Bantam Doubleday, 1993. An overview of the origin, development, and impact of blues music.

Lorde, Audre. *Cables to Rage.* London: Paul Breman, 1970.

———. *Sister Outsider: Essays and Speeches.* New York: Crossing, 1984. The essential writings of the late Black lesbian poet and feminist writer.

Lott, Tommy L. *African American Philosophy: Selected Readings.* New York: Pearson/ Prentice Hall, 2002. A topically organized collection of articles on a wide range of social and political issues.

———. *The Invention of Race: Black Culture and the Politics of Representation.* Malden, MA: Blackwell, 1999. A classic examination of the visual construction of race in America.

Love, Janice. *The U.S. Anti-apartheid Movement: Local Activism in Global Politics.* Westport, CT: Praeger, 1985. An evaluation of the effect of the sanctions used to pressure the South African government to end apartheid.

Macionis, John J. *Sociology.* New York: Pearson/Prentice Hall, 2013. A wide-ranging examination of community life in the United States specifically based on the interpersonal intimacy in families, effective teaching, humor, new information technologies, and the importance of global education.

Madhubuti, Haki, ed. *Confusion by Any Other Name.* Chicago: Third World, 1990. A collection of commentaries on the sometimes complex relationship between African American women and men.

Maffly-Kipp, Laurie F., and Kathryn Lofton, eds. *Women's Work: An Anthology of African American Women's Historical Writings from Antebellum America to the*

Harlem Renaissance. New York: Oxford University Press, 2010. A description of how several key and important African American women saw and critiqued the racism and sexism in society.

Magubane, Bernard M. *Ties That Bind: African American Consciousness of Africa.* Trenton, NJ: Africa World, 1988. An analysis of the phenomenon of ambivalence so persistent in the African American consciousness of Africa.

Malcolm X. *The Autobiography of Malcolm X: As Told to Alex Haley.* New York: Ballantine, 1965. A classic chronicle of the life and transformation of Malcolm X.

Marable, Manning, ed. *The New Black Renaissance: The "Souls" Anthology of Critical African American Studies.* Boulder, CO: Paradigm, 2005. A multicultural and Afrocentric approach to Black studies.

Mays, Benjamin E. *The Negro's God as Reflected in His Literature.* Boston: Chapman & Grimes, 1938. A collection of speeches and sermons by African American religious leaders.

Mbiti, John S. *African Religions and Philosophy.* Garden City, NY: Anchor, 1970. A systematic study of the mind-sets and beliefs that have evolved in different African societies.

McAdoo, Harriette P., ed. *Black Families.* Beverly Hills, CA: Sage, 1981. An interdisciplinary approach to African American families.

McAfee, Ward. *Religion, Race, and Reconstruction: The Public Schools in the 1870s.* Albany: State University of New York Press, 1998. A consideration of the public education system in the decade or so after the Civil War.

McClellan, B. Edward, and William J. Reese, eds. *The Social History of American Education.* Urbana: University of Illinois Press, 1988. A collection analyzing the educational history of the United States through the 1970s.

McKenzie, Vashti M. *Not without a Struggle: Leadership Development for African American Women in the Ministry.* Cleveland: United Church Press, 1996. An examination of the role and impact of African American religious leaders.

McMillan, Terry. *Five for Five: The Films of Spike Lee.* New York: Stewart, Tabori & Chang, 1991. A discussion of the filmmaker Spike Lee.

McPherson, August. *Negro Thought in America.* Ann Arbor: University of Michigan Press, 1963. An overview of the main themes of African American political thought from the War of Independence through the 1950s.

McPherson, James. *Battle Cry of Freedom: The Civil War Era.* 1988. New York: Oxford University Press, 1988. A comprehensive study of the Civil War.

Meier, August. *Negro Thought in America, 1880–1915.* Ann Arbor: University of Michigan Press, 1967. A study tracing African American political thought around the turn of the twentieth century.

Menzie, Nicola. "TD Jakes Breaks Down the Trinity, Addresses Being Called a 'Heretic.'" *Christian Post,* January 26, 2012. An examination of the early history of Bishop T. D. Jakes.

Meyers, Debra, and Burke Miller, eds. *Inequity in Education: A Historical Perspective.* New York: Rowman & Littlefield, 2009. A collection of essays on the history of inequality in the American educational system.

Miller, Floyd J. *The Search for Black Nationality: Black Colonization and Emigration, 1787–1863*. Urbana: University of Illinois Press, 1975. A study linking the origins and development of Black nationalism to the colonization and emigration movements in the United States.

Mirel, Jeffrey. *The Rise and Fall of an Urban School System—Detroit, 1907 to 1981*. Ann Arbor: University of Michigan Press, 1993. A detailed examination of Detroit's public education system.

Moikobu, Josephine Morra. *Blood and Flesh: Black American and African Identification*. Westport, CT: Greenwood, 1981. An examination that links the topics of African identity and African Americans.

Moore, Jacqueline M. *Booker T. Washington, W. E. B. Du Bois, and the Struggle for Racial Uplift*. Wilmington, DE: SR, 2003. A reconsideration of the Washington/Du Bois debate.

Morgan, Marcyliena. *The Real Hip Hop: Battling for Knowledge, Power, and Respect in the LA Underground*. Durham, NC: Duke University Press, 2009. An ethnographic approach to the LA underground rap music world within the context of hip-hop culture generally.

Morrison, Toni. *The Bluest Eye*. New York: Holt, Rinehart & Winston, 1970. This important author's first novel.

Morrison, Toni, Nellie McKay, and Michael Thelwell. *Race-ing Justice, En-gendering Power: Essays and Speeches on Anita Hill, Clarence Thomas, and the Construction of Social Reality*. New York: Pantheon, 1992. A collection examining the intersection of race and gender during Supreme Court justice Clarence Thomas's confirmation hearing.

Morrison-Reed, Mark D. *Black Pioneers in a White Denomination*. Boston: Beacon, 1984. An account of two pioneering Black American ministers.

Moses, Wilson J. *The Golden Age of Black Nationalism, 1850–1925*. New York: Oxford University Press, 1988. An examination of the origins and development of Black nationalism.

Moynihan, Daniel P. *The Negro Family: The Case for National Action*. Washington, DC: US Department of Labor, 1965. A report on Black poverty in the United States.

Murray, Andrew. *Presbyterians and the Negro: A History*. Philadelphia: Presbyterian Historical Society, 1966. A history of African Americans in the Presbyterian church.

Myers, Linda J. *Understanding an Afrocentric World-View: Introduction to an Optimal Psychology*. Dubuque, IA: Kendell/Hunt, 1998. A detailed discussion of the field of Afro-centered psychology.

Myrdal, Gunnar. *An American Dilemma*. New York: Harper & Bros., 1944. A classic examination of race relations in the United States.

Nash, Gary B. *Forging Freedom: The Formation of Philadelphia's Black Community, 1720–1840*. Cambridge, MA: Harvard University Press, 1988. An analysis of the creation of the African American community in Philadelphia.

———, ed. "Petitions of New England Slaves for Freedom, 1773–1779." In *Race and Revolution*, 171–76. Lanham, MD: Madison House, 1990.

Nelsen, Hart M., and Ann Kusener Nelsen. *Black Church in the Sixties.* Lexington: University Press of Kentucky, 1975. A description of the transformation of many African American churches during the 1960s.

Neville, Helen A., Brendesha M. Tynes, and Shawn O. Utsey, eds. *Handbook of African American Psychology.* Thousand Oaks, CA: Sage, 2008. A presentation of the theoretical, empirical, and practical issues that are foundational to African American psychology.

Newman, Richard S. *Freedom's Prophet: Bishop Richard Allen, the AME Church, and the Black Founding Fathers.* New York: New York University Press, 2008. A powerful and straightforward interpretation of Richard Allen.

Nobles, Wade. "African Philosophy: Foundation for Black Psychology." In *Black Psychology,* ed. R. Jones, 18–32. New York: Harper & Row, 1972. A path-breaking study of the origins of Black psychology.

———. *African Psychology: Towards Its Reclamation, Re-ascension, and Revitalization.* Oakland, CA: Black Family Institute, 1986. A detailed discussion of Black American psychology.

Nobles, Wade, and L. L. Goddard. *Understanding the Black Family: A Guide to Scholarship and Research.* Oakland, CA: Black Family Institute, 1984. An overview of the then-current literature and research methodology.

Norment, Nathaniel, Jr., ed. *The African American Reader.* Durham, NC: Carolina Academic, 2007. A comprehensive Black studies anthology.

Oliver, Paul. *Songsters and Saints: Vocal Traditions on Race Records.* New York: Cambridge University Press, 1984. An overview of the origins and impact of African American–led religious music.

Oliver, Ronald. *The African Experience: From Olduvai Gorge to the 21st Century.* Boulder, CO: Westview, 2000. An analysis of cultural relationships in Africa.

Olson, Lynee. *Freedom's Daughter: The Unsung Heroines of the Civil Rights Movement from 1830 to 1970.* New York: Simon & Schuster, 2001. The first comprehensive book on the vital role that both Black and White American women played in the civil rights movement.

O'Toole, James M. *Passing for White: Race, Religion, and the Healy Family, 1820–1920.* Amherst: University of Massachusetts Press, 2002. A chronicle of the transformation of the construction of the concept of race.

Palmer, Robert. *Deep Blues.* New York: Viking, 1995. The story of the history of blues music told through the lives of several great musicians.

Parham, Thomas A. *The Psychology of Blacks: Centering Our Perspectives in the African Consciousness.* New York: Pearson/Prentice Hall, 2010. An examination of the field of Black psychology.

Parham, Thomas A., Joseph L. White, and Adisa Ajamu. *The Psychology of Blacks: An African Centered Perspective.* 3rd ed. New York: Pearson/Prentice Hall, 1999. A brief but detailed discussion of the field of Black psychology.

Patterson, James T. *Brown v. Board of Education: A Civil Rights Milestone and Its Troubled Legacy.* New York: Oxford University Press, 2001. A step-by-step account of the 1954 *Brown* decision and its aftermath.

Patton, Sharon F. *African American Art*. New York: Oxford University Press, 1998. A reassessment that sets African American art in the context of the African American experience.

Perman, Michael L. *Emancipation and Reconstruction, 1862–1879*. 2nd ed. Arlington Heights, IL: Harlan Davidson, 2003. A survey of the Reconstruction period.

Perry, Imani. *Prophets of the Hood: Politics and Poetics in Hip Hop*. Durham, NC: Duke University Press, 2004. An analysis of song lyrics that focuses on the art, politics, and culture of hip-hop.

Pinkney, Alphonso. *Black Americans*. Pearson/Prentice Hall, 2000. A contemporary assessment of the lives of African Americans in the United States.

Platt, Anthony M. *E. Franklin Frazier Reconsidered*. New Brunswick, NJ: Rutgers University Press, 1991. A reassessment of the work of E. Franklin Frazier.

Plummer, Brenda Gayle. *Rising Wind: Black Americans and U.S. Foreign Affairs, 1935–1960*. Chapel Hill: University of North Carolina Press, 1996. An articulation of a new perspective on Black Americans' engagement with international issues, from the Italian invasion of Ethiopia in 1935 through the wave of African independence movements of the early 1960s.

Powell, Richard J. *Black Art and Culture in the 20th Century*. New York: Thames & Hudson, 1997. A comprehensive study of Black American art.

Pratt, Robert A. *The Color of Their Skin: Education and Race in Richmond, Virginia, 1954–1989*. Charlottesville: University Press of Virginia, 1992. An examination of the hectic process of integrating the public schools of Richmond, Virginia, and integration's aftermath.

Quarles, Benjamin. *Black Abolitionists*. New York: Oxford University Press, 1969. An examination of the relationships between Black and White abolitionists.

———. *The Negro in the American Revolution*. New York: W. W. Norton, 1973. A comprehensive overview of the participation of African Americans in the American Revolution.

Rabinowitz, Howard N. *Race Relations in the Urban South, 1865–1890*. New York: Oxford University Press, 1978. An examination of African American life in Atlanta, Montgomery, Nashville, Raleigh, and Richmond.

Raboteau, Albert J. *Slave Religion: The "Invisible Institution" in the Antebellum South*. New York: Oxford University Press, 2004. A chronicle of the transformation of African religions into evangelical Christianity.

Rainwater, Lee. *Behind Ghetto Walls: Black Family Life in a Federal Slum*. Chicago: Aldine, 1970. A relation of the lives of the children and adults who lived in an all-Black public housing project in St. Louis during the 1960s.

Rediker, Marcus. *The Slave Ship: A Human History*. New York: Viking, 2007. An account of life aboard slave ships in the eighteenth century.

Reed, Adolph, Jr. *The Jesse Jackson Phenomenon: The Crisis of Purpose in Afro-American Politics*. New Haven, CT: Yale University Press, 1986. An examination of the religious leader's two failed attempts to become the Democratic Party's presidential nominee.

Reimers, David. *White Protestantism and the Negro.* New York: Oxford University Press, 1965. A consideration of the impact of Protestant churches on the lives of African Americans.

Richardson, Harry V. *Dark Salvation: The Story of Methodism as It Developed among Blacks in America.* Garden City, NY: Doubleday, 1976. A discussion of Methodism as it developed in the United States and the role it played in the lives of Black Americans.

Richardson, Marilyn, ed. *Maria W. Stewart, America's First Black Woman Political Writer: Essays and Speeches.* Bloomington: Indiana University Press, 1987. A solid account of the life and work of this important early nineteenth-century African American writer.

Robeson, Paul. *Here I Stand: Paul Robeson.* Boston: Beacon, 1958. Paul Robeson's autobiography.

Robinson, David. *Muslim Societies in African History.* New York: Cambridge University Press, 2004. An examination of the many Muslim societies that have existed in Africa over the last thousand years.

Rodee, C. C., T. J. Anderson, and C. Q. Christol. *Introduction to Political Science.* New York: McGraw Hill, 1967. A basic introductory text.

Rojas, Fabio. *From Black Power to Black Studies: How a Radical Social Movement Became an Academic Discipline.* Baltimore: Johns Hopkins University Press, 2007. An examination of the origins and development of various Black studies programs, especially on the West Coast.

Rose, Jerry D. *Introduction to Sociology.* Chicago: Rand McNally College, 1980. A comprehensive overview of the field of sociology.

Rose, Tricia. *Black Noise: Rap Music and Black Culture in Contemporary America.* Hanover, NH: University Press of New England, 1994. A comprehensive look at the lyrics, music, cultures, themes, and styles of rap's highly rhythmic, rhymed storytelling.

Rosenberg, Jonathan. *How Far the Promised Land: World Affairs and the African American Civil Rights Movement from the First World War to Vietnam.* Princeton, NJ: Princeton University Press, 2006. An exploration of the relationship between the struggle for racial justice in the United States and overseas developments.

Ruiz, Dorothy S., ed. *Handbook of Mental Health and Mental Disorder among Black Americans.* New York: Greenwood, 1990. An examination of the impact of social structures and conditions on the mental health of Blacks.

Schubert, Frank N. *Voices of the Buffalo Soldiers: Records, Reports, and Recollections of Military Life and Service in the West.* Albuquerque: University of New Mexico Press, 2003. An overview of African American military life from the Civil War to World War I.

Schuller, Gunther. *Early Jazz: Its Roots and Musical Development.* New York: Oxford University Press, 1986. An exploration of the history and musical contribution of jazz from its origins to the 1930s.

Schulz, Duane P., and Sydney Ellen Schulz. *A History of Modern Psychology.* San Diego: Harcourt Brace Jovanovich, 1987. A comprehensive overview of the field of psychology.

Scott, William R. *The Sons of Sheba's Race: African Americans and the Italo-Ethiopian War.* Bloomington: Indiana University Press, 1993. A consideration of the place Ethiopia and Ethiopianism held in the African American imagination and the role of the Italian crisis in crystallizing the image of Ethiopia as a bastion of Black resistance to Western/White hegemony.

Scott, William R., and William G. Shade, eds. *Upon These Shores: Themes in the African American Experience, 1600 to the Present.* New York: Routledge, 2000. A collection of essays on topics ranging from African American history, to Black feminism, to African American religion, to African American educational history.

Sennett, Richard, and Jonathan Cobb. *The Hidden Injuries of Class.* New York: W. W. Norton, 1993. A sociological perspective on the lives and conflicts of people near the bottom of the socioeconomic scale.

Sernett, Milton C. *African American Religious History: A Documentary Witness.* Durham, NC: Duke University Press, 1999. A collection of documents offering a view of African American religious history from Africa and early America, through Reconstruction, to the rise of Black nationalism, the modern civil rights movement, and contemporary Black theology.

Shadd Cary, Mary Ann. "A Plea for Emigration; or, Notes of Canada West" (1852). In *Let Nobody Turn Us Around: An African American Anthology* (2nd ed.), ed. Manning Marable and Leith Mullings, 68–70. New York: Rowman & Littlefield, 2009. Drawn from a powerful collection of writings and speeches by African American leaders, this document outlines several reasons for migration to Canada during the antebellum period.

Shade, William G., and Roy C. Herrenkohl, eds. *Seven on Black: Reflections on the Negro Experience in America.* Philadelphia: Lippincott, 1969. Discussions of the religious experience of important African American religious leaders.

Shannon, Sandra. *The Dramatic Vision of August Wilson.* Washington, DC: Howard University Press, 1995. A decade-by-decade account of the playwright's career.

Sharpley-Whiting, T. Denean. *Pimps Up, Ho's Down: Hip Hop's Hold on Young Black Women.* New York: New York University Press, 2007. An account of how African American women interrogated the complexities of hip-hop culture, which is characterized by masculinism and misogyny.

Simpson, Alphonso, Jr. *Mother to Son: A Collection of Essays and Readings in African American Studies.* San Diego, CA: Cognella, 2011. A comprehensive overview of Black studies.

Singh, Nikhil Pal. *Black Is a Country: Race and the Unfinished Struggle for Democracy.* Cambridge, MA: Harvard University Press, 2004. An examination of the declining visionary goals of many leaders of the modern civil rights movement.

Singleton, G., ed. *The Life, Experience, and Gospel Labors of the Rt. Rev. Richard Allen—by Richard Allen.* Nashville: Abingdon, 1960. A volume that includes many of Allen's speeches.

Sitkoff, Harvard. *A New Deal for Blacks: The Emergence of Civil Rights as a National Issue: The Depression Decade.* New York: Oxford University Press, 2009. A comprehensive examination of the experience of African Americans from the Great Depression to the start of the modern civil rights movement.

Small, Christopher. *Music of the Common Tongue: Survival and Celebration in Afro-American Music.* 1987. Reprint, New York: Riverrun, 1994. An exploration of how African American music developed from the collision of African and European traditions that occurred in the Americas.

Smiley, Tavis. *The Covenant with Black America.* Chicago: Third World, 2006. A collection outlining the ways African Americans can move beyond their current economic, political, and social circumstances.

Smith, Barbara, ed. *Home Girls: A Black Feminist Anthology.* New York: Kitchen Table, 1983. An anthology of writings by Black feminists and lesbian activists.

Smith, Valerie. *Not Just Race, Not Just Gender: Black Feminist Readings.* New York: Routledge, 1998. A collection of Black feminist writings from the early nineteenth century through the end of the twentieth.

Sobel, Michael. *Trabelin' On: The Slave Journey to an Afro-Baptist Faith.* Princeton, NJ: Princeton University Press, 1988. A history of the Black American Baptist church movement.

Solomon, Mark. *The Cry Was Unity: Communists and African Americans, 1917–1936.* Jackson: University Press of Mississippi, 1998. The first study of the relationship between African Americans and Communists in both its national and its international contexts.

Solomon, R. Patrick. *Black Resistance in High School: Forging a Separate Culture.* Albany: State University of New York Press, 1992. An examination of the link between learning and cultural norms for people of African descent in the United States, Canada, and Great Britain.

Southern, Eileen. *The Music of Black Americans: A History.* 3rd ed. New York: W. W. Norton, 1997. A fascinating narrative of how various intense musical activities not only played a vital role in the lives of Black Americans but also deeply influenced performance in the United States and many other parts of the world.

———, ed. *Readings in Black American Music.* New York: W. W. Norton, 1983. Includes quotations from John F. Watson, *Methodist Error or Friendly Christian Advice to Those Methodists Who Indulge in Extravagant Religious Emotions and Bodily Exercises* (Trenton, NJ: D. and E. Fenton, 1819).

Spear, Allen H. *Black Chicago.* Chicago: University of Chicago Press, 1967. A sociological examination of the development of several African American communities in Chicago.

Spring, Joel. *The American School, 1642–1993.* New York: McGraw Hill, 1994. A short but comprehensive history of education in the United States.

Stack, Carol B. *All Our Kin: Strategies of Survival in a Black Community.* New York: Basic, 1996. A debunking of the misconception that poor families are unstable and disorganized.

Stanley, A. Knighton. *The Children Is Crying: Congregationalism among Black People.* New York: Pilgrim, 1979. A chronicle of the impact of Congregationalism on African Americans.

Stanlie, James, and Abena P. A. Busia, eds. *Theorizing Black Feminism: The Visionary Pragmatism of Black Women.* New York: Routledge, 1994. A collection of essays on Black feminism that pushes the boundaries of social theory.

Staples, Robert, ed. *The Black Family: Essays and Studies.* Belmont, CA: Wadsworth, 1978. A combination of empirical research and scholarly essays on various aspects of the African American community.

———. *Introduction to Black Sociology.* New York: McGraw Hill, 1976. The work that introduced the topic of Black sociology to a general audience.

Stein, Judith. *The World of Marcus Garvey: Race and Class in Modern Society.* Baton Rouge: Louisiana State University Press, 1991. A detailed examination of the effectiveness of Marcus Garvey and the Universal Negro Improvement Association.

Stewart, Jacqueline Najuma. *Migrating to the Movies: Cinema and Black Urban Modernity.* Berkeley: University of California Press, 2005. A detailed look at the numerous early relationships between African Americans and cinema.

Stuckey, Sterling. *Slave Culture: Nationalist Theory and the Foundations of Black America.* New York: Oxford University Press, 1988. A discussion of how different African peoples interacted during the nineteenth century to achieve a common culture.

Synan, Vinson. *The Holiness-Pentecostal Movement in the United States.* Grand Rapids, MI: William B. Eerdmans, 1971. An examination of the influence of the Pentecostal church movement on African Americans.

Tatum, Beverly Daniel. *Assimilation Blues: Black Families in a White Community.* New York: Greenwood, 1987. An in-depth look at the realities of being a middle-class Black parent living, working, and raising children in a predominantly White community.

Taylor, Quintard. *In Search of the Racial Frontier: African Americans in the American West, 1528–1990.* New York: W. W. Norton, 1998. The first book-length study of African American life in the American West.

Taylor, William E., and Harriet G. Warkel. *A Shared Heritage: Art by Four African Americans.* Bloomington: Indiana University Press, 1996. A presentation of four African American artists with shared Indiana roots.

Teachout, Terry. *Pops: A Life of Louis Armstrong.* New York: Houghton Mifflin Harcourt, 2009. The most comprehensive account of the life and times of Louis Armstrong.

Terry-Thompson, Arthur C. *The History of the African Orthodox Church.* New York: Beacon, 1956. A classic account of the African Orthodox church.

Thomas, Lamont D. *Rise to Be a People: A Biography of Paul Cuffe.* Urbana: University of Illinois Press, 1986. The most comprehensive study of Paul Cuffe.

Thompson, Daniel C. *Sociology of the Black Experience.* Westport, CT: Greenwood, 1974. An examination of the history of African America from a sociological perspective.

Travis, Dempsey J. *Autobiography of Black Jazz.* Chicago: Urban Research, 1983. A collection covering both famous and little-known Chicago-based African American jazz musicians.

Truth, Sojourner. "A'n't I a Woman?" (1851). In *Let Nobody Turn Us Around: An African American Anthology* (2nd ed.), ed. Manning Marable and Leith Mullings, 66–68. New York: Rowman & Littlefield, 2009.

Turner, James E. *The Next Decade: Theoretical and Research Issues in Africana Studies.* Ithaca, NY: Africana Studies and Research Center/Cornell University Press, 1984. An overview of the theoretical framework and research methodologies of Africana studies programs.

Von Eshen, Penny. *Race against Empire: Black Americans and Anti-colonialism, 1937–1957.* Ithaca, NY: Cornell University Press, 1997. A vivid portrayal of the African diaspora in its international heyday, from the 1945 Manchester Pan-African Congress to early cooperation with the United Nations.

Walker, Alice. *In Search of Our Mothers' Gardens.* San Diego: Harcourt Brace, 1983. Alice Walker's first nonfiction collection, in which she speaks out as a Black woman, writer, mother, and feminist in pieces ranging from the personal to the political.

Walker, David. *An Appeal in Four Articles; Together with a Preamble, to the Coloured Citizens of the World, but in Particular, and Very Expressly, to Those of the United States of America.* Boston, 1830. A powerful and important document on the views of an African American leader during the antebellum period.

Wallace, Michele. *Invisibility Blues.* New York: Verso, 1990. A landmark history of Black feminism.

Wallace, Ruth A., and Alison Wolf. *Contemporary Sociological Theory.* New York: Pearson/Prentice Hall, 1991. An examination of the five major contemporary sociological theories and their classical roots.

Walters, Ronald W. *Pan-Africanism in the African Diaspora: An Analysis of Modern Afrocentric Political Movements.* Detroit: Wayne State University Press, 1995. A collection of important case studies of Black political movements since the 1960s and the impact of those movements on the African American community.

Ward, Brian. *Just My Soul Responding: Rhythm and Blues, Black Consciousness, and Race Relations.* Berkeley: University of California Press, 1998. A detailed examination of the relationship between rhythm and blues, Black consciousness, and race relations within the larger context of the modern civil rights movement.

Washington, James M. *A Testament of Hope: The Essential Writings and Speeches of Martin Luther King, Jr.* New York: Harper One, 2003. A collection of both famous and obscure speeches and writings.

Washington, Joseph R., Jr. *Black Religion: The Negro and Christianity in the United States*. Boston: Beacon, 1964. A classic examination of the religious experience of African Americans in the United States.

Washington, Margaret, ed. *Sojourner Truth: The Narrative of Sojourner Truth*. New York: Vintage, 1993. An edition of the memoir that also contains a selection of the writings and speeches.

Watkins, Mel. *On the Real Side: Laughing, Lying, and Signifying*. New York: Simon & Schuster, 1994. A comprehensive history of African American humor from the antebellum South to the Apollo Theater.

Watkins, William H. *The White Architects of Black Education: Ideology and Power in America, 1865–1954*. New York: Teachers College Press, 2001. A historical and sociological perspective on the history of the education of African Americans from the mid-nineteenth century to the 1950s.

Watkins, William H., James H. Lewis, and Victoria Chou, eds. *Race and Education: The Roles of History and Society in Educating African American Students*. Boston: Allyn & Bacon, 2001. A collection of essays on the progress of the education of African Americans since the 1954 *Brown* decision.

Weber, Max. *Basic Concepts in Sociology*. Westport, CT: Greenwood, 1976. One of the first comprehensive studies of the field of sociology.

Welsing, Frances Cress. *The Cress Theory of Color Confrontation and Racism (White Supremacy)*. Washington, DC: C-R, 1970. A classic study linking skin color and psychology.

Werner, Craig Hansen. *Playing the Changes: From Afro-Modernism to the Jazz Impulse*. Urbana: University of Illinois Press, 1994. A consideration of the relationship between two superficially distinct musical and cultural traditions: European (post)modernism and African American culture in both literary and musical forms.

West, Cornel. *Race Matters*. New York: Vintage, 2001. A classic treatise on race that discusses a variety of issues, including the crisis in leadership in the Black community, Black conservatism, Black-Jewish relations, myths about Black sexuality, and the legacy of Malcolm X.

Whelchel, L. H. *The History and Heritage of African American Churches: A Way Out of No Way*. Saint Paul, MN: Paragon, 2011. An examination of the origins of the Black American church movement from its cultural heritage in Africa to the present.

White, Deborah Gray. *Ar'n't I a Woman? Female Slaves in the Plantation South*. New York: Norton, 1999. An examination of the lives of enslaved African American women.

———. *Too Heavy a Load: Black Women in Defense of Themselves*. New York: W. W. Norton, 1999. An exploration of the lives of African American women during the twentieth century.

White, Joseph. "Toward a Black Psychology." *Ebony* 25 (1970): 44–53. A landmark study that challenged orthodox psychology.

Williams, Eric. *Capitalism and Slavery.* Chapel Hill: University of North Carolina Press, 1994. The first detailed study of the linkage between the capitalist system and slavery.

Williamson, Joy Ann. *Black Power on Campus: The University of Illinois, 1965–75.* Champaign: University of Illinois Press, 2003. An examination of the development of the Black Power movement on America's campuses during the 1960s and 1970s, with special attention paid to the University of Illinois.

Willie, Charles Vert. *A New Look at Black Families.* 2nd ed. Bayside, NY: General Hall, 1981. Case studies of the varieties of the Black family experience and how that experience varies with socioeconomic status.

Willis, Deborah. *Reflections in Black: A History of Black Photographers, 1840 to the Present.* New York: W. W. Norton, 2000. A powerful and comprehensive history of African American life using famous and little-known photographs.

Wilmore, Gayraud S. *Black Religion and Black Radicalism: An Interpretation of the Religious History of African Americans.* Maryknoll, NY: Orbis, 1988. A collection of essays by leading scholars on the origin, development, and impact of Black theology on African Americans and other racial and ethnic groups.

Wilson, Amos N. *The Developmental Psychology of the Black Child.* New York: Africana Research, 1978. An important study of the psychology of African American children.

Wilson, William Julius. *The Bridge over the Racial Divide: Rising Inequality and Coalition Politics.* Berkeley: University of California Press, 1999. A presentation of new ways to discuss America's class and racial divisions with an eye toward resolving them.

———. *The Declining Significance of Race.* Chicago: University of Chicago Press, 1979. A controversial book contending that class has become more of a deciding factor in the life chances of Black Americans than race.

———. *The Truly Disadvantaged: The Inner City, the Underclass, and Public Policy.* Chicago: University of Chicago Press, 1987. A controversial book claiming that poverty in urban America greatly increased because of a massive shift in the nation's manufacturing sector.

Wolff, Kurt H., ed. *The Sociology of Georg Simmel.* New York: Free Press, 1964. An examination of the life, times, and ideas of one of the pioneering figures in the field of sociology.

Womack, Ytasha L. *Post Black: How a New Generation Is Redefining African American Identity.* Chicago: Chicago Review Press, 2010. A fresh look at the dynamics shaping the lives of African Americans in the twenty-first century.

Wood, James A., ed. *Problems in Modern Latin American History: Sources and Interpretations.* New York: Rowman & Littlefield, 2014. A unique and comprehensive approach, based on both primary and secondary sources, to the modern era in Latin America.

Wood, Peter H. *Black Majority: Negroes in Colonial South Carolina from 1670 through the Stono Rebellion.* New York: W. W. Norton, 1974. One of the best studies of slavery in South Carolina and the origins of the Stono Rebellion.

Woodson, Carter G. *The Education of the Negro prior to 1861.* Washington, DC: Associated Publishers, 1915. One of the first studies on African American education.

———. *History of the Negro Church.* Washington, DC: Associated Publishers, 1945. One of the first comprehensive studies of the origin and development of the African American church.

———. *The Mis-education of the Negro.* Washington, DC: Associated Publishers, 1933. A classic and seminal study examining the plight of African American education from its inception in the United States to the 1930s.

Woodward, C. Van. *The Strange Career of Jim Crow.* New York: Oxford University Press, 1955. A description of the evolution of legal segregation in the South.

Wright, Bobby E. *The Psychopathic Racial Personality.* Chicago: Third World, 1975. A thought-provoking examination of the group personality of Europeans as manifested in their behavior toward Black people.

Wright, Donald R. *African Americans in the Colonial Period: From African Origins through the American Revolution.* Arlington Heights, IL: Harlan Davidson, 2000. A brief but well-written survey of African American life during the colonial period.

Wright, Lawrence. *Saints and Sinners: Walker Railey, Jimmy Swaggart, Madalyn Murray O'Hair, Anton LaVey, Will Campbell, Matthew Fox.* New York: Alfred A. Knopf, 1993. A penetrating study of the triumphs and failures of the life of faith featuring portraits of six religious leaders.

Wright, Richard. *Native Son.* New York: Harper & Bros., 1940. A classic novel tackling African American history and identity.

Yee, Shirley J. *Black Women Abolitionists: A Study in Activism, 1828–1860.* Knoxville: University of Tennessee Press, 1992. One of the first studies of female African American abolitionists.

Young, Henry J. *Major Black Religious Leaders since 1940.* Nashville: Abingdon, 1979. An examination of the impact of various African American religious leaders.

Index

abolition movement: absence of collaboration between Black and White abolitionists, 44; Black feminists and, 127, 130–33; Black nationalism and, 88; the Civil War and, 46; colonization and, 44–45; creation of independent Black churches and, 43; Frederick Douglass and, 177; key early influences on, 43–44; rise of following the American Revolution, 40

abstract artists, 218

accommodation, 73–74

Addiction, The (film), 210

Africa: African Americans and African consciousness, 87; American colonization movement and, 44–45 (*see also* emigration); ancient civilizations in, 31–32; Atlantic slave trade and, 34–35; family structures and the African American family, 154; origin of humans and, 30–31; presence of Islam and Christianity in, 99; religious traditions and concepts, 98–99, 100; Rwandan genocide, 95; slavery in, 32; South Africa and the antiapartheid movement, 92–93; World War II and, 67

African American artists: Black Arts movement and, 69–70, 214, 218–19; Diahann Carroll, 213–14; dominance of Eurocentric aesthetics and, 214–15; Harlem Renaissance and, 65, 216–18; during the post-Reconstruction period, 60; Paul Robeson, 18, 85–86, 216–17;

visual and performance art after World War II, 218–20; visual and performance art through the Civil War and Reconstruction, 215–16; visual and performance art through World War II, 216–18. *See also* African American music

African American Baptist church: Nannie Burroughs and, 109, 111; current state of, 122; First African Baptist Church of New York, 106; growth in the post–Civil War period, 112

African American community: Black studies and promoting the welfare of, 23; class divisions in the late twentieth century, 157–58; northern Black churches and, 106, 108

African American culture: Black sociology and, 144, 148; Black studies and the preservation of, 23; in the colonial period and following the American Revolution, 39–40; Harlem Renaissance and, 65, 216–18; music and, 199 (*see also* African American music)

African American education: African American political power during the 1970s and, 191–92; in the antebellum period, 76–79; *Brown v. Board of Education* and school desegregation, 66, 69, 82–84, 162; Du Bois–Washington debate over, 80; Thomas Fuller and, 73–74; historically Black colleges and universities, 59, 79,